Cognitive Humanistic Therapy

Cognitive Humanistic Therapy

Buddhism, Christianity and Being Fully Human

Richard Nelson-Jones

SAGE Publications
London • Thousand Oaks • New Delhi

First published 2004

SAGE Publications Ltd
1 Oliver's Yard
55 City Road
London EC1Y 1SP

SAGE Publications Inc.
2455 Teller Road
Thousand Oaks, California 91320

SAGE Publications India Pvt Ltd
B-42, Panchsheel Enclave
Post Box 4109
New Delhi 110 017

British Library Cataloguing in Publication data

A catalogue record for this book is available
from the British Library

ISBN 1 4129 0074 3
ISBN 1 4129 0075 1 (pbk)

Library of Congress Control Number: 2003112274

Typeset by C&M Digitals (P) Ltd., Chennai, India
Printed in India at Gopsons Papers Ltd, Noida

Contents

Practices

Preface

Cognitive humanistic therapy, or CHT for short, aims to bring the insights and methods of the cognitive behavioural, cognitive and humanistic psychotherapies and of religion to help clients, therapists and others to become and stay more fully human. Being more fully human entails possessing and demonstrating high levels of mental cultivation and human sympathy or, more simply, of reason and love. In the past, stipulating such qualities as goals has been more a feature of the world's religious traditions than of psychotherapeutic approaches, the latter concentrating mainly on helping patients and clients to attain normal functioning.

Cognitive humanistic therapy represents an integrative or crossover approach in a number of different ways. For example, psychotherapy meets with religion, especially Buddhism and Christianity, in that humane religious aspirations are approached through therapeutic methods. West meets with East in that the approach is heavily influenced by Buddhist ideas of how to be a good human being, without making any demands on the reader to adopt Buddhist ideas like multiple rebirths, which many find unconvincing. An aspect of the Buddhist religious tradition central to the book's structure and content is the importance of cultivating positive qualities at the same time as curbing negative qualities. Normal functioning meets with supra-normal functioning, because humans cannot bypass problems and poor human-being skills related to deficiencies in their upbringing and move directly to working on superior functioning. Psychotherapy meets with continuing personal practice because being fully human involves a lifelong commitment to service and to working to attain and maintain high levels of mental cultivation and human sympathy. Finally, therapists' personal levels of mental cultivation and human sympathy meet with what they can offer clients. Becoming a better therapist means being more fully human oneself.

One way to indicate the integrative nature of cognitive humanistic therapy is to name the sources that have inspired it. The following is a list of the ten people who have most influenced the creation of the approach: Alfred Adler, Aaron Beck, the Buddha, Jesus Christ, the current Dalai Lama, Charles Darwin, Albert Ellis, Erich Fromm, Abraham Maslow and Carl Rogers.

For whom is this book intended? I hope that the book resonates with all those who, like me, feel that there is something missing in contemporary psychotherapy and counselling, which tends to be unnecessarily pessimistic about human nature and offers few specific strategies and practices for those clients and others wanting to lead meaningful lives by becoming and remaining more other-centred and less self-centred. Readers may be at different stages along their journeys as psychotherapists and counsellors, for instance as students, beginning or experienced practitioners, trainers, supervisors or supervisors of supervisors. Possibly, the book may be of interest to some clients and lay people who want to address issues in their own lives that are touched on here. Although I am an agnostic myself, I hope that the book will appeal to many religiously committed people who may then fruitfully integrate some of its insights and methods into their practice.

The book is divided into two overlapping parts: understanding being fully human (mainly theory) and cultivating being fully human (mainly practice). The first chapter – 'What is cognitive humanism?' – defines humanism, discusses it in relation to philosophy, religion and psychotherapy, and mentions some distinctive features of the cognitive humanistic approach. Chapter 2 looks at what Darwin really said and presents a cognitive humanistic view of the nature of human nature and motivation. Chapter 3 develops the concept of human-being skills, with the two main areas being mind skills and communication/action skills. The chapter also looks at some other basic CHT concepts. Chapter 4 explores what it means to be fully human, in particular in terms of human sympathy and mental cultivation. Chapter 5 presents some of the main processes by which people learn and maintain skilful and unskilful behaviour, including reviewing seven contemporary dehumanizing contexts.

Chapter 6 overviews CHT, breaking it into two overlapping components: *adaptation* CHT for normal functioning, and *mental cultivation* CHT for supra-normal functioning. This chapter also examines the processes of CHT, the therapeutic relationship and some applications of the approach. Chapter 7 presents a three-stage skilled client model of the therapeutic process, each stage having three phases. Chapter 8 reviews skills for calming and focusing the mind and looks at ways of challenging the illusions of an independent self and of permanence. Chapters 8 to 15 end with skills-building practices or activities that may be performed either as part of therapy or in personal practice independent of therapists.

Chapter 9 looks at how the heart may be awakened further by challenging the illusions of differentness and of human badness. Chapters 10 and 11 present some mind skills and communication skills for curbing anger and aversion, and greed and craving, respectively. Curbing negative qualities and cultivating positive qualities interact. Chapters 12 to 14 review mind skills and communication skills for cultivating goodwill/lovingkindness, sympathetic joy, gratitude, compassion, equanimity, generosity and helping. The final chapter on personal practice encourages therapists, clients and others to cultivate a service-oriented mentality in which they curb negative qualities and develop positive ones for the sakes of themselves, others and the human species.

I thank my publishers, Sage, for having the courage to publish a book like this that falls somewhat outside conventional writing about psychotherapy and counselling. In particular I thank my editor, Karen Haynes, for her support and feedback. When asked to comment on an outline of the proposed book, I appreciated a very kind letter of encouragement from Dr Albert Ellis, President of the Albert Ellis Institute, New York City, USA. I have also been exceptionally fortunate in having two excellent consultants who acted as friendly critics during the writing process. My heartfelt thanks go to the Reverend John Butt, Director, Institute of the Study of Religion and Culture, Payap University, Chiang Mai, Thailand, and to Professor Danny Wedding, Director, Missouri Institute of Mental Health, St Louis, USA, and co-editor of *Current Psychotherapies*. Both the Reverend John and Professor Danny performed their tasks well above and beyond the call of duty. My thanks also to Andrew Chua, a counselling psychologist and Victorian Executive Officer of the Boys' Brigade in Australia, for providing feedback on the book's practices.

In a nutshell, this is a book about how to use therapeutic tools to develop reason and love in the interests of oneself, others and humankind. Some may view the cognitive humanistic approach and its advocacy of connecting at deeper levels to the better natures of oneself and one's fellow humans as something akin to 'small r' religion. Many readers may prefer to place the approach within the context of a divine ultimate reality. Whatever readers' therapeutic and religious orientations, I hope they will gain something of professional and personal value from the book.

I encourage readers to give me feedback about the book and to make suggestions about improving the theory and practice of cognitive humanistic therapy. To ease communicating with me, below I provide my postal and email addresses.

Richard Nelson-Jones
Director, Cognitive Humanistic Institute
Suite 715, Supakit Condominium
Suthep Road, Soi 4,
Chiang Mai,
THAILAND 50200
Email address: rnjchi@loxinfo.co.th

PART ONE

UNDERSTANDING BEING FULLY HUMAN

ONE   What is Cognitive Humanism?

What does it mean to be fully human? Most people consider that they are being human just by virtue of being members of the species *Homo sapiens*. However, a simple biologically based answer 'I am because I breathe' does not really describe what it is to be fully human. Neither does a simple answer based on the French philosopher Descartes' famous quote 'I think, therefore I am'. Still less does a modern-day parody 'I consume, therefore I am'. Being human is a process that continues throughout life and at each stage people are influenced by others and make choices that can enhance, diminish or, if very unlucky, irreversibly cripple their capacity to attain more of their essential humanity. Although the mind–body distinction is somewhat artificial, being human is a psychological process that takes place in the context of the biological process of being a living organism. Being fully human entails accessing and demonstrating at a very high level the better parts of one's human potential.

This book explores what it is to be fully human and how psychotherapy and personal practice can enhance that process. It is assumed throughout that being human is a full-time occupation that takes place at every moment of people's waking lives right up until the moment of death. Furthermore, that being human is a process involving people's relationships with themselves, with those with whom they come into face-to-face contact, the broader human family, and also with the natural environment that they will bequeath to future generations. Life is tragic in that most people could be much more fully human than they and their circumstances allow. People always have to struggle to attain high levels of humanity, sometimes against great odds. This book is intended as a small contribution in the search for a more human and humane world.

What is humanism?

Humanism can be defined by the combination of the following three ways of *thinking*. First, humanism is a secular outlook or system of thought concerned with human rather than divine or supernatural matters. Humanists neither hold religious beliefs nor look outside or inside of themselves for a relationship with God or some other supernatural being. Second, humanism emphasizes the primacy of reason for approaching and solving human problems. Humankind is viewed as having the potential to think responsibly and rationally. Inasmuch as this is the case, the term 'cognitive humanism' is something of a tautology, although it is still useful in making the distinction with humanistic psychology and psychotherapy as commonly defined in the West. Third, humanism is concerned with the welfare of humankind and with developing the better aspects or higher potentials of human beings.

Although it is interrelated with thoughts, humanism can also be viewed in terms of the *feelings* or emotions characteristic of humanists. Here, the term 'humanitarian' applies in that the main feelings associated with humanism are humaneness, benevolence and compassion or, to use Darwin's term, the instinct of sympathy. The reverse side of the coin is that, alongside cultivating positive feelings, humanists seek to curb negative feelings such as greed and anger. Humanism can also be viewed in terms of *actions*. Ideally the actions of humanists express their humanitarian feelings and are concerned with improving their capacity to think and feel benevolently so as to synergistically affirm their own and other people's welfare.

Humanism may be viewed from the perspectives of its philosophical background, as a tradition within the world's religions, as influential in psychotherapy, and grounded in evolutionary biology, a discussion of the latter being deferred until Chapter 2.

Philosophy and humanism

In philosophy the term 'humanism' has its roots in devotion to those studies that promote human culture, especially the revival of interest in Greek and Roman classics, which came into vogue at the time of the fifteenth-century Italian Renaissance (Oxford English Dictionary, 2001). Noted philosopher Bertrand Russell (1945) observed that the Renaissance was not a popular movement, but rather a movement of a small number of scholars and artists, encouraged by liberal patrons. During the Renaissance, these people substituted the authority of the ancient Greeks and Romans for that of the Church. For example, Plato and his student Aristotle, who lived in the fifth and fourth centuries BC, espoused both virtue and reason, placing the intellectual virtues above all other virtues. Aristotle considered the man who exercised his reason and cultivated it to be both in the best state of mind and most dear to the gods. The kind of humanism advocated by the ancient Greeks assumed a leisured class that could engage in contemplative activity and philosophical debates. Such humanism was not for the masses.

Stoicism, whose leading figures lived during the period from the third century BC to the second century AD, is another important philosophical influence on the development of Western humanism. Virtue is the sole good and consists in a will that is in agreement with Nature. The Stoics valued using reason in a disciplined way to assume control of their inner lives. Others may have power over external events, but everything good or bad in one's life depends entirely on oneself. The Roman philosopher Epictetus, who was born about 60 AD and died about 100 AD, was one of the most prominent of the Stoics. The Stoic outlook is well summed up in his statement: 'Men are disturbed not by things, but by the views which they take of them.' Much of the period in which the Stoics lived was chaotic and dangerous and Stoicism may have provided a bulwark against the darkness outside.

Humanism became prominent again in Europe in the seventeenth and eighteenth centuries, which have been described as the Age of Enlightenment. As with the Renaissance, a significant factor was that people moved beyond superstition and religious dogmas to trust in the powers of reason and humanity. Human beings could use their reason to harness the forces of nature, and create a more fair, humane and enlightened world. However, in the twentieth century, people became less optimistic about the use of reason and the dawn of a new enlightened era. The reasons for this more pessimistic outlook include the horrors of the two world wars, of Stalinism, of the Khmer Rouge and of the numerous armed conflicts that still exist at the start of the twenty-first century. Further reasons are the threat of man-made catastrophes from nuclear war, terrorism and global warming, and the realization that material affluence has the power to create alienation in the midst of plenty. In addition, there is a distinct fear that human beings in future may be controlled by the machines that they are creating. The fact that humankind throughout history has been shown to be highly fallible and that it now faces some daunting challenges to global survival is an urgent imperative for people to become more fully human.

The philosophical background to humanism encompasses both East and West. For example, the leading text of Confucianism, *The Analects of Confucius* (Confucius, 1994), has been immensely influential throughout the Chinese world, although sometimes honoured more by word than by deed. Compiled some 2,400 years ago, it emphasizes the relationship between politics and morality, with special emphasis on benevolence. The writings of Confucius and his disciples also stressed the virtues of integrity, loyalty, forbearance, love of knowledge, wisdom, self-improvement and filial piety.

The philosophical movement known as the Romantic Movement merits attention as it is important for understanding the philosophical base for Western humanistic psychotherapy. The Romantic Movement has influenced politics, art, literature and, as shown later in this chapter, psychotherapy. The Romantic Movement aimed at liberating people from the fetters of social morality and conventions. The leading figure of this movement was the Frenchman Jean-Jacques Rousseau, who lived from 1712 to 1778. In Rousseau's time, restraint in the expression of passion was the mark of a gentleman and, as such, an important aim of education. Whereas the ancient Greeks valued the cultivation of reason, the aim for the Romantics was to be as natural as possible – Rousseau's 'natural man'. Rousseau thought that human beings were naturally good and that only institutions made them bad and the first sentence of his book on education *Emile* reads: 'God made all things good: man meddles with them and they become evil' (Rousseau, 1993, p. 5). Rousseau heavily emphasized learning by experience, preferably in the countryside. Acknowledging the existence of a God, he advocated a 'natural religion' in which human beings would discover rules of conduct in the depths of their hearts. By following their feelings rather than reason, human beings would be virtuous and serve the common interest.

Christianity, Buddhism and humanism

This section focuses on humanistic elements in two of the world's great religious traditions: Christianity and Buddhism. Each religious tradition may be viewed as involving a total response and commitment of one's existence to events and experiences that are interpreted and expressed by a belief system and a set of ethics. Most Christians understand the key experiences in human life to be related to a transcendent reality expressed as the trinity of God the Father, Jesus the Son and the Holy Spirit. Though questioned by some, central Christian beliefs are that human beings are born in a state of sin, their sins are forgiven and they are reconciled with God through the life and death of Jesus Christ. Another key belief is that, at the Day of Judgment, those people who have made a sincere effort in trying to follow the example of Christ's life shall be saved by God's grace and those who have not made this effort shall fail to receive salvation. Christian denominations vary greatly in the degree to which they require their adherents to believe in the authority of the Church to interpret Christian faith. The notion of papal infallibility shows that, although the 'Kingdom of God' may be within human beings, in the Roman Catholic Church there is limited appeal to the authority of individual conscience.

As a manifestation of faith in God, a strong humanistic tradition exists within the area of Christian ethics. This tradition runs throughout both the Old and the New Testaments. An outstanding example of humanism in the New Testament is the second of the two main commandments given by Jesus. The first main commandment directs Christians to love God with heart, soul and mind whereas the second main commandment states that one must love one's neighbour as oneself. The Christian message has often been distorted by religious bigotry, but compassionate concern for the less fortunate has been a central feature of Christian ethics and practice. Throughout the four Gospels, Jesus is presented as a compassionate role model performing healing miracles and preaching the need to help the hungry, the thirsty, strangers, the naked, the sick and those in prison. The reason that Jesus is important and is viewed as a role model is that he is understood to embody and reveal in his life the transcendent dimension of human experience that is God.

Christians are at the forefront of compassionate service in many countries. Something of the motivation of committed Christians to help those less fortunate can be seen from the following saying of Mother Teresa: 'Do you want to do something beautiful for God? There is a person who needs you. This is your chance' (Chalika and Le Joly, 1996, p. 47). Another example of Christian motivation is that of Mother Teresa experiencing feelings of repugnance passing by, seeing and smelling an old woman in Calcutta whose face and feet were eaten by rats. However, she also saw the face of Jesus in this distressing disguise and, therefore, was moved to pick her up and take her to a local hospital. For Mother Teresa seeing Jesus was seeing the incarnation of God. One of the side effects of the decline of Christianity in Western countries is that a principal source of motivation for compassionate service to others and for restraining individual egocentricity has become correspondingly weakened.

Buddhism, named after the Buddha – 'the enlightened one' – is another world religious tradition with a strong humanistic emphasis. For many non-Buddhists, elements of its belief system, such as multiple rebirths, are unconvincing. However, this is a predominantly non-theistic religious tradition with no god as creator or saviour. Individuals create their own destinies with their present condition being the result of actions in past lives and their future destiny influenced by actions in this life. Thus people are their own creators. The core of Buddhist teaching is the Four Noble Truths:

1. all is suffering;
2. craving arising from ignorance causes suffering;
3. the cessation of suffering, or Nirvana and enlightenment, results from the elimination of ignorance and craving; and
4. ignorance and craving are eliminated and Nirvana and enlightenment attained by following the Noble Eightfold Path.

To a Buddhist, like the current Dalai Lama, suffering consists of two elements. There is the suffering that is a part of the human condition connected with sickness, aging, death, and tragic events. There is also self-created suffering that is the result of ignorance, craving and hatred, the three 'poisons of the mind', which interfere with human beings accessing and developing their underlying pure and radiant Buddha nature. Such suffering consists of any form of mental discomfort, unhappiness or distress, however large or small. The eight principles of the Noble Eightfold Path to enlightenment are contained in three groupings relating to the cultivation of ethical conduct, mental discipline and insight-wisdom.

There are two main traditions within Buddhism, Theravada, which is the Buddhism of South and South-East Asia, and Mahayana, a later form, which is the Buddhism of East Asia (China, Korea and Japan) and Tibet. Both traditions exemplify compassion, but the motivation in the Theravada tradition is more focused on the attainment of wisdom and concerned with individual liberation and enlightenment. However, the motivation of the Mahayana tradition is that provided by the *bodhisattva* ideal exemplified by the Buddha himself and other enlightened beings who defer attaining their own Nirvana to serve as teachers and helpers for others on the path.

The Dalai Lama is so concerned with the suffering in the affluent West that he has attempted to teach some of the main principles of Buddhism as a version of humanistic ethics for non-believers (Dalai Lama, 1999, 2000, 2001, 2002; Dalai Lama and Cutler, 1998). He often describes the essence of Buddhist teaching in two sentences: 'If you can, help others, serve others. If you cannot, at least refrain from harming others.' Buddhist ethics contain two overlapping parts: overcoming tendencies to ignorance, craving and hatred and cultivating the good. The latter includes transforming one's heart, mind and actions so as to embody The Four Divine Abodes of lovingkindness, compassion, sympathetic joy and equanimity. Lovingkindness means wishing the happiness of all sentient beings, oneself and others; compassion, seeing and wanting to relieve the suffering of others; sympathetic joy, being glad about others' happiness; and equanimity, possessing a balanced and composed mind.

As with those who practise Christian ethics, the issue of what motivates people to attain more of their innate Buddha nature is important. Buddhist believers would say that they find strength and take refuge in the three pillars of the religion. These pillars are the life and example of the Buddha, the *dhamma* or teachings concerning the truth about ultimate reality as interpreted by the Buddha, and the Sangha or community of Buddhist monks and others who have committed themselves fully to following the Buddha's teaching. The Buddhist religion can provide some useful insights for humanism in a number of ways. These include its positive view of true human nature, its emphasis on mental cultivation both to lessen negative qualities and develop and strengthen good qualities, its stress on compassion for all sentient beings, and the notion of the *bodhisattva* or person devoted to advancing the welfare of others.

Probably all the major world religious traditions emphasize the ethic of compassionate service. For example, alms giving or giving away a portion of one's goods is one of the core religious duties or five pillars of Islam (Jones, 1994). Good thoughts and deeds are essential aspects of the religious duties of pious Hindus (Loewenthal, 2000).

A final point is that many Christians and Buddhists see themselves as Christian humanists and Buddhist humanists. It is sometimes forgotten that both Jesus Christ and the Buddha were human beings. A strand in Christian thinking, first propounded in the last century by the Protestant theologian Paul Tillich, views God neither as the 'old man in the sky' nor 'out there' but as the 'ground of our being' (Robinson, 1963; Tillich, 1952). Tillich replaces images of height with images of depth to reflect more accurately the truth about God. The love revealed in Christ's life shows what it means to be deeply human. The contemporary theologian and former student of Tillich, Bishop Spong advises Christians to live fully, love wastefully and have the courage to be themselves (Spong, 1998). For Buddhists, committed adherence to the Buddha's teachings can be viewed as helping themselves and others to become more fully human by revealing more of the essential Buddha nature at the depths of their being.

Psychotherapy and humanism

Given the earlier definition of humanism, there are two main humanistic schools or traditions within psychotherapy: the humanistic psychotherapies and the cognitive behavioural psychotherapies, the latter sometimes indicated by the letters CBT. Both of these important traditions are discussed, followed by some suggestions about how cognitive humanistic therapy attempts to fill a gap left by each of them.

Humanistic psychotherapy

Throughout the 1950s, in the USA, Abraham Maslow and like-minded people laid the groundwork for what is now known as the humanistic psychology movement. In 1961 Maslow and Anthony Sutich launched the *Journal of Humanistic Psychology* for those authors finding difficulty in publishing articles dealing with the wider possibilities of the human potential in the then established journals. Sutich summarized the nature of humanistic psychology in the journal's first editorial.

The *Journal of Humanistic Psychology* is being founded by a group of psychologists and professional men and women from other fields who are interested in those human capacities and potentialities that have no systematic place either in positivistic or behavioristic theory or in classical psychoanalytic theory, e.g. creativity, love, growth organism, basic need-gratification, self-actualization, higher values, ego-transcendence, objectivity, autonomy, identity, responsibility, psychological health etc. (Sutich, 1961: viii–ix)

In 1963, the founding meeting of the American Association of Humanistic Psychology (AAHP) took place with James Bugenthal as its first president – in 1969, the word 'American' was dropped from the title and the AHP became international. In 1964, Bugental organized an eminent group of humanistically oriented psychologists and scholars to meet at Old Saybrook in Connecticut to clarify the development of the movement up until then and formulate a vision for this new orientation in psychology. At the front of current copies of the *Journal of Humanistic Psychology* there is a statement of the five basic postulates of humanistic psychology, adapted from an article about the 'third force in psychology' written by Bugenthal shortly after the conference (Bugenthal, 1964). The five postulates are:

1. Human beings, as human, supersede the sum of their parts. They cannot be reduced to components.
2. Human beings have their existence in a uniquely human context, as well as in a cosmic ecology.
3. Human beings are aware and aware of being aware – i.e., they are conscious. Human consciousness always includes an awareness of oneself in the context of other people.
4. Human beings have some choice and, with that, responsibility.
5. Human beings are intentional, aim at goals, are aware that they cause future events, and seek meaning, value and creativity.

Humanistic psychotherapy covers a broad range of therapies, so some of its defining elements apply to some approaches more than to others. Working with the whole person is a central feature of humanistic psychotherapy. Rowan writes: 'The main plank in humanistic psychology is the integration of body, feelings, intellect, soul and spirit, and it says so very clearly in all the introductory leaflets put out by AHP affiliates around the world' (Rowan, 2000, p. 23).

Probably the two main humanistic psychotherapies are person-centred therapy, developed by Carl Rogers (Rogers, 1961, 1980), his colleagues and more recent contributors, and gestalt therapy, developed by Fritz Perls (Perls, Hefferline and Goodman, 1951), his colleagues and more recent contributors. Rogers, in particular, stressed the importance of therapists creating humane relationships with clients in which they can learn to listen to themselves more clearly. Person-centred and other humanistic therapies emphasize authenticity, getting in touch with one's body and with the flow of one's inner experiencing, and uncovering and releasing the real self rather than one that is inhibited and distorted by upbringing and social convention. Such work can include expressing and working through strong feelings as well as accessing and understanding the meaning of underlying 'felt senses'. Sometimes body work, including bioenergetics, is used to help clients release energy and feel grounded in their bodies. Action-oriented techniques based on Moreno's psychodrama are also used to help clients experience, express and work through important feelings blockages.

Existential therapy is a strand both within and outside of humanistic psychotherapy. Notable existential therapists such as Viktor Frankl, the founder of logotherapy, and Rollo May, who with Irvin Yalom developed a dynamic form of existential therapy, have served on the *Journal of Humanistic Psychology*'s board of editors.

The notion of self-actualization is important in humanistic psychotherapy. Approaches such as person-centred therapy aim to help clients become more authentic and to get in touch with their real selves rather than with a false sense of self based on inhibitions, distortions and denials due to unfortunate aspects of their family, social and cultural upbringing. Rogers assumed that the more people get in touch with their real selves, the more rational they become because they are more open to their experience and less defensive. Furthermore, the more centred they are in their real selves, the deeper the quality of their relationships and capacity to care for others.

Transpersonal therapy is a further strand within humanistic psychotherapy. Maslow was particularly interested in what he termed peak experiences, which are 'ordinarily brief and transient moments of bliss, rapture, ecstasy, great happiness or joy' (Hoffman, 1996, p. 206). In such moments people can feel reverence, awe and in touch with the sacred. Towards the end of his life Maslow was promoting transpersonal psychology focusing on the spiritual dimensions of the human potential. British humanistic psychotherapist John Rowan echoes Maslow's espousal of the transpersonal when he asserts that the actual experience of the real self is a mystical experience of being in touch with the self that lies beyond all self-concepts, self-images and sub-personalities (Rowan, 2000).

How humanistic is Western humanistic psychotherapy in terms of the three defining characteristics of humanism stipulated earlier? First, there is the criterion that humanism is not concerned with divine or supernatural matters. Addressing transpersonal issues is a strand within Western humanistic psychology that is of major concern to some of its main theorists and practitioners. However, although Rogers allowed the possibility of altered states of consciousness and of spiritual development, probably most clients seeing person-centred therapists do so without bringing up transpersonal issues. The same holds true for gestalt therapy clients. To the extent that humanistic therapists deal with clients' problems concerning the divine or the supernatural, they not only engage in transpersonal therapy, but in 'trans-humanistic' therapy as well. Historically, as in the Italian Renaissance and the Age of Enlightenment, humanism has been a counterweight against the main traditional forms of religion in the West.

In relation to the criterion that humanism emphasizes the primacy of reason for approaching and solving human problems, humanistic psychology and psychotherapy have both strengths and much room for improvement. Humanistic therapists tend to see the development of reason as a by-product of the development of the capacity to experience, feel and be in touch with the energy of one's body. Clients who feel safer, more energetic, more open to their experience and inner valuing process, and more authentic are also often, as part of this process, able to become more rational. However, when cognitive weaknesses are not addressed directly, they may not be addressed at all. Furthermore, if one of the goals of therapy is to assist clients to live their lives more rationally, this outcome is probably more expeditiously achieved if therapists address mental processes directly rather than place their trust in less direct methods. Most major humanistic psychology and psychotherapy authors do not even mention leading cognitive therapy theorists, like Albert Ellis or Aaron Beck, let alone try to integrate their contributions into their writing and work.

Humanistic psychology and psychotherapy also have strengths and much room for improvement in relation to the third criterion for humanism, that of developing the better aspects or higher potentials of human beings. Again the assumption is that higher potentials of human functioning are attained as a by-product of a process that focuses on experiencing the real self more deeply. The quality of the relational depth established between humanistic therapist and client often enables clients to relate with less hostility and more honesty and caring outside of therapy. However, human beings may become better at relating more quickly and maintain their changes if they have directly worked on the mental and communication processes involved in high quality relationships. Even legends of the humanistic movement have experienced trouble with mature detachment and forgiveness. For instance, towards the end of his life Rogers was still apt to blame his parents for having made him feel that he did not deserve to be loved (Cohen, 1997). Maslow also felt intensely hostile towards his mother, was never reconciled with her and refused to attend her funeral

(Hoffman, 1999). Furthermore, although many humanistic psychologists and psychotherapists are extremely committed to the betterment of humankind, humanistic psychotherapy does not directly address issues of helping people to feel more compassionately and act more generously to those less fortunate.

To summarize, when Western humanistic psychotherapy veers into the transpersonal which is most often not the case, it transgresses one of the main criteria for humanism. Contemporary humanistic psychology and psychotherapy appear to be based more on Rousseau-like Romanticism in which enhancing qualities like reason and compassion are mainly by-products of releasing the 'natural person' than on the kind of humanism that involves developing such qualities more directly, albeit still within the context of caring human relationships (Howard, 2000).

Cognitive behaviour therapy

Probably most readers approach the terms 'humanistic psychology' and 'humanistic psychotherapy' with the assumption of their advocates' strong, if not impeccable humanistic credentials. However, humanistic psychotherapy's claim to represent humanism is only to some extent credible. The reverse may be the case with cognitive behaviour therapy in that probably many readers do not associate it with humanism. The author begs to differ and so do many humanists: for example, in 1971, Albert Ellis, the originator of rational emotive behaviour therapy (REBT), received the prestigious Humanist of the Year award from the American Humanist Association.

The 25 years from 1940 to 1965 can be viewed as the period in which humanistic psychotherapy became established. The cognitive element of cognitive behaviour therapy became prominent in the 25 years from 1955 to 1980. Both humanistic psychotherapy and the cognitive element of cognitive behaviour therapy were attempts to develop better forms of psychotherapy than psychoanalysis and behaviour therapy. The two most significant proponents of cognitive behaviour therapy, Albert Ellis, whom some consider the father of CBT, and Aaron Beck, the originator of cognitive therapy (CT), were trained in psychoanalysis and went on to discard it (Beck, 1976; Beck and Weishaar, 2000; Ellis, 2000, 2001). Another prominent cognitive behaviour therapist, Arnold Lazarus, the originator of multimodal therapy (MMT), rebelled against the narrowness of traditional behaviour therapy and broadened his approach to contain cognitive and other elements (Lazarus, 1984, 1997).

A misconception concerning cognitive behaviour therapy is that it insufficiently values the importance of feelings and physical reactions. The approach to feelings in the humanistic psychotherapies emphasizes uncovering them and using experiential techniques to assist clients in acknowledging, releasing and expressing them. The approach to feelings in the cognitive behaviour therapies focuses more on identifying and altering the mental processes that create negative feelings and that interfere with clients being able to experience and express appropriate feelings. Much of Albert Ellis's early work was in helping clients to release and enjoy their sexual energy and Aaron Beck's seminal work was in assisting depressed patients to become more energetic and happy – hardly the track records of people who undervalue feelings and physical reactions.

As with humanistic psychotherapy, the 'three criteria for humanism test' can be applied to cognitive behaviour therapy. In regard to the first criterion, cognitive behaviour therapists make no mention of the divine or supernatural in their work. Regarding the second criterion – the primacy of reason in solving human problems – this is the central message of the cognitive part of cognitive behaviourism. A distinctive feature of *Homo sapiens* is the genetically based potential to be *Homo rationalis*, although for psycho-biological, socio-cultural, family and personal reasons all human beings need to struggle to attain this potential. Ellis's rational emotive behaviour therapy focuses on altering people's tendencies to make irrational demands on themselves, others and the environment by replacing these self-defeating thoughts with more rational ones. The cornerstone of Beck's cognitive therapy is helping people to correct systematic biases in how they process information by assisting them to become more skilled at testing the reality of the thoughts that they create. Both Ellis and Beck emphasize the need to take a scientific approach to thinking about one's thinking and to amending it accordingly, if necessary. Lazarus's multimodal therapy is a comprehensive approach, but he has made a particularly useful contribution in showing how people can create and alter unhelpful visual images.

Two important issues connected with an emphasis on reason in solving human problems are whether using reason to address human problems is a solely rational process and, related to this, the extent to which helping clients to become more rational is best approached by focusing directly on their mental processes. The second criterion for humanism, concerning the primacy of reason in addressing human problems, assumes that the use of reason is a matter of heart as well as of head. This assumption leads into the issue of the extent to which humane values are part of the current psycho-biological inheritance of the human species, a question insufficiently addressed to date in the cognitive behavioural literature. Reason needs to be grounded in values that affirm humanity or else it can be positively dangerous, as is shown when it is used to support religious bigotry, excessive nationalism, corrupt elites and the unethical use of scientific discoveries.

The issue of whether helping clients to become more rational is best approached by directly addressing their mental processes is more a matter of means than ends. Cognitive behaviourists acknowledge that thinking is a complex process that can involve emotional and behavioural components and feedback processes. Cognitive behaviour therapists often attempt to get clients to think more rationally about problems by focusing on altering their behaviour, for instance Beck's attempts to encourage depressed patients to engage in some actions first to loosen up how they think about their ability to influence their environment. The emphasis in humanistic therapy on providing clients with safe and/or emotionally challenging human relationships can also help some clients to become more rational. However, probably in most instances the most sensible way of addressing the human problem of how to help clients to think more rationally is to focus directly on their mental processes, albeit within the context of mutually respectful collaborative working relationships.

The third criterion for defining humanism relates to commitment to the welfare of humankind and to developing its better or higher potentials. Cognitive behavioural theorists acknowledge humankind's potential for thinking in ways that display enlightened altruism by rationally taking into account the needs and preferences of others. However, when they mention evolution and genetics, they emphasize that the human organism is highly vulnerable to irrational tendencies, holding primitive core beliefs, and jumping to false conclusions. Possibly because of the distressed nature of their clientele, the main focus of the cognitive behaviour therapies is more on eliminating and reducing the negative mental processes and behaviours that interfere with loving and compassionate interaction than on cultivating these qualities in their own right. Furthermore, when a major theorist like Beck addresses the issues of anger, hostility and violence in the world, the thrust of his message is on how people individually and collectively become and stay hostile. Beck has far less to say about how people can develop what he terms the 'altruistic mode' which will leave them less vulnerable to falling into the trap of becoming prisoners of hate (Beck, 1999).

Cognitive behaviour therapy has been developed mainly by psychiatrists and clinical psychologists who are dealing with either severely disturbed people or with those needing assistance so that they can function at a level considered normal in current society. Even when advocating such qualities as acceptance of others and expressing appreciation it is more with the aim of communicating better in conventional terms rather than of attaining genuinely supra-normal levels of human functioning. The author has yet to come across a single CBT article on how to cultivate a deep level of compassion for humankind. Furthermore, there is insufficient acknowledgement within CBT of the pathological elements in Western culture that are part of everyday life, for example consumerism and excessive competitiveness, which interfere with people being able to develop and show more human sympathy. Such pathology often requires addressing if people are to transcend the insidious nature of their cultural conditioning.

To summarize, the cognitive behavioural therapies all espouse humanism to the extent that they do not deal with the divine or supernatural. Cognitive behavioural therapy's emphasis on reason is also a key feature of humanism. Although CBT has much to offer in helping people to access their higher human potentials, to date its major focus has been more on the problems and issues of the seriously disturbed clients and of those whom Ellis terms the 'nicely neurotic'. The thrust of CBT's efforts at bettering humankind has been more on curbing its negative than on cultivating its positive potential, especially at the higher or supra-normal levels.

Cognitive humanistic therapy

Therapy is derived from the Greek word *therapeia,* meaning healing. Cognitive humanistic therapy (CHT) uses the word 'therapy' in two different but overlapping ways. The conventional approach to psychotherapy mainly views it as a healing process for helping seriously and moderately distressed clients to attain normalcy. However, even for those who function normally, another way of looking at healing is to view it as closing the gap between their current levels of functioning and their potential for full humanity. In varying degrees and with different levels of awareness of the nature and extent of their suffering, everyone is alienated from their capacity for being fully human. Cognitive humanistic therapy attempts to find ways of addressing this as well as the more commonly acknowledged need for human healing. However, healing can only be partially obtained as the result of psychotherapy because, where psychological problems are concerned, the idea of total cure is total nonsense. This is for two reasons. First, presence or absence of psychological problems is never totally black and white. Second, even after successful therapy, clients always have to keep healing themselves to maintain their gains afterwards.

An overriding goal of cognitive humanism is to cultivate and merge reason and love or, to put it another way, head and heart. All people suffer from being slaves to negative aspects of their minds that interfere with their capacity for reason and love, although this is more true of some than others. The place to start searching to understand the human potential for so-called good and evil is to examine the evolutionary basis of *Homo sapiens.* As Darwin pointed out, human beings contain within them 'an impulsive power widely different from a search after pleasure or happiness; and this seems to be the deeply planted social instinct' (Darwin,

1998a, p. 124). Cognitive humanism regards the need to cultivate this social instinct, a precious part of the human evolutionary inheritance, as central to its outlook. Given that human beings have a social instinct and a capacity for sympathy and for supporting the good of their community, reason and love have the potential to merge rather than to be separate processes. The challenge to the human species is to enhance the likelihood of this happening more frequently. The cultivation of qualities such as compassion, reflecting the social instinct, require special attention since humans have other instincts and instinct remnants that provide an evolutionary foundation for their less social and more destructive tendencies.

Cognitive humanistic therapy (CHT) is an attempt to fashion an approach to psychotherapy, self-therapy and personal practice that fulfils each of the three criteria for humanism. The approach is grounded in human rather than in divine or supernatural matters. Many human beings have what Maslow called peak experiences and also yearn for a way of understanding the human predicament with a spiritual transpersonal explanation, but this does not prove the existence of the divine or supernatural. Accepting that there are supernatural forces requires a leap of faith inconsistent with both strict cognitive humanistic or humanistic outlooks. Cognitive humanism approaches the issue of the divine or supernatural with an open scientific mind and a willingness to examine impartially any confirmatory evidence that emerges over time. However, without accepting aspects of their belief systems, cognitive humanism acknowledges the sincerity and fellowship of Christian humanists, of Buddhist humanists, and indeed of humanists from all other religious faiths. Indeed the qualities of being fully human reviewed later in this book are derived mainly from and emphasized more in religious than secular sources.

Cognitive humanistic therapy, which in many respects rests on cognitive behavioural foundations, shares CBT's emphasis on the primacy of reason and on the importance of directly addressing clients' mental processes. Along with many CBT therapists, CHT acknowledges that assisting some badly wounded clients to become more rational is best achieved within the context of highly empathic, gentle and safe therapeutic relationships, at least until they feel less threatened. This may especially be the case for clients who have never been truly loved when growing up. Some clients may also be helped to become more rational by direct emotional-experiential and behavioural interventions, which are features of CBT approaches as well.

A major difference between CHT and CBT is that CHT emphasizes the concept of mind and regards various mental processes, such as reality-testing perceptions and altering irrational beliefs, as mind skills requiring improvement. Cognitive humanistic therapy possibly goes further than some CBT approaches in attempting to address the hidden anti-human cultural agendas that, like water surrounding fish, are so much a part of people's non-conscious thinking that they take them for granted. Furthermore, CHT is more similar to Buddhism than to CBT as commonly practised in the West in focusing on mental cultivation beyond that needed for everyday survival. As such, ongoing personal practice becomes an important part of the approach.

Cognitive humanistic therapy is dissimilar to CBT in its major emphasis on cultivating human sympathy or innate goodness. It consists of two parts: *adaptation* CHT for attaining normal functioning in terms of Western societies and *mental cultivation* CHT for those who want to attain supra-normal levels of functioning. The two areas overlap, but adaptation CHT for normal functioning is akin to CBT in that often learning to communicate and act better entails working through faulty mental processes that sustain hostile and inappropriate behaviour. Even within adaptation CHT, direct attention to positive mind and communication skills, like showing goodwill and expressing gratitude, can be very important.

It is in the area of mental cultivation CHT that the practice of cognitive humanistic therapy differs most from CBT. Mental cultivation CHT is also dissimilar to the practice of humanistic psychotherapy in that it views attaining supra-normal levels of development as far too important and difficult to be just a by-product of high-quality experiential relationships. Mental cultivation CHT aims to develop one's mind and human sympathy beyond that which is needed for normal adaptation. Its goals are not being nice, popular or manipulating the environment to get something for oneself. Instead its goal is to cultivate the social instinct so that one's own personal betterment becomes synergistically aligned to that of the betterment of everybody one meets and of the human species. The author prefers not to use terms like selfless service or altruism to describe the outcomes of progressing along this therapeutic personal development path. At the higher levels, human functioning service for other people's welfare becomes a form of self-service in which a deep-seated evolutionary predisposition receives satisfaction.

TWO   Human Motivation

In the last chapter it was mentioned that, because of the atrocities of the twentieth century, which continue into this century, many people are now disillusioned with the power of reason to solve human problems. This chapter, which emphasizes the evolutionary and psycho-biological aspects of human nature, makes the case that human beings, along with their primitive aggressive instinct remnants, also have residues of social instincts that allow for sympathy and ethical actions towards other humans. Such positive instinct remnants, when aligned with reason, provide the foundation for humanism.

What Darwin really said

Charles Darwin's *The Descent of Man* (1998a), originally published in 1871, should be mandatory reading for all counsellors, therapists and anyone who wishes to conduct an informed discussion about the nature of human nature. When penning his autobiography towards the end of his life, Darwin (1809–82) observed: 'As soon as I had become, in the year 1837 or 38, convinced that species were mutable productions, I could not avoid the belief that man must come under the same law' (Darwin, 1958, p. 130). From 1842, supported by abundant personal wealth and surrounded by an increasingly big family, Darwin worked as a gentleman scholar pursuing his love of science. Despite proneness to nausea, weakness, headache and palpitations (Miller and Van Loon, 1992), Darwin continued being industrious, patient, meticulous and extremely dedicated.

Contrary to popular perception, Darwin may be the most important humanist in the last 200 or more years. One reason for Darwin's outstanding humanist credentials is that his theory of evolution demolished religious myths about the creation of human life. A considerable period elapsed between his epic 1831–6 voyage around the world as a naturalist on *HMS Beagle* and the 1859 publication of his seminal book *The Origin of Species*. An explanation for the book's delay and for his omitting to include humankind in it may have been his fear of the consequences of blasphemy, then taken much more seriously in Britain than now. A second important humanist credential is that Darwin extended his theory of evolution to provide explanations of human beings' intellectual faculties and their moral sense. Most notably he considered that humankind was capable of improving itself by taking more control over its thinking and by becoming more sympathetic.

Evolutionary theory asserts that the five great vertebrate classes of mammals, birds, reptiles, amphibians, and fishes descended from one prototype. This early progenitor was most likely some fishlike animal with the two sexes united in the same body and with the most important organs of the body, such as the brain and the heart, imperfectly or not at all developed. Over the course of thousands of generations, the process of human evolution has been through a long line of diversified forms through some amphibian-like creature, through an ancient marsupial animal, and then through a hairy-tailed probably arboreal quadruped mammal, to the human species as it is now. However, Darwin cautioned against assuming that the early progenitors of the whole Simian stock, including humans, were identical to or even closely resembled any existing apes or monkeys.

Evolution follows from the principle of natural selection. Natural selection means that, in the struggle for existence involving competition for scarce resources, individuals having any advantage, however slight, over others have the best chance of surviving and of reproducing their kind. Natural selection entails the preservation of favourable variations and the extinction of injurious variations. Among many animals, natural selection is accompanied by sexual selection. Sexual selection consists of two components. First, same-sex individuals, usually males, drive away or kill their rivals, in order to gain access to desirable sexual partners. Second, individuals struggle to excite and charm those of the opposite sex, usually females, so that they will select them as agreeable partners. In sum, *natural selection* depends on the success of both sexes, at any age, in relation to the struggle for existence. *Sexual selection* depends on the success of certain individuals over others of the same sex in relation to the propagation of the species.

Human beings are social animals and primeval man and his ape-like progenitors probably lived in groups. The basis of the social instincts stems from parental and filial affection, which is a trait largely gained from natural selection based on individual advantage. However, natural selection operates at the level of the group or the tribe as well as of the individual. With social animals, natural selection sometimes acts on the individual through the preservation of variations that are beneficial to the community. The social instincts were probably developed in order that those animals that had most to gain from living as a group should be induced to do so.

The small strength and speed of early man, coupled with his want of natural weapons, have contributed to his need to become a social animal, which, in turn, has contributed to the development of his intellectual powers and social qualities, such as giving and receiving aid from his fellows. Darwin observed: 'And natural selection arising from the competition of tribe with tribe … together with the inherited effects of habit, would, under favourable conditions, have sufficed to raise man to his present high position in the organic scale' (Darwin, 1998a, p. 66).

Darwin considered that there was no fundamental difference between human beings and the higher mammals in terms of their mental faculties. Both possess the same faculties of imitation, deliberation, choice, memory, imagination and the association of ideas, although in varying degrees. Language is common to lower animals and human beings: for instance, both use inarticulate cries to express meaning aided by gestures and facial movements. However, human beings are alone in the habitual use of articulate language, their capacity for logical reasoning, in self-consciousness and in their ability to reflect on past and future, life and death and so on. As their intellectual powers became more highly developed, the various parts of the emerging human brain must have become connected by very intricate channels allowing the freest intercommunication. A consequence of this development was that each separate part of the brain would probably react less well in an instinctive manner to particular sensations and associations. Nevertheless, human beings still possess a few instincts in common with the lower animals, for instance self-preservation, sexual desire, the love of the mother for her new born offspring, and the offspring's desire to suck.

Darwin considered the moral sense or conscience to be the most important difference between human beings and lower animals. Moral beings are those capable of reflecting on their actions and motives and of approving of some and disapproving of others. The foundation of the moral qualities lies in the social instincts, the most important elements of which are love and sympathy. Animals endowed with such instincts enjoy one another's company, warn of danger, and defend and look after one another in other ways. However, such social tendencies only extend to their community or tribe, and not to other members of the same species.

The moral sense of human beings is influenced by the approval and disapproval of others. Such moral judgements rest in turn on sympathy, one of the most important elements of the social instincts that evolved due to natural selection. Furthermore, human sympathy, although gained as part of the social instincts, can also be considerably strengthened by exercise or habit – in other words, by practising benevolent thoughts and actions. Ultimately human beings do not accept the praise or blame of their fellows as their sole guide, although they are influential for most people. Instead their usual convictions, controlled by their reason, are more important. Individual conscience then becomes the supreme judge and monitor.

Natural selection, although still important, is not the most important agency in developing humankind's moral qualities. These qualities are advanced much more through the effects of habit, reasoning, instruction and religion. Regarding religion, Darwin saw no evidence that human beings were originally endowed with the belief in the existence of an omnipotent God, although belief in unseen spiritual agencies was universal among the less-civilized races.

Far from possessing a narrow deterministic 'survival of the fittest' explanation of the human condition, Darwin was acutely sensitive to humankind's capacity to improve both its intellectual faculties and its moral sense. As animals move further up the evolutionary scale, they control themselves less by strong instincts and more by learning and thinking. Human beings share some instincts with the lower animals, for instance self-preservation. However, human beings' power of self-consciousness and logical reasoning, coupled with their capacity for sympathy and benevolent actions open the possibility of developing and evolving the species of *Homo sapiens* to greater levels of perfection than attained heretofore.

Evolution of the human forebrain

The human brain, which possesses about 3 lb or 1.5 kg of cells and neural juices, is about triple the size of the nearest non-human primates. The human brain has three regions: hindbrain, midbrain and forebrain. In the 1960s an evolutionary perspective on the development of the human forebrain was proposed by Dr Paul MacLean, Chief of the Laboratory of Brain Research and Evolution at the US National Institutes of Health (MacLean, 1991; Stevens and Price, 2001). MacLean proposed that, over countless millions of years, the human forebrain has evolved and expanded to its great size while retaining commonalities of three neural assemblies reflecting an ancestral relationship to reptiles, early mammals, and late mammals. Together these three assemblies, each of which is very different in their structure and chemistry, represent a unity of three forebrains in the one brain, called by MacLean the *triune brain*.

The innermost core of the human brain is the *reptilian forebrain*, which evolved in humankind's reptilian ancestors about 300 million years ago. Now no reptiles exist directly in line with the mammal-like reptiles regarded as the ancestors of mammals. The reptilian forebrain, whose main structural components are the basal ganglia, contains nuclei vital to the maintenance of life, such as those controlling the cardiovascular and respiratory systems. Furthermore, the reptilian forebrain may be associated, in land animals, with the behaviour involved in their daily routine and in social communication in four main areas, namely signature, challenge, courtship, and submissive displays.

The reptilian forebrain is covered by a layer, called the *paleo-mammalean forebrain*, which is made up of cortical structures that comprise the limbic system. The limbic system is involved in feeling and expressive states essential for self-preservation – namely searching for food, feeding, fighting and self-protection. This system is also implicated in the feeling and expressive states conducive to procreation. By this evolutionary stage of the brain, the feelings and behaviours associated with fear, anger, love and attachment have emerged. Another subdivision of the limbic system possesses a representation of a behavioural triad characterizing the evolutionary transition from reptiles to mammals:

1. nursing in conjunction with maternal care
2. audio-vocal communication for maintaining maternal-offspring contact, and
3. play behaviour.

The innermost two layers of the forebrain are covered by a third layer, which is called the *neo-mammalean forebrain*. This is the neo-cortex, whose expansion has brought about a progressive capacity for solving problems, learning, and memorizing details. The pre-frontal cortex, which is one of the last areas of the human neo-cortex to have undergone great expansion, provides a capacity for insightful identification with other human beings. In addition the pre-frontal cortex is also instrumental in anticipation or foresight and in planning. Behaviour arising in the neo-cortex is usually described as 'conscious', 'voluntary', and 'rational' (Stevens and Price, 2001).

Thus the human forebrain is composed of three central processing assemblies that, although extensively interconnected, can operate somewhat independently. An important problem for humankind is that the two older assemblies are not wired and programmed for the exchange of verbal information. Regarding the paleo-mammalean forebrain, MacLean observed: 'It is profoundly significant that a primitive system of the brain with an incapacity for verbal communication may generate feelings of conviction that we attach to our beliefs, regardless of whether they are true or false' (MacLean, 1991, p. 186).

MacLean goes even further than Darwin, who saw the social instincts as only advancing the interests of the tribe or group, in speculating on the possibility that, through the neo-frontal connections, a parental concern for the young might be expanded to empathy and concern for other members of the human species. If so, this psychological development would amount to an evolution from a primal sense of responsibility to what might be termed human conscience. Furthermore, this concern might extend beyond the human family to all living organisms (Franck, 1991).

When describing the brain's development in his book *Emotional Intelligence*, Daniel Goleman notes the work of Paul MacLean (Goleman, 1995). Goleman considers that human beings can be viewed as having two minds: an emotional mind, related to the brain's limbic system (the paleo-mammalean forebrain), and a rational mind, related to the neo-cortex (the neo-mammalean forebrain). Since the limbic system is the root from which the newer forebrain grew, the emotional areas it houses are inter-connected by a huge number of circuits to all parts of the neo-cortex, which gives it enormous influence over it. Ordinarily, both emotional minds and rational minds work in balance and being in touch with one's emotions can provide vital information for being truly rational. However, when passions surge, the balance can tip so that the rational mind can become hijacked by the emotional mind.

This eruption of more primitive thinking reflects Darwin's final sentence in his book *The Descent of Man*. After extolling human beings' qualities of sympathy and benevolence and their god-like intellect, he then concludes that 'with all these exalted powers – Man still bears in his bodily frame the indelible stamp of his lowly origin' (Darwin, 1998a, p. 643). Sometimes contemporary evolutionary psychology uses the concept of 'evolutionary time lags' to explain the fact that existing human beings are necessarily designed for the previous environments of which they are a product rather than being optimally designed for their current environment (Buss, 1999). Nevertheless, as the cognitive behavioural psychotherapy theorists show, human beings can develop their minds so they are less at risk of being at the mercy of inappropriate primal 'knee-jerk' emotional reactions.

Maslow's humanistic biology

Of all the humanistic writers, the American psychologist Abraham Maslow (1908–70) is possibly the most insightful when it comes to exploring the psycho-biological origins of human motivation. It is a curious and unfortunate gap that Maslow neither cites any Darwin references in the bibliographies of his major books nor in a posthumous collection of his hitherto unpublished papers (Maslow, 1962, 1970, 1971; Hoffman, 1996). Furthermore, some of Maslow's remarks about instinct theory are inaccurate: for example, mentioning that Darwin overlooked co-operation in the animal world and that the theory failed to look at instincts unique to the human species (Maslow, 1970). Nowadays, with the growing prominence of evolutionary psychology and psychiatry, such gaps in his knowledge would have been less likely. The reality is that Maslow would probably have found Darwin's work sympathetic to some of his important propositions.

Maslow was concerned about the extent to which human beings were motivated by their instincts, whether destructiveness was instinctive, whether there were some higher level instinctual remnants in humans, and the relationship between individuals' motivations and the wider societies in which they lived. He distinguished between basic needs and meta-needs, or needs that go higher or beyond basic needs (Maslow, 1969). The basic needs refer to safety and protection, belongingness, love, respect, self-esteem, identity and self-actualization. For animals, instincts are powerful and unmodifiable, yet this is not true for humankind. For human beings, such basic needs or urges are instinctoid, in that, although they may be innately given to at least some appreciable degree, they are nevertheless instinct remnants. Some basic needs may be easily repressed or otherwise controlled. For instance, needs can be easily masked or modified or even suppressed by habits, suggestions, cultural pressures, guilt and so on. Furthermore, as in the case of the psychopathic personality, the instinctoid impulses for loving and being loved can disappear altogether, which is not the case in non-human animals.

A distinction may be made between a good-animal and a bad-animal interpretation of human inner nature (Maslow, 1970). Western civilization has generally believed that the most primitive animal instincts in human beings were bad ones, such as greed, selfishness and hostility. Maslow queries this pessimism without saying that there are no instinctoid tendencies to bad behaviour or to destructiveness. His caution arises partly because there is insufficient knowledge and partly because some evidence exists to contradict such an assertion.

Arguments from animal to human beings should always be held suspect. Aggressiveness in many animals is not primary, but secondary to various determinants, such as threat to territory. When higher animals are studied attacking appears correlated more with dominance, which is related to competition for biological satisfactions such as food and mating, than with aggression. The closer the approach up the phyletic scale to human beings, the evidence for a primary instinct of aggressiveness becomes progressively weaker. The behaviour of anthropoid apes, humankind's closest animal relatives is on the whole pleasant and likeable. Thus, if anything, comparative psychology supports a good-animal rather than a bad-animal interpretation of human nature.

Regarding human beings, what child data existed at the time seemed to show that normal children could be both hostile and selfish and also co-operative and generous. The evidence suggested that there was less destructiveness in children who were basically loved and respected than in those less fortunate. As such, the latter's destructiveness might represent a thwarting of their basic needs. Anthropological data show that in primitive cultures the presence of hostility and destructiveness has a huge range from being nearly absent to being very much present. Maslow's first-hand experience of the co-operative Northern Blackfoot Indians before the Second World War convinced him that destructiveness and aggression were largely culturally determined.

Clinical experience reported in the psychotherapy literature shows that anger, hatred, destructive wishes, and wanting revenge exist in great quantity in practically everyone. Generally, the result of successful therapy is that clients' approach to anger becomes more like Maslow's sample of superior human specimens that he called self-actualizing people. Such superior specimens experienced hostility much less than did average people, could channel their aggression into healthy forms such as self-affirmation and resistance to exploitation, and were able to express their anger more wholeheartedly if and when they did express it. For Maslow, human aggression was more likely to be a secondary or derived behaviour rather than, in whole or in part, the result of some instinct of destructiveness. Maslow adopted a good-animal interpretation of human nature. If anything, humankind's weak instinctoid tendencies are 'good, desirable, and healthy rather than malign or evil' (Maslow, 1970, p. 129). The basic needs of safety and protection, belongingness, love, respect, self-esteem, identity, and self-actualization are biologically based. As such, loss of these basic need satisfactions produces illnesses and deficiency diseases. The basic need deficiency diseases can be termed the neuroses and the psychoses.

Maslow speculates that all human beings also have meta-needs that are biologically based (Maslow, 1969, 1971; Hoffman, 1996). Like the basic needs, the meta-needs – otherwise known as being-needs or growth needs – are instinctoid in that they are rooted in the fundamental structure of the human organism, however weak this genetic connection may be. Motivation based on satisfying or gratifying these being-needs entails a commitment to being-values, including truth, beauty, justice, order, law, and unity. Each person is born with an innate need to experience such higher values. This may be most clearly seen in people already self-actualizing and gratified in their basic needs, who are strongly motivated by their higher needs. Such people invariably have a vocation or calling to some form of beloved work that is outside of themselves.

Both the basic needs and the meta-needs are in the strictest sense biological needs in that their deprivation produces disease or illness. Lack of, or insufficient gratification of, the meta-needs or being-needs produces meta-pathologies. It is as though people have a biologically rooted intrinsic conscience that, if they violate any of the being-values, produces intrinsic guilt. These meta-pathologies are not like normal medical diseases that invade an otherwise intact organism. Instead they are systemic diseases that invade the individual's whole mind and body. For example, definite emotional pathologies have arisen in societies denied truth and justice, for instance in Nazi Germany or in the Soviet Union under Stalin. Furthermore, if people violate any of the being-values, they feel intrinsic guilt because they have transgressed their biologically rooted intrinsic or humanistic conscience.

If human beings are to fulfil their instinctoid potential as good persons, they require good societies in which to do so. Ultimately the good society needs to encompass the whole world. Some societies have social arrangements that set human beings against each other unnecessarily, for instance being based on zero-sum law of the jungle assumptions in which someone's gain is another's loss. Instead it is necessary to create societies that are synergistic in that people can help themselves and others at the same time, be this altruistic or not.

Psychotherapy represents an uncovering, encouraging and releasing of the basic instinctoid needs at the same time as weakening or expunging neurotic needs representing deficiencies in basic need satisfaction. Psychotherapy can also focus on meta-counselling that assumes the active presence in everyone of instinctoid meta-needs for being-values and then provides specific methods for manifesting these values. Maslow pointed out that people often repress their higher as well as their lower potentials. The ultimate goal of therapy is that of authentic people, who have discovered and accepted their own biological, temperamental and constitutional signals from within – their inner voices – and have the courage to act on them. Maslow thought that only about 1 per cent to 3 per cent of the human species had attained person-hood or full humanness (Hoffman, 1996).

Within humanistic psychology, and perhaps psychology in general, Maslow was a pioneer in emphasizing and analysing the instinctive nature of human motivation and behaviour. Maslow did not focus directly on what Darwin called the social instincts and sympathy, but his benign view of human nature provided a welcome relief from those who considered human motivation largely determined mainly either by the environment or by their sexual and aggressive instincts. Maslow emphasized the psychotherapist's role in uncovering clients' basically positive animal nature. Despite advocating a disciplined approach to life, he omitted to mention any direct focus on developing clients' powers of reasoning. In the last fifteen years of Maslow's life, cognitive behaviour therapy, focusing on helping clients to develop their mental process and manage their emotions and behaviour to better effect, was gaining in prominence. However, the author found no references to its two leading proponents, Aaron Beck and Albert Ellis, in the bibliographies of Maslow's main publications.

Cognitive behaviourism and motivation

This section presents the views on the evolutionary and biological basis of human nature and functioning of Burrhus (B. F.) Skinner (1904–90), probably the leading behaviourist experimental psychologist and theorist, Albert Ellis (1913–), who originated rational emotive behaviour therapy, and Aaron Beck (1921–), the founder of cognitive therapy.

Skinner thought that human behaviour was shaped and maintained by its consequences. Behaviour can be either overt or covert. Thinking is covert behaviour, with the most common example being verbal behaviour or internal talking. There is a direct link between covert and overt behaviour in that 'Covert behavior is almost always acquired in overt form, and no one has ever shown that the covert form achieves anything that is out of reach of the overt' (Skinner, 1974, p. 103). The concept of mind is a myth or invention to explain part of the behaviour of an evolving organism.

Skinner, who was familiar with Darwin's work, made a number of observations pertinent to the role of evolution in understanding human behaviour. Where instinctive behaviour leaves off, the process of conditioning takes over. He thought that a capacity to be reinforced by any feedback from the environment would be biologically advantageous (Skinner, 1953). Acknowledging that all reinforcers eventually derive their power from evolutionary selection, Skinner distinguishes between primary and secondary reinforcers. Primary or unconditioned reinforcers are those that have obvious survival value, such as food, water, sexual contact, escape from a dangerous situation and other reinforcers of evident biological significance. Most behaviour is emmited in response to secondary reinforcers that have become associated with or conditioned to primary reinforcers. Secondary reinforcers include money, attention, approval and affection.

Skinner, unlike Darwin, thought that it could not be assumed that the good represented by survival would generally prevail. Human behaviour may have to be explicitly put right by environmental design. Humankind needs to look at the conditions under which people govern, give help, teach and arrange incentive systems in particular ways (Skinner, 1974).

Skinner made a major contribution to psychology by highlighting the role and processes of reinforcement in shaping behaviour. However, he was an experimental psychologist whose subjects tended to be pigeons and rats. Arguably Skinner underestimated the influence of human instincts and instinct remnants. However, conditioning within families, societies and cultures can be so powerful that it has the potential to drown out weak, but adaptive, emotional inner voices, including the instinct remnant of human sympathy. Skinner is inconsistent in saying that there is no such thing as mind at the same time as advocating designing environments for the general good. The latter endeavour both involves mental processes that go beyond conditioned reactions and requires sensitivity to the better parts of humans' underlying animal nature.

Ellis considers that, in all of humankind, a tension exists between two opposing biological creative tendencies (Ellis, 1993, 2000). On the one hand, people have innate tendencies to create, develop and actualize themselves as healthy goal-attaining human beings. They have a great potential to be rational and pleasure producing. On the other hand, they have innate tendencies to create, develop and implement irrational cognitions, unhealthy emotions and dysfunctional behaviours. Rational emotive behavioural therapy (REBT) theorizes that often people are 'biologically predisposed to strongly, passionately, and rigidly construct and hold on to their disturbance-creating musts and other irrational beliefs' (Ellis, 1993, p. 199). Thus, they possess a huge potential to be destructive of themselves and of others, to be illogical and continually to repeat the same mistakes.

Ellis believes that all the major human irrationalities exist in virtually all humans regardless of culture and educational level. Human fallibility has an inherent source. The facts that people seem so easily conditioned into dysfunctional thinking and behaviour and that it is so hard to modify are both viewed as evidence for an innate tendency to irrationality (Ellis, 1980). People's failure to accept reality almost always causes them to manifest the characteristics of emotional disturbance. However, differences exist in genetic predisposition to irrationality.

People can use their biological tendencies to have some degree of free choice to help as well as to damage or disturb themselves. First, they can choose to think differently and more effectively about what is going on. Second, because they possess the capacity to think about how they think, they can choose to acquire and maintain the cognitive skills for containing and counteracting their tendencies to irrationality.

Beck's cognitive therapy starts from the premise that the processing of information is crucial for the survival of any organism. Human beings need to adapt to changing environmental circumstances. Cognition includes the processes involved in identifying and predicting complex relations among events for the purposes of adaptation. Human beings have the capacity both for primal or primitive processing and for higher level cognitive processing.

Schemas are structures that consist of people's fundamental beliefs and assumptions. They are relatively stable cognitive patterns that influence, through people's beliefs, how those people select and synthesize incoming information. Schemas are meaning-making cognitive structures. There are two categories of meaning: first, the objective or public meaning of an event, which may have few significant implications for the individual; and second, its personal or private meaning. Schemas are not pathological by definition – they may be adaptive or maladaptive. Psychopathology is characterized not only by the activation of inappropriate schemas but, in all probability, by their crowding out or inhibiting more adaptive schemas.

Contemporary cognitive theory stresses the concept of modes. Modes are networks of cognitive, affective, motivational and behavioural schemas. Modes are fundamental to personality because they interpret and adapt to emerging and ongoing situations (Beck and Weishaar, 2000). In earlier writings, cognitions were viewed as the mediating variable that triggered people's affective, motivational and behavioural systems. Now, instead of a linear relationship, all aspects of human functioning are viewed as acting together as a mode. Alford and Beck (1997, p. 10) observe: 'The operation of a mode (for example, anger, attack) across diverse psychological systems (emotion, motivation) is determined by the idiosyncratic schematic processing derived from an individual's genetic programming and internalized cultural/social beliefs.'

Modes can be primal, which means that they are universal and linked to survival. Anxiety is an example of a primal mode. Primal modes include primary process thinking that is primitive and that conceptualizes situations in global, rigid, biased and relatively crude ways. Primal modes of thinking may originally have been adaptive in an evolutionary sense, yet they can become maladaptive in everyday life when triggered by systematically biased thinking and misinterpretations. Even personality disorders may be viewed as exaggerated versions of formerly adaptive strategies: for example, the dependent disorder exaggerates attachment and the paranoid disorder exaggerates wariness (Beck, Freeman *et al.*, 1990).

Human beings are also capable of higher levels of cognitive processing to test reality and correct primal, global conceptualizations. However, in psychopathology, these corrective functions become impaired and primary responses can escalate into full-blown psychiatric disorders. Nevertheless, conscious or higher level thinking can override primal thinking and make it more flexible and realistic. Cognitive therapy approaches dysfunctional modes by deactivating them, modifying their content and structure, and by constructing adaptive modes to neutralize them.

The ideas of Beck and Ellis have a different emphasis, but a common theme runs through them. Humans are capable of primitive or highly irrational thinking that is very deeply embedded in their psyche. Such thinking is related to maladaptive or highly inappropriate emotions and behaviour. However, human beings are also capable of higher level or rational thinking. Furthermore they are capable of developing these higher level or rational capacities so as to process information, feel and behave much more adaptively.

Possibly another way of making these points is to say that human beings can be heavily influenced by the primal emotions and pre-verbal 'thoughts' of their paleo-mammalean forebrain together with the insufficient development of their neo-mammalean forebrain so that they become irrational, process information rigidly and behave inappropriately. However, human beings can develop and be helped to develop the reasoning ability of their neo-mammalean forebrain or neo-cortex to counteract such primitively based irrational tendencies and thus to exercise more control over their thinking, emotions and behaviour.

Cognitive humanism and motivation

The following points attempt to clarify a cognitive humanistic view of the nature of human nature and motivation.

1. Human beings possess relatively strong instincts or instinct remnants in relation to the four Ps of genetic survival: namely, procreation, preservation, protection and power. These four functions overlap and combine to serve the common purpose of perpetuating the species within the broad framework of evolutionary theory. For example, power to select mates leads to procreation, the offspring of which require preservation, for instance food and shelter, and protection from external threats, as do those responsible for maintaining their lives. Important human motivators associated with procreation, preservation, protection and power include sexual urges, attachment needs of parents and offspring, impulses to gather food, aggression and dominance.

2. Human beings are social animals, who possess what Darwin called the social instincts, important amongst which are sympathy and love. Humans are also tribal animals whose social instincts have a tendency to extend mainly, if not exclusively, to members identified as being of their own group. Over time, co-operation between human beings and their less-evolved forebears has served numerous functions connected with preservation and protection, such as group hunting, providing calls warning of threats, and group attacks on predators. Co-operation is also involved in sexual activity, rearing of offspring and in play. Humankind's primitive forebears communicated by means of pre-verbal vocal language and by body language.

3. Human beings are feeling animals, with the most fundamental basis of their feelings stemming from their instincts and instinct remnants. For example, the feeling of anxiety is associated with threats to procreation, preservation, protection and power. Probably, the underlying

source of anxiety is fear of death. The paleo-mammalean forebrain (limbic system) is involved in important feelings and expressive states related to self-preservation and preservation of the species. Prior to the development of verbal language, any thinking connected with feelings would probably have been visual.

4. Unlike Maslow, the author would answer his question 'Is destructiveness instinctoid?' (Maslow, 1970) with a definite 'yes'. Both for purposes of natural selection and sexual selection, competitive destructiveness formed part of the behaviour of *Homo sapiens*' less-evolved forebears and remains an instinctive derivative in the paleo-mammalean forebrain.

5. Human beings are thinking animals, whose mental processes now take place in words as well as images. The evolutionary expansion of the neo-mammalean forebrain (neo-cortex) has afforded a progressively greater capacity for reasoning, self-consciousness, memory, learning, foresight and sympathetic identification with other individuals. The higher up the phyletic scale organisms are, the less their feelings and behaviour are controlled by instincts and instinct remnants. The way human beings think can greatly influence how they feel and communicate/act. Human beings are the only animals that possess the capacity to think about how they think. This capacity provides them with the opportunity to assume greater control over how they think, which they may use for either life-affirming or destructive purposes. In the next chapter it is proposed that the way human beings think is best thought of in terms of a repertoire of mind skills.

6. Human motivation can take place at various levels of consciousness. Think of a pyramid consisting, from the top down, of the three levels of consciousness, preconsciousness and the unconscious. The top tip is a tiny area of here-and-now awareness or consciousness. Beneath that is a much, much larger preconscious level of material that, although potentially accessible, may not be in awareness at any given moment because it is not thought particularly relevant, or because it is being partially distorted, or perhaps even being denied. The kind of thinking in this second level includes automatic thoughts that take place below the level of consciousness and repetitive sub-vocalizations of varying levels of rationality. The pyramid's third and largest area consists of the unconscious. Jung divided the unconscious into the personal unconscious and the collective unconscious (Jung, 1966). Perhaps a better way of viewing the collective unconscious is to think of it as the species unconscious consisting of the deeper evolutionary foundations of the human psyche. Human beings can use repression to remain unaware of not just their personally, socially and culturally disapproved motivations but of their social instincts as well.

7. Human motivation is shaped by learning that can take place in numerous contexts, such as families, peer groups, schools, and wider societies and cultures. Three main avenues for such learning are conditioning, or learning from consequences, modelling, or learning from observation, and instruction, or learning from direct and indirect teaching. External learning can influence the growth and development of the human organism for good or ill. Human diminution, consisting of a crippling of or weakening of the capacity to develop life-affirming innate potentials, can result from a range of possible negative learning experiences. Cultures and societies are very powerful in either motivating people to become or hindering them from becoming more fully human. The new communication technologies, such as television and the Internet, provide avenues for enhancing or retarding humanity.

8. The seeds for the development of a humanistic conscience exist in the social instincts, including human sympathy, and in human beings' capacity to improve their mental processes. However, as human history so amply attests, the widespread development of people with humane consciences that allow them to feel compassionate sympathy with the other members of the human species and to act benevolently towards them cannot be left to chance. Because of their highly developed cognitive capacities, human beings are at a stage of their development as a species where they can assume considerable responsibility for how they evolve. The challenge of cognitive humanism is to uncover and release the human potential for sympathy and to cultivate reason both to strengthen this constructive potential and to curb destructive instinct remnants. It is imperative that the human species shapes its future motivation so as to ensure its survival and enhancement. Reason and love must be developed together in the interests of present and future generations.

THREE Human-being Skills

Human beings are distinguished from other animals by the weakness of their instincts and by the extent of their mental capacities. However, to take full advantage of their capacity to evolve themselves, they require a conceptual framework or language with which to do so. This chapter explores some of the basic concepts of the cognitive humanistic approach to psychotherapy, self-therapy and personal practice.

Cognitive humanism and skills

The issue of what constitutes a skilled human being is fundamental to counselling and psychotherapy and, accordingly, the concept of skills is central to the cognitive humanistic approach. To date, strangely enough, the theory and practice of psychotherapy have not placed a major emphasis on explicitly identifying and imparting skills to clients. Psychoanalysis, analytical therapy, person-centred therapy and gestalt therapy do not clearly advocate teaching skills to clients. Even the psychological education approaches to therapy, such as Ellis's rational emotive behavior therapy, Beck's cognitive therapy and Lazarus's multimodal therapy are not predominantly framed in the language of training clients in skills. However, in the cognitive-behavioural literature references are made to skills, such as assertion and friendship, but rarely to cognitive or mind skills. The multicultural counselling and therapy literature stresses therapist competencies or skills (for example, Sue *et al.*, 1998) independently of training clients in skills. Furthermore, professional training in the West heavily emphasizes teaching clinical and counselling skills to students without acknowledging that therapists and counsellors are only skilled to the extent that they can impart skills to their clients. If we can have skilled therapists and counsellors, why can't we have skilled clients too?

There are many potential advantages to thinking about human beings, clients and their problems in skills terms. First, attempts can be made to identify and define the skills that people and clients require if they are to function effectively. Second, the concept of skills provides a focus for training people in human-being skills. Already much successful training takes place without using the concept of skills. For example, children reared in loving and nurturing environments are more likely to possess the skills of relating to other people warmly than those children who are emotionally abused or deprived. Nevertheless, further work in identifying and articulating what are desirable human-being skills might lead to better child-rearing practices. Third, in therapy, the use of skills language provides a framework for assessing clients and for identifying the mind skills and communication/action skills they need to improve. Furthermore, derived from such assessments, therapists and clients can select interventions designed to build clients' skills. Fourth, the concept of skills provides both clients and non-clients alike with a self-help framework for monitoring, improving and, where necessary, self-correcting how well they use their mind skills and communication/action skills.

Given such advantages, why has there not been a rush by therapists to use the concept of skills? This is explicable from a humanistic psychotherapy viewpoint in that humanistic approaches emphasize dealing with whole persons. These psychotherapies are terrified of anything that might seem to dehumanize clients by taking a mechanical approach to them, paying insufficient attention to their feelings and bodily sensations, and so undermining their basic authenticity. However, dealing with wholes and parts need not be mutually exclusive. Sometimes the best way to integrate the parts may be to work with the whole person. On other occasions the best way to help people to become integrated wholes may be to strengthen the parts. Furthermore, some clients may require a whole person focus and also a focus on particular skills, although not necessarily at the same time.

The resistance to using the concept of skills in the psychodynamic approaches may partly lie in their major emphasis on the expertise of the therapist to work with clients' unconscious processes. However, some client-focused activities, such as Jung's use of active imagination, lend themselves to being imparted as self-help skills (Jung, 1968).

The fact that the concept of skills in the cognitive behaviour therapies has mainly been restricted to overt behavioural skills rather than to cognitive skills is harder to explain. There is some evidence that this state of affairs may be changing. For instance, the prologue to Greenberger and Padesky's popular cognitive therapy client self-help manual *Mind Over Mood* (1995) explicitly states that the book teaches *skills* (author's italics) necessary for making fundamental changes in moods, behaviours, and relationships.

Defining human-being skills

Apart from such obviously biological functions as breathing, virtually all human behaviour can be viewed in terms of human-being skills. One meaning of the word 'skills' pertains to *areas* of skill. For instance, albeit overlapping, broad areas of skills include: relating skills, study skills, leisure skills, health skills and work skills. A second meaning of the word skills refers to *level of competence* or expertise. For instance, in a specific area of skill people can be skilled, unskilled or a mixture of the two. The third meaning of the word 'skills' is less common. This meaning relates to the knowledge and *sequence of choices* entailed in implementing a skill. The concept of skills is best viewed not in either/or terms in which a person either possesses or does not possess a skill. Rather, in any area of skill, it is preferable to think of people as possessing either good skills or poor skills, or a mixture of the two. If they make good choices, this is a strength. If they make poor choices, this is a deficiency. In all areas of skill, in varying degrees, human beings are likely to possess elements of both good skills and poor skills.

The term 'human-being skills' in itself is a neutral concept. Human-being skills may be positive or negative depending on the extent to which they help people to survive and to maintain and develop potentials. A neutral definition is that *'Human-being skills are sequences of choices that people make in specific areas of skill'*. However, the above can be transformed into a positive cognitive humanistic definition: namely, *'Human-being skills are sequences of choices characterizing the good person that people make across a range of areas.'*

The two broad areas of human-being skills are communication/action skills and mind skills. Feelings and physical reactions are not skills in themselves as they reflect the underlying animal nature of humans. The distinction between thoughts and mental processes, external communications and actions, and feelings and physical reactions can be complex because they interact with and influence each other. For example, a specific external communication can produce consequences that generate thoughts and feelings that may or may not increase the probability of the original communication being repeated. Another example is that suggested in the previous chapter where primal feelings, reflecting the paleo-mammalean forebrain, become activated so as to cause highly inappropriate thinking and communication/actions. A further example is that people's thoughts can be viewed as either hot, or warm or cool depending on the intensity of anger attached to them.

Communication/action skills

Communication and action skills involve observable behaviours. They are what people do and how they do it rather than what and how they feel and think. For instance, it is one thing to feel human sympathy, and another to act on this feeling. People need to communicate and act if they want to show their sympathy and compassion for other human beings. Communication and action skills vary by area of application: for instance, relating, study, work, leisure, health and social participation. Box 3.1 presents the five main ways in which human beings can send communication/action skills messages.

Box 3.1: Five main ways of sending communication/action skills messages

Verbal messages: messages that people send with words.

Voice messages: messages that people send through their voice: for example, through volume, articulation, pitch, emphasis and speech rate.

Body messages: messages that people send with their bodies, for instance through their gaze, eye contact, facial expression, posture, gestures, physical proximity and clothes and grooming.

Touch messages: a special category of body messages. Messages that people send with their touch through the part of body that they use, what part of another's body they touch, how gentle or firm they are, and whether or not they have permission.

Action-taking messages: messages that people send when they are not face-to-face with others, for example sending flowers or a legal writ.

How people communicate and act can never be divorced from how they think. For example relationship skills such as becoming more outgoing, listening better, showing caring, sharing intimacy, enjoying sex together, managing anger and communicating assertively, and managing relationship problems each contain two elements: creating skilful communications and creating skilful thinking to support and guide the skilful communications (Nelson-Jones, 1999).

Mind skills

The previous chapter mentioned the evolution of the human brain. To alter one's own or another's behaviour without recourse to drugs or surgery, it is useful to have the concept of 'mind'. While a person's mind is a central integrating concept in Buddhist psychology, it is curiously absent in Western cognitive and cognitive behavioural psychology. A person's mind is a complex entity ultimately based on physical processes located mainly in the brain. It is the seat of awareness, thought, imagery, volition, feeling and of personal identity and agency.

People's minds are subject to a flow of experiencing and, as such, the mind has the function of a thought, imagery, sensation and feeling generator of its own accord. However, human beings also have the capacity to influence and to create their minds. The mind possesses a super-cognitive capacity that enables individuals to think about their thinking. To a large extent, human beings can choose the content of their minds, what they think about. In addition, they can exert control over their mental processes. Furthermore, human beings can consciously train their minds to develop and engage in mental processes that cultivate happiness and lessen or eliminate self-created suffering.

Mind skills are mental processes in which people can be trained and train themselves. Box 3.2 provides brief descriptions of seven central mind skills derived from the work of leading cognitive therapists, such as Aaron Beck and Albert Ellis.

Box 3.2: Seven central mind skills

Creating awareness: people develop their capacity to become aware of their feelings, physical sensations and thoughts. They can observe, listen to and become mindful of the flow of their inner and outer experiencing and allow it to unfold without feeling the need to direct it in any way. Unlike the other mind skills, which are more active, creating awareness can be a receptive or passive mind skill.

Creating rules: people's rules make irrational and unrealistic demands on themselves, others, and the environment. For instance, 'I must always be happy', 'others must look after me', and 'my environment should not contain any suffering'. Instead they can develop preferential rules: for instance, 'I prefer to be happy much of the time, but it is unrealistic to expect this all the time.'

Creating perceptions: people can avoid perceiving themselves and others either too negatively or too positively by testing the reality of their perceptions. They can distinguish between fact and

---

inference and make their inferences as accurate as possible. Furthermore, they can create compassionate rather than negative perceptions of the human race.

Creating self-talk: instead of talking to themselves negatively before, during and after specific situations, people can acknowledge that they have choices and make coping self-statements that assist them to stay calm and cool, establish goals, coach themselves in what to do, and affirm the strengths, skills and support factors that they possess.

Creating visual images: people can use visual images in ways that calm them down, assist them in acting competently to attain their goals, and help them to resist giving in to bad habits.

Creating explanations: people can explain the causes of events accurately. They avoid assuming too much responsibility by internalizing, 'It's all my fault', or externalizing, 'It's all other people's fault'.

Creating expectations: people can be realistic about the risks and rewards of future actions. They can assess threats and dangers accurately and avoid distorting relevant evidence with unwarranted optimism or pessimism. Their expectations about how well they will communicate and act are accurate.

In reality, some of the mind skills overlap. For instance, all of the skills, even visualizing, involve self-talk. However, here self-talk refers to self-statements relevant to coping with specific situations. Interrelationships between skills can also be viewed on the dimension of depth. Arguably, people who believe in the rule 'I must always be happy' are more prone to perceiving events as negative than those who do not share this belief.

Levels of human-being skills

There is nothing new about viewing levels of human functioning in skills terms. Buddhist psychology does not use the noun skills as such, but contemporary Buddhist writers, including the current Dalai Lama, frequently use the adjective 'skilful'. Joseph Goldstein, a prominent American teacher of Buddhist insight meditation, observes that 'skilful' in the

Buddhist sense refers to that which leads to happiness or freedom, whereas 'unskilful' refers to that which leads to suffering (Goldstein, 1994). Echoing the above distinction between mind skills and communication/ action skills, Goldstein distinguishes between skilful states of mind, comprising both thoughts and feelings, and skilful actions.

Approaches to discussing and assessing levels of human-being skills can range from focusing on the general or overall skill levels of individuals to identifying their levels of competence in specific skills areas. Generally speaking people can be divided into three levels of overall human-being skills: sub-normal, normal, and supra-normal. People with sub-normal skills function below the level of the population of which they are a part, people with normal skills function at or around the average, whereas people with supra-normal skills function well above the average. Take the broad area of relating to others. A person with subnormal mind skills and communication skills may consistently act out of narrow self-interest, often at the expense of others. Those with normal mind skills and communication skills might act considerately much of the time to those within their family, social and cultural group and probably even to those outside it, although less so. The person with supra-normal mind skills and communication skills might have compassion and benevolence as a way of life, yet act assertively to protect self and others when necessary.

Towards the end of Chapter 1 it was mentioned that cognitive humanistic therapy consists of two kinds of therapy, albeit somewhat overlapping: adaptation CHT for attaining normal levels of functioning and mental cultivation CHT for those who want to attain supra-normal levels of functioning. At the commencement, during and at the end of each kind of therapy, therapist and client can assess levels of specific mind skills and specific communication/action skills and identify any requiring improvement. In addition, after therapy, clients can monitor their levels of specific skills and, as necessary, modify how they think and communicate. Furthermore, monitoring one's levels of and use of specific human-being skills can form an integral part of personal practice independent of therapists.

Species-wide or universal human-being skills

Are there species-wide or universal human-being skills? Apart from a personal contribution (Nelson-Jones, 2002c), nowhere in the psychotherapy theory and the multicultural literature has the author seen the issue addressed of whether there are species-wide human-being skills that underlie and transcend cultural diversity. Species-wide or universal human-being skills can be defined as skills that characterize good or effective people regardless of the culture or country in which they live.

Arguably the widespread possession of such skills throughout the world is fundamental to creating happiness and avoiding suffering on a daily basis. Furthermore, the survival of the species depends on the existence of sufficient good or skilled human beings to protect the interests of future generations. Currently human beings, in their dealings with one another, are not nearly as skilled as they should be to make the world a happier and safer place. Not to apply the concept of skills to human functioning leaves a huge gap in thinking about how to improve the human condition.

Almost certainly there are species-wide human-being skills. Furthermore, human beings have the potential to develop such skills to a high level. Family and social environments differ across cultures, but certain values and skills of the good person almost certainly transcend culture (Schwartz, 1992). One possible reason for this is that such skills are ultimately grounded in human biology and the evolutionary imperative to protect the survival of the species.

It is probably more important to define universal mind skills than universal communication/action skills. One of the Buddha's sayings is 'As the shadow follows the body, as we think, so we become.' Put another way, most skilful communication and action follow from skilful thinking. For instance, compassionate actions are likely to follow from compassion-enhancing perceptions and beliefs. When identifying what are universally desirable mind skills, one can draw upon the wisdom and traditions of Eastern and other cultures as well as those of the West. Partly because they are observable, human beings may have more latitude for cultural diversity in communication/action skills than in mind skills. Much more effort needs to be put into identifying what are universal human-being skills before it is too late. The human species' capacity to destroy itself seems to be increasingly outreaching its ability for skilful and harmonious living. A starting point is to gain much more widespread recognition that psychotherapy and counselling, as well as everyday life, can profit from being viewed within a human-being skills framework.

Mind, feelings and physical reactions

People are human animals. Cognitive humanistic therapy does not ignore feelings and physical reactions. Quite the reverse: it actively encourages people to feel happy and fulfilled and to avoid suffering. In addition, the approach encourages people to get in touch with their instinctually derived tendencies towards goodness and sympathy. An overriding goal of CHT is to help humans to experience themselves and others compassionately and deeply and to communicate and act appropriately. Nevertheless feelings and physical reactions, however low or lofty, are not in themselves skills, but rather part of humankind's animal nature. The way people can influence how they experience, express and manage their feelings is through altering their minds and by changing how they communicate and act.

A focus on developing the mind enhances people's abilities to experience a range of emotions that manifest their underlying animal nature. It can liberate rather than stifle the capacity to feel fully human. Generally people feel better and enjoy enhanced health when they feel genuine affection for others rather than anger and alienation. The way people can increase their chances of feeling more affection and less anger is through cultivating their minds and altering their communication/actions. Another example of the connection between mind, feelings and physical reactions comes from sexual behaviour. How people think about sex strongly influences how well they perform. Noted sex therapists and sexual behaviour researchers Masters and Johnson stated that inhibitions and guilt, performance anxiety, erotic boredom, and blind acceptance of sexual misinformation accounted for about 80 per cent of sexual dissatisfaction in American society (Masters, Johnson and Kolodny, 1986).

Further concepts in cognitive humanism

The self

The Western construct of self can be viewed within the framework of mind. There are three main components. First, there is the natural self or a person's underlying animal nature, instincts, instinct remnants and unique propensities. Second, there is the learned self, which is the product of parental, social, cultural and other learning influences as well as of what the individual has made of them. This learned self consists of mental self-conceptions, what the person refers to as 'I' or 'me'. The learned self also consists of mind skills and communication/action skills, which are often not clearly acknowledged as part of the self because most people do not think of themselves in skills terms. Third, there is the choosing self or executive self, which represents people's capacities to make their lives through their present and future choices. Thus people not only have existing mental concepts of themselves but they can use their minds to create different self-concepts and to think and act more skilfully.

Buddhist psychology, with its concept of *anatta* or no-self, raises at least two important issues. The first issue is that of whether it is desirable to attain what might be termed a selfless or ego-less state of being. If this is not the case, the second issue becomes that of the extent to which people should place limits on their attachments and identifications with various aspects of their view of themselves. Unlike Buddhism, cognitive humanistic therapy does not seek to do away with the concept of the self, but rather to refine it. Both the adaptation and the mental cultivation parts of CHT seek to make the self or ego more efficient by limiting and/or attempting to eliminate unwholesome attachments and identifications related to one's concept of oneself, such as excessive craving for money, status and approval.

Innate goodness

Every person has a biologically based inner nature comprised of elements that are common to the species and those that are unique to the individual. Much of Western thinking sees this inner nature as egotistic, selfish and destructive, summed up in one of Freud's favourite quotes, which came from the Roman writer Plautus: 'Man is a wolf to man.' This 'bad-animal' view of humankind tends to be based on those who are not functioning at a high level rather than on the psychologically healthiest human beings (Maslow, 1971). Furthermore, it ignores the ample evidence that human beings can be co-operative and caring as well as hostile and uncaring (Argyle, 1991; Beck, 1999).

As indicated in the previous chapter, the matter of instincts and instinct remnants is complex. Human instincts overlap, can be of varying degrees of strength, are inter-connected to different parts of the evolving brain, and those instincts and instinct remnants with positive and negative outcomes can be mixed together. The position taken here regarding the basic 'goodness' or 'badness' of human nature is neutral in that, at its deepest levels, human nature is both sublime and savage. Consequently, human beings have the potential to act constructively and destructively in their daily lives. How well people handle their inner nature is largely a matter of training and mental development, and of how much this nature is encouraged or frustrated by the larger groupings in which they live.

It is vitally important to acknowledge humankind's innate goodness and not just to focus on aggressive and destructive tendencies. Allport (1964) observed that debasing theoretical assumptions degrade human beings and generous assumptions exalt them. Innate goodness refers to the positive core of one's being, which encompasses instinctual tendencies towards affirming life, affiliation, attachment, co-operation, compassion, nurturing, caring and benevolence. At its most highly developed level, innate goodness is striving to cultivate the happiness and eliminate the suffering of oneself, others and the human species. People who are truly in touch with their core of innate goodness are capable of transcending the boundaries between self, others and the human species to act in the interests of all.

The capacity for human sympathy is a central element in the concept of innate goodness. Darwin (1998a) saw sympathy as one of the cardinal social instincts. An important goal of cognitive humanistic therapy, especially of mental cultivation CHT, is to foster human sympathy. Human sympathy can be defined as identifying and feeling a sense of fellowship with others who are made of the same human clay, go through the same cycle of birth, life and death, and who want to be happy and to avoid suffering just like oneself. Human sympathy entails the capacity for compassion and for enhancing oneself and others through giving.

Adler's concept of social interest comes close to describing human sympathy. Social interest means community spirit, a sense of human fellowship and identity with the whole of humanity. Social interest begins with the ability to empathize with fellow human beings, and leads to the striving for an ideal community based on co-operation and personal equality (Adler, 1998). Beck (1999) has also noted the human capacity for sympathy. He contrasts the altruistic mode, favouring others, with the narcissistic mode, favouring the self. In the altruistic mode people obtain gratification from subordinating their needs to others and are vigilant about protecting the rights of underdogs, the underprivileged and the disadvantaged. However, people can alternate between narcissistic and altruistic modes depending on circumstances.

Suffering

To some extent suffering and happiness are two sides of the same coin. To the extent that people are not suffering, they are happy and vice versa. Suffering is defined here as experiencing any form of dissatisfaction or discomfort, however minor or major. Suffering may range from undergoing life's minor upsets and hassles to its major tragedies. As suffering is inextricably woven into the fabric of all lives, it may be better to see the aim of life as the reduction of suffering rather than the pursuit of happiness. Certainly a balance needs to be struck between these two overlapping objectives.

There are numerous causes of suffering, which can overlap and interact. Existential suffering is the lot of all human beings who are faced with universal processes of birth, aging, dying and the death of themselves and their loved ones, friends and others. Loss of physical powers and poorer health can be part of the process of growing older. Pain is a form of suffering produced by illness, injury or other strong or harmful physical contact. Physical deprivation is another form of suffering caused by insufficient access to such basic requirements as food, shelter and rest. Fate or being the victim of uncontrollable events, such as natural disasters or car crashes, can also cause suffering.

Suffering can be psychological as well as physical or a mixture of the two. Existential suffering frequently involves coming to terms with loss:

for instance, the death of others and the weakening of one's own capacities. Physical pain can have a large psychological component in creating the pain, for instance ulcers, and in dealing with it well or poorly. The effects of physical deprivation and the exigencies of fate can also be influenced by the mental attitude adopted towards them. An inspiring example is that of the founder of logotherapy, Viktor Frankl (1905–97), who found the inner strength to triumph mentally over the tragedy of being incarcerated in a series of Nazi concentration camps (Frankl, 1963).

Psychological suffering can also be caused by emotional crippling and human diminution resulting from others' actions. Tragically, in families this deprivation can extend over generations with the poor parenting skills of one generation creating emotional problems in the next generation which contribute to them using poor parenting skills with their offspring and so on. Furthermore, people in all walks of life from the lowly to the most powerful can possess poor human-being skills that cause others to suffer.

Much suffering is self-created in that people fail to use good mind skills and communication/action skills and, in so doing, harm themselves and others who may then harm them back in return. Greed for such things as money, possessions, status and reputation can be a major cause of self-created suffering. Uncalled-for anger and aggression is another cause. Self-created suffering mainly results from an insufficiently disciplined mind, the causes of which may be many and varied: for instance, never having learned the importance of and some key skills for disciplining one's mind.

Two further forms of suffering are inability to find meaning and alienation. Viktor Frankl stressed the need for all human beings to find meanings in their lives. He used the term 'existential vacuum' to describe the widespread difficulty many in the West experience in finding any meaning in their lives and 'existential neurosis' to describe the resultant suffering (Frankl, 1963, 1975). The existential vacuum describes a state in which people feel an inner void and suffer from a sense of meaninglessness, emptiness and futility. Related to meaninglessness, increasingly many people feel alienated, isolated and estranged from the wider societies in which they live. Religious leaders like the current Dalai Lama and Mother Teresa have observed that people in the affluent West can suffer intensely because of the way in which these cultures fail to meet their basic instinctually derived human needs: for example, someone or some group that genuinely cares for them.

Another form of suffering is that of failing to fulfil one's potential for innate goodness. People can lead narrow and selfish lives instead of being a positive force in their own and others' lives, transcending and fusing the boundaries between self-interest and human sympathy. Resultant forms of suffering can include diminished self-esteem, lack of self-respect, inability to form genuinely deep relationships with others, lack of respect from others, obtaining too few of the satisfactions and joys of giving, and diminished zest for life. Arguably, in varying degrees, all but the most emotionally crippled of people develop some form of humanistic conscience with rules about safeguarding the welfare of others and the human species. Humanistic guilt, with accompanying feelings of discomfort and lowered self-esteem, can be a further form of suffering for those who narrowly pursue their own agendas at others' expense.

An issue related to suffering is the extent to which people are aware of it when it happens. In an area of suffering, like not having enough to eat, people's bodies give them loud and clear signals that they are suffering. However, becoming aware of forms of suffering like one's own poor personal relationships, meaninglessness, alienation and fulfilling too little of one's potential for innate goodness can be much more difficult. People can build up varying defenses against acknowledging both the shadow and brighter sides of their nature. Furthermore, societies and cultures can collude in obscuring sources of suffering, for instance by placing too high a value on the pursuit of personal happiness rather than by taking a more balanced approach to life.

Happiness and fulfilment

Happiness tends to be a word applied to many states, perhaps the main ones being pleasure and contentment. Happiness can consist of absence of negative experiences as well as presence of positive experiences. In regard to the satisfaction or removal of a deprivation it can incorporate anticipation, the act of removing the deprivation, and remembrance: for example anticipating eating, eating, and remembering eating. However, there are also states where the process of attaining an outcome is rewarding rather than just the outcome itself. Furthermore, people can follow a way of life that is rewarding, although at times it may not bring happiness.

One form of happiness is *survival happiness* in which basic needs for protection, food and shelter are being met. Happiness to a Third World peasant may be a full belly. Another form of happiness is *hedonic happiness* based on pleasurable or rewarding experiences. For the rich person, it is not only the quantity but the quality of food that is important. Hedonic happiness can cover a range of gratifying experiences such as sex, vacations, aesthetic pleasures, food, spending money on desired objects, getting other people's approval for doing something, and so on. An important feature of hedonic happiness is that it tends not to last – the car that was wonderful last year may not be experienced as so exciting this year. There is a large mental component in hedonic happiness. One mental consideration is that such happiness often tends to be more a matter of how people perceive their situations rather than of the absolute conditions in their life, such as being rich or poor. Both survival and fulfilment happiness often involve the temporary satisfaction of a need or craving that is likely to recur.

Fulfilment happiness tends to involve longer term and deeper sources of satisfaction, which are not necessarily associated with hedonic happiness. People can obtain fulfilment happiness in many areas of life such as from mutually rewarding relationships and finding meaningful challenges in their work. A prime source of fulfilment happiness consists of feelings of contentment, self-worth, self-respect and wellbeing arising from connecting with the positive core of one's own or of another's being. As such fulfilment happiness exists in being, over a period of time, the generator, giver or recipient of thoughts and actions reflecting innate goodness. This source of fulfilment happiness may be more aligned to the meeting of underlying social instincts than to short term considerations of pleasure. An example of the difference between fulfilment and hedonic happiness is that of parents who willingly experience less hedonic happiness in order to gain the deeper fulfilment happiness of helping their offspring to obtain some chances in life that they never had.

People may have varying levels of awareness about how happy and fulfilled they are. Sometimes, because of the pressure to seem happy in Western cultures, they try to convince themselves and others that they are happier than is really the case. On other occasions, they may only realize how happy and fulfilled they were when they no longer receive one or more former satisfactions. Many people extend their conceptions of themselves to include what they perceive as their possessions, for instance money, property, clothes, cars and even people. They then attach their happiness to these possessions and, if they are not careful, set themselves up for being very unhappy when there is a diminution or loss of any of these so-called possessions.

Impermanence, interdependence and insignificance

Humanism requires humility about the role of human beings both collectively and as individuals in the grand scheme of nature. Awareness of impermanence, interdependence and insignificance may contribute to people having a more realistic view of themselves and of the limitations and existential boundary conditions of the human species. Humanism is not about making human beings into idolatrous objects but about striving to maximize the human potential with all its inherent fallibility and strengths.

The Buddhist religious tradition stresses being mindful of *impermanence* or of the transitory nature of everything in life. All human beings go through the process of birth, maturation, decline and death. Even in life their bodies are continually changing as their cells are regularly replaced. Furthermore, people's thoughts are in a continual process of change: for instance, the content of consciousness is always changing. In the surrounding environment, all natural organisms, be they animals, plants or whatever, eventually die. The natural environment is always changing, sometimes slowly as over the course of evolutionary history, and sometimes much more rapidly. Similarly, nothing is permanent in people's relationships to one another and the societies in which they live. Recently, the pace of technological change has highlighted issues of change and obsolescence.

The meaning of *interdependence* can be viewed in at least two ways. Firstly, all things have causes. Regarding this kind of interdependence the Dalai Lama observes: 'This implies that there is no creator; things depend only on their own causes and those causes in turn have their own causes, with no beginning' (Dalai Lama, 2000, p. 30). On the level of the individual, how people feel, think and behave at any given moment both have their causes and in turn act as causes for other causes and so on. Secondly, interdependence can mean that all individuals depend throughout their life-span on other individuals, on the fruits of their efforts, and on nature to provide the necessities of living for them. For instance, when young, very sick and old, humans are dependent on others for care. As social animals, they need one another as mates, parents, friends and mutual protectors. Furthermore, especially with the increase in world trade, much of what people consume involves the labour of others to garner, transform and transport nature's bountifulness.

Regarding *insignificance*, at the same time that each human being is precious, everyone is just a small part of the earth's currently more than six billion people and rapidly growing overall population. Each generation is a miniscule part of the evolution of the human species. Furthermore the earth itself is just a minute part of a seemingly infinite cosmos, the immensity of which most people's minds cannot even begin to grasp. A light-year is the distance at which light will journey in a year, travelling at the approximate rate of 186,000 miles per second. Spong observes 'The nearest star to our sun, Alpha Centauri, is about 4.3 light-years away. The large Magellanic cloud, the nearest galaxy to our galaxy, is about 150,000 light-years away. Andromeda, the nearest clearly defined galaxy is 2,000,000 light-years away' (Spong, 1998, p. 33). In the face of nature's vast scope, humility on the part of humankind is clearly in order. Nature is indifferent to and capricious about the existence of individual human beings and, quite conceivably, about the continued existence of the human species.

FOUR   Being Fully Human

Reason and love, or head and heart, are the twin pillars of the cognitive humanistic approach to being fully human. Human beings possess the potential to cultivate their minds so that they can influence and control their primitive destructive urges and release and develop their social instincts. As such, being fully human can be seen in terms of attaining personal excellence in two main areas: namely, human sympathy and mental cultivation. Human sympathy and mental cultivation are closely related in that external communications and actions showing human sympathy are important manifestations of internal mental cultivation. Good deeds tend to follow from and represent good thoughts.

Human sympathy

Human sympathy may be viewed in terms of different levels or stages. Discussing what absence or insufficiency of human sympathy means can help to illuminate it. It is also important to try to define what the higher levels of human sympathy are, to show human capabilities, and to look at the stars as well as at the ground. Furthermore, human sympathy can be viewed as a progressive scale in which each person functions predominantly at a certain level during a given period of time, with movement in either direction being possible. When some people gain insight into – and possibly dissatisfaction with – their current level of human sympathy they may be motivated to go further along the path of transcending and transforming themselves to become more sympathetic and loving.

Box 4.1 presents five levels of human sympathy: egocentric, restricted, reciprocal, enhanced and committed. These levels are just approximate signposts along the range of possibilities from egocentricity to synergistically caring for the welfare and wellbeing of oneself, others and the human species. A number of themes are implicit or explicit in the five levels of human sympathy. An important theme relates to Maslow's (1962, 1970) distinction between deficiency-motivation and growth-motivation.

At the lower end of the human sympathy scale, people's deficiencies in self-love motivate them to become inward looking and selfish. At the higher end, their level of self-love is such that they can transcend themselves by identifying with and being truly loving to their fellow human beings. Thus, there are many ways of relating ranging from being almost solely self-centred to being other-centred and species-centred as part of valuing and expressing one's humanity.

A connected theme is the movement from viewing people as objects to be used and manipulated for one's own need gratification to celebrating and prizing them as unique individuals in their own right. There is a progression from an emphasis on taking, receiving, and getting towards a mature mutuality of giving and receiving. A further theme is that from being egocentrically unconcerned about others' approval, to being heavily dependent on others' approval, and next to being largely autonomous from others' approval in pursuing higher values as ends in themselves. A theme that emerges at about the middle of the five levels is that of developing a humanistic conscience in which people judge their behaviour not just by how affirming it is for them, but for humanity as well.

Box 4.1: Levels of human sympathy

Level 1: Egocentric
Such emotionally stunted and crippled individuals relate to others almost solely as objects for their personal need gratification. These people, who are often very angry, emphasize getting, receiving, manipulating and taking advantage of others.

Level 2: Restricted
Such individuals possess some sympathy for others, but this mainly depends on how useful they are to them. Too easily threatened, these people are motivated by insufficient self-esteem in how they relate to others. Sometimes restricted human sympathy individuals camouflage their insufficiency by professing to care for others much more than they do.

Level 3: Reciprocal
Feeling moderately secure, such individuals feel and show sympathy for others in their intimate partnerships and in their family, social and national groupings, but still depend heavily on receiving sympathy in return. They may show high levels of

affection for and attention to those who can validate their self-images. However, such people have limited ability to feel sympathy and act compassionately towards those outside of their immediate spheres of interest. Often their emphasis is on seeming to be good rather than on actually being good.

Level 4: Enhanced
For the most part feeling secure themselves, such individuals possess a widened human sympathy that extends beyond their immediate family and social groupings. These people demonstrate on a fairly regular basis a capacity to act compassionately both within and beyond their immediate circle, even though the costs in time, effort, money and emotional involvement may be reasonably high.

Level 5: Committed
These are well balanced and autonomous individuals who possess a broad identification with their fellow humans, highly developed humanistic consciences, and powerful commitments to the preservation and enhancement of humankind. Such people synergistically help themselves and others to attain more of their human potential. Often such highly committed people are leaders, at various levels of society, with the mental discipline and courage to keep fighting for a better world.

Presenting levels of human sympathy definitely does not imply a rush to judge those functioning at lower levels as bad people. The levels of people's egocentricity and absence of genuine human sympathy often reflect the extent of their emotional deprivation and suffering, both past and present. An unfortunate fact is that those who suffer emotionally almost invariably inflict suffering on others too. Such persons are insufficiently skilful rather than intrinsically bad. Another point is that ordinary people can have great hearts and exhibit high levels of human sympathy.

Mental cultivation

Mental cultivation is the *camino real*, the royal road, to human sympathy. The two go hand in hand and progress in showing human sympathy can also influence and reinforce mental cultivation. The Buddha laid heavy stress on mental cultivation, especially as it pertained to meditation. Three of the eight principles in his Noble Eightfold Path to the reduction of suffering and attainment of enlightenment pertain to this goal: namely, right effort, right mindfulness and right concentration. In the Christian religious tradition, despite its stress on showing commitment to God and Jesus through developing oneself ethically and morally, the recognition that focusing on mental cultivation is a vehicle for achieving such ends is less explicit and detailed than in Buddhism. In Western psychotherapies, for the most part, mental cultivation has been viewed largely in terms of helping people overcome deficiencies to attaining normal functioning rather than of helping those who are already functioning reasonably well to become better human beings.

Charles Darwin observed 'The highest possible stage in moral culture is when we recognize that we ought to control our thoughts' (Darwin, 1998a, p. 127). Box 4.2 presents five levels of mental cultivation: namely, primitive, limited, adapted, superior and enlightened. As with human sympathy, each level is a signpost along a range of possibilities where any individual may be at a given moment of time.

A number of themes run through the levels of mental cultivation. One theme is that the more mentally developed people become, the more access they have to their finer emotions. At the lowest level, emotions are often punitive and hostile, whereas at the superior and enlightened levels, reason increasingly merges with love to facilitate demonstrating human sympathy. Put another way, at the lower levels head may be separated from heart, while at the higher levels head is increasingly fused with heart. A feature of this progression is that at lower levels of mental cultivation conscience tends to be primitive and rigid, whereas at the higher levels an individual's conscience becomes much more humane. A related feature is that at the lower levels individuals identify mainly with their own interests, whereas at the higher levels their boundaries are widened to enable them to identify with others and with the human species.

Another theme is that of the movement from thinking others' thoughts to thinking one's own thoughts. At the lower levels, people are dominated by their conditioning, whereas at the higher levels people become increasingly autonomous and free to think critically and constructively. Related to this development is a progression from the need for self-protective mental processes to being secure enough to be open to new experience and ideas whether these come from internal or external sources. A further theme is that of a progression from closed mindedness and jumping to conclusions on the basis of inadequate evidence to thinking rationally and being able to absorb and evaluate past and emerging information.

Box 4.2: Levels of mental cultivation

Level 1: Primitive
Such individuals demonstrate rigid and absolutistic thinking allied to primitive emotional reactions. These people possess no real awareness of their own and others' mental processes and are unable and/or unwilling to control how they think. Their conscience is rigid, undeveloped and often punitive. Their degree of self-protective thinking can be very high.

Level 2: Limited
Such individuals possess a limited ability to test the reality of their thoughts and to examine their rules and beliefs. Their thinking is heavily dominated by what they have incorporated, without much reflection, from their families, societies and cultures. Frequently, these people are somewhat out of touch with the gentler and more affectionate aspects of their human potential. Their need to protect their self-image leaves them vulnerable to self-protective mental processes and to communicating poorly.

Level 3: Adapted
Such individuals, who are generally well adjusted to their societies, have some insight and skills in influencing and controlling how they think. Furthermore, they possess a conceptual framework that allows them to think with some validity about their thoughts, feelings, actions and experiences. They show evidence of developing humanistic consciences, although they often attach little importance to cultivating their minds. Their thinking is often heavily dominated by excessive attachments to approval, status and money.

Level 4: Superior
Such well-balanced individuals value mental and emotional cultivation and are prepared to expend some effort in improving their minds and mental processes. They are insightful and skilful in generating, creating and influencing how they think, feel, physically react and communicate/act. They are also reasonably autonomous in understanding and resisting pressures to be less than human from the societies and cultures in which they live. Furthermore, their humanistic consciences often allow them to sympathize with the suffering and happiness of others and to act appropriately.

Level 5: Enlightened

Such individuals are deeply committed to mental training, discipline and personal excellence. They possess an exceptionally high degree of wisdom, equanimity, insight and skills in influencing and controlling how they think. Having highly developed humanistic consciences and a strong core of inner strength, they can be largely autonomous in resisting and fighting against dehumanizing pressures in contemporary life. They are very mindful of the needs of other humans and of the welfare of the planet. At the highest levels of mental cultivation, reason and love, head and heart are fused, so that people can relate to themselves, others and the human species in rational, loving and life-affirming ways.

The description of an enlightened level of mental cultivation approximates a counsel of perfection that is extremely difficult to attain and maintain. Nevertheless, no apology is made for providing it, because it is important to try to define human heights as well as human depths. Again a rush to judge individuals at lower levels of mental cultivation as bad people should be avoided. Many reasons exist why people do not develop their minds and, therefore, those insufficiently skilled should be viewed as such. Another issue relates to whether people whose intellectual intelligence is not great can be highly mentally cultivated. Mental cultivation is a matter both of heart and of head. Intellectually intelligent people can be highly stupid and destructive, and less intellectually intelligent people can think in ways that are highly constructive and emotionally intelligent. However, leaders who are outstanding in raising the levels of mental cultivation and human sympathy of others are likely to be of above average intellectual intelligence.

Mental cultivation cannot be seen independently of emotional cultivation, not least because the mind is the seat of wishing and feeling as well as of awareness and thinking. The starting point of mental cultivation is acknowledging that such an activity is both possible and necessary. People need to shed their illusions of their own adequacy and autonomy and become humble enough to realize that, for their own and others' sakes, they need to make strenuous efforts to think more effectively and humanely.

Acknowledging the need for mental cultivation is one aspect of possessing a rich conceptual framework and an adequate language to think and converse about how to face life's challenges. All people are personality theorists who possess their own worldviews consisting of the concepts that they have been taught, thought about in varying degrees, and found valuable in communicating with others and in explaining their lives. Psychology, with its emphasis on trying to present itself as a science, has insufficiently addressed the need to develop conceptual frameworks or worldviews for everyday use. This book attempts to provide a framework and language that describes some central elements of a humanistic worldview that has relevance for sub-normal, normal and supra-normal functioning.

In the previous chapter on human-being skills, mention was made of seven central mind skills, namely creating awareness, rules, perceptions, self-talk, visual images, explanations and expectations. In the cognitive humanistic approach, the concept of mind skills is central to achieving and maintaining higher levels of mental cultivation. It is possible to describe many desirable mental characteristics of being fully human. However, specific ways are also needed for people to become more mentally cultivated. Approaches like meditation, prayer, persuasion and exhortation are often insufficient to help people move to higher levels of mental cultivation and human sympathy. The second part of this book addresses how people can develop their mind skills and communication/action skills to become more fully human.

The skilled or good human being

Another way to address the question 'what does it mean to be fully human?' is to try to identify some of the main skills people require to fulfil their potential. This discussion mainly refers to Western cultures, but arguably many of the points made about desirable human-being skills are universal.

In the psychological literature, the term 'self-actualizing' is often used to describe those persons who are functioning at superior levels (for instance, Ellis, 1991; Maslow, 1970). Here the term 'skilled' or 'good' human being is used. The emphasis on goodness attests to a widespread value across cultures of being compassionate and benevolent. It draws together the emphases on human sympathy and mental cultivation already reviewed. Furthermore, skills and goodness are simple everyday concepts, whereas the term 'self-actualizing' is psychological jargon.

An emphasis on people developing their humanity by being skilled or good human beings provides a framework for viewing how humans function that transcends the boundary between the non-religious and the religious. Cognitive humanism involves 'a fresh commitment to the conventional, disciplined and artistic use of the language of the educated layman' (Szasz, 1973, p. xx). Though for certain mental disorders a medical framework may be appropriate, for the vast majority of people it can be constricting. Such a framework can over-emphasize the contributions of medical professionals and medication and place too little emphasis on self-reliance and building psychological self-help skills.

Box 4.3 presents the five Rs of skilled or good human beings: responsiveness, realism, relating, rewarding activity, and responsibility for others. Put simply, responsiveness focuses on having access to one's animal nature and feelings; realism focuses on using one's mind skilfully and mental cultivation; relating focuses on possessing skills for being connected to other human beings; rewarding activity focuses on spending and structuring time beneficially; and responsibility for others focuses on the compassion and service dimensions of being human. The five dimensions are interrelated: for example, emotionally responsive people have a strong base for being skilled in the other four Rs. Responsiveness differs from the other dimensions in that instincts and feelings are not skills in themselves. To become more responsive, individuals need to use the mind and communication/action skills represented in the other four dimensions.

Box 4.3: The five Rs of skilled or good human beings

Responsiveness includes openness to instincts/instinct remnants, accurate experiencing of feelings, physical reactions and sensuality, spontaneity and naturalness, ability to listen to 'inner voices', identification with others and the human species, and sensitivity to anxiety and guilt.

Realism skills include possessing a rich conceptual framework, existential awareness, curiosity and creativity, rational or scientific thinking and developing and using the mind skills of creating awareness, rules, perceptions, self-talk, visual images, explanations and expectations.

Relating skills refer to developing and using person-to-person communication skills including initiating contact, conversing, disclosing, listening, showing caring, sharing intimacy, cooperating, asserting oneself, and managing anger and conflict.

Rewarding activity skills include identifying interests, work skills, entrepreneurial skills, study skills, leisure skills, and looking after physical health skills.

Responsibility for others skills are grounded in humanistic consciences and include demonstrating compassion and showing human sympathy through a service orientation within one's immediate environment and in the wider community.

To conclude, being fully human is mainly characterized by demonstrating human sympathy and mental cultivation. To become more human, people require better human-being skills. The five Rs for being skilled or good human beings provide an easily memorized framework for identifying some of the skills required for being fully human.

FIVE Learning and Losing Humanity

Unable to rely solely on instincts, people need to learn to become more fully human. Nurture must complement and supplement nature, but unfortunately nurture can be for ill as well as for good. All too often, in the process of growing up, individuals learn to think and behave in unskilful rather than in skilful ways and then repeat their mistakes. Almost everyone undergoes experiences that can lead them too much in the direction of personal insecurity, selfishness, short-term hedonism, and craving external affirmation and status. Important questions therefore include 'How can skilful human qualities be acquired and maintained?' and 'What are the circumstances and pressures that lead so many people to suffer and fall short of being fully human?'

Psychotherapy and counselling theoretical approaches may be viewed as possessing four main dimensions if they are to be stated adequately.

1. a statement of the *basic concepts* or assumptions underlying the theory;
2. an explanation of the *acquisition* of skilful and unskilful behaviour;
3. an explanation of the *maintenance* of skilful and unskilful behaviour;
4. an explanation of how to help clients *change* their behaviour and *consolidate* their gains when therapy ends.

A possible fifth dimension is that of *personal practice for supranormalcy.* Here, the idea is that reasonably well functioning individuals assume responsibility for a lifelong process of cultivating their humanity.

The first four chapters of this book, on humanism, human motivation, human-being skills and being fully human, presented some of the basic concepts of cognitive humanistic therapy. This chapter identifies and reviews some processes whereby people acquire and maintain good and/or poor human-being skills. These skills are on two overlapping levels: those for conventional adaptation within most Western, and probably many Eastern, societies and enhanced skills for higher levels of human functioning, such as being mentally well cultivated and consistently showing human sympathy.

Acquisition: Learning to live skilfully and/or unskilfully

A brief overview is now provided of some processes whereby people learn to live skilfully and/or unskilfully.

Supportive relationships are crucial to human beings of all ages. The development of human sympathy and a cultivated mind begins in the cradle. Infants and children require 'the blissful certainty of being wanted' (Horney, 1937, p. 89). They need a good start in life that lays a solid foundation for self-esteem and for acquiring good human-being skills. Life is a lottery and unfortunately many children do not receive the quality of love that is their birthright because of the poor skills of those upon whom they rely for psychological as well as physical sustenance. From the beginning of life, when they are small, vulnerable and psychologically defenceless, children may start receiving messages that undermine their fragile self-esteem. Those responsible for their care can be too anxious, hostile and enmeshed in their own agendas and unhappiness to provide consistently warm and secure emotional climates. Furthermore, there are a host of verbal, physical and social skills that require the support of good parenting to be learned properly. Parents and significant others who inadequately support infants and young children can deprive them of essential early experiences for learning confidence, trust in themselves and others, and human-being skills.

Though differing in resilience, infants and children seem to need at least one primary supportive relationship in which they are loved, celebrated as beautiful and receive much human warmth just for being alive. British child psychiatrist John Bowlby (1979) emphasized the concept of a secure base, otherwise referred to as an attachment figure. He noted accumulating evidence that humans of all ages are happiest and most effective when they feel that standing behind them is a trusted person who will come to their aid should difficulties arise. Rogers (1959) stressed the importance of parents offering children empathy, unconditional positive regard and respect. Parents and surrogate parents who offer these conditions become secure bases from which children can explore and learn from their environments and develop their capacity for listening to their feelings and inner voices. Furthermore, high quality parental affection and attention early in life lay the basis for children developing good attachment skills for later rather than avoiding attachment or becoming very conflicted about it.

Learning from example or from observing others is a major way by which people learn to live skilfully or unskilfully (Bandura, 1986). How to think, feel, communicate and act can be learned from others' examples.

Frequently people remain unaware of behaviours that they demonstrate to children. If either or both parents are emotionally inexpressive, children miss opportunities for learning how to experience and express emotions. Families in which the parents are skilled at showing affection and allowing open communication provide invaluable examples for children to observe and develop these skills themselves. On the other hand, families where parents demonstrate human sympathy at egocentric and restricted levels not only insufficiently model positive communication but, even worse, show children how to communicate destructively.

Parents, surrogate parents, teachers and peer group members implicitly as well as explicitly demonstrate either good or poor mind skills, or a mixture of both. Parents whose own level of mental cultivation is primitive or limited can demonstrate how to think in self-protective and aggressive ways – for instance by possessing demanding rules and by jumping to unwarranted conclusions. By observing such thinking, young people can become skilled at mentally disturbing themselves by creating and sustaining problems rather than calmly and rationally preventing and solving them. Though fortunately the transmission of unskilful thinking from one generation's example to the next generation is not automatic, parents unskilful at creating rules, perceptions, self-talk, visual images, explanations and expectations significantly increase the likelihood of their children being similarly unskilful both during childhood and in later life.

From the examples of parents and significant others children may be helped to acquire poor mind and communication skills in such areas as relationships, study, work, leisure, healthcare and participating responsibly in the wider community. The converse is also true in that skilful mental processes, communications and actions can be acquired from good role models. Just as teaching by example is often unintentional, especially when it comes to mind skills, so is learning by example. Children may absorb from others' examples unskilful ways of thinking, feeling, communicating and acting and then possess the added barrier of remaining unaware that this has happened. Furthermore, children can learn from others' examples the kind of self-protective processes that make it hard later in life to gain insight into any unskilful mental states and patterns of communication that they possess.

Learning skilful or unskilful behaviour from observing examples is frequently intermingled with *learning from rewarding or unrewarding consequences*. For example, parents poor at expressing their emotions may also be poor at receiving their children's emotions. Rewarding consequences can be either primary or secondary. Primary rewarding consequences are rewards independent of people's learning histories – for instance, food, shelter, sex and human warmth. However, only a small portion of behaviour is immediately reinforced by rewards of evident biological significance. Most behaviour is emitted in response to secondary rewards such as approval or money, which have become associated or conditioned to primary rewards (Skinner, 1953). In addition, people do not just receive rewarding or unrewarding consequences; they think about past consequences they have received, present consequences they are receiving, and make rules and predictions to guide their future behaviour.

Children are explorers and experimenters as they interact with their environments and learn which behaviours and ways of thinking help them to deal with life. Just as parents can model either skilful or unskilful ways of thinking and communicating, so they can use rewards well or poorly. For example, either or both parents may choose to reward or discourage children for being assertive, showing sympathy to others, telling the truth, thinking for themselves, controlling their anger, to mention but some possibilities for learning good or poor skills. A danger here is that thoughts and behaviours that show humanity and concern for others may go unrewarded or get discouraged so that children become progressively out of touch with their potential for innate goodness. In addition, children frequently receive mixed messages, with 'Do as I say not as I do' being an example of an inconsistent attitude toward providing rewards. Furthermore, poor skills can be fostered and self-esteem undermined by children receiving unrewarding messages that their whole personality is bad rather than that specific behaviours are insufficiently skilled.

Another way to view the use of rewards is to see growing up in terms of a continual process of two-way power and influence in which children reward their parents as well as the reverse. Such power and influence processes extend to all significant people in their environments, be they older relatives, siblings, other children, teachers or whoever. Children are not just passive recipients of the rewards others provide or fail to provide for their behaviour, though sometimes they may be engulfed or overwhelmed by oppressive environments. They can be active agents in trying to assert and define themselves. Sometimes family life, like the remainder of life, resembles Thomas Szasz's aphorism: 'In the animal kingdom, the rule is to eat or be eaten; in the human kingdom, define or be defined' (Szasz, 1973, p. 20). Many children find it more difficult to become truly skilled because some of their thoughts and communications/actions are negatively defined resulting from discrimination because of their biological sex, sexual orientation, race, social class or culture. Such negative messages can become internalized in ways that make people the instruments of their own oppression, albeit often unawares.

Psychologists researching animal behaviour stress the importance of learning from example and consequences. However, humans are unique in possessing the capacity for symbolic thought and communication. Hence, they can *learn from instruction and from self-instruction.*

However, this avenue for learning to live skilfully is woefully underutilized, especially when it comes to mind skills and mental cultivation. Western countries for the most part emphasize developing young people's minds intellectually. They insufficiently stress helping them to learn good mind skills for managing their own and others' emotions and for communicating effectively. Where courses on effective thinking do exist they tend to focus on such topics as overcoming negative emotions like excessive anxiety or on how to become more successful in work and business. Unless they are very lucky, few young people are trained to think systematically about their personal problems and relationships. In addition, sound and affordable instruction in how to become more mentally cultivated is rarely available, especially outside of large cities. In secondary schools, there may be courses on moral development, but these are not part of the examinable curriculum for entry into higher education and consequently students' main efforts are placed elsewhere. Furthermore, such courses are more likely to be grounded in philosophy and religion rather than the kind of applied psychology that forms the core of this book.

Children and young people are more likely to receive instruction in communication and action skills than in mind skills. Much of this instruction is informal and provided by parents, relatives and peer groups. Sometimes courses are offered in educational institutions in such areas as assertion skills, friendship skills and interview skills, but probably a minority of children and students attend them. Even at the start of the twenty-first century, much sex education is left to peer groups to impart as best as they can. Relatively few people attend marriage preparation and parenting courses, despite the importance of sound family relationships in developing skilful human beings in the next generation.

In both informal and formal contexts, poor as well as good skills can be imparted by trainers who are deficient in the skills they try to impart. Furthermore, for various reasons, including differences in preferred teaching and learning styles, those instructed may resist instructors. Sometimes family members, peers and even qualified trainers are poor at drawing out learners and building on their motivation and knowledge base rather than just telling them what to do. Basic and more advanced human-being skills need to be communicated clearly enough for learners to instruct themselves afterwards. Much instruction in both mind and communication/action skills falls far short of this preparation for personal coaching objective.

The degree to which people learn good or poor human-being skills is also influenced by their *access to information and opportunity*. Missing information and misinformation hamper children and adults alike in developing their humanity. In regard to absence of information, many people do not view their relationships in skills terms, have never clearly identified the components of skilful relating, and lack the knowledge base to improve how they function. Ignorance about what it takes to be a successful human being is pervasive. Few people have a good grasp about how they can influence their feelings and physical reactions by altering their thinking. Furthermore, many children grow up ignorant of the basic facts in such crucial areas as death and sexuality, partly because of the problems of many adults in dealing with such issues honestly in their own lives. Even well-intentioned adults often relate to their children on the basis of lies, omissions of truth and partial truths.

The conditions in which reliable information is missing form a fertile breeding ground for misinformation. The socialization of boys and girls into gender roles often ignores the huge similarities in psychological characteristics between the sexes. The result of this misinformation can lead to both sexes losing touch with some important parts of their humanity – obvious examples being some boys' and men's difficulties in showing affection and some girls' and women's difficulties in being assertive. Such difficulties can impede genuine intimacy that involves both partners in being emotionally intelligent and expressive. At worst gender-role misinformation can lead to crude sexism on the part of either or both sexes. All areas of difference between people – for instance, biological sex, sexual orientation, culture, race and social class – provide the potential for unskilful mental states and communication based on missing information and misinformation.

Children, adolescents and adults alike need opportunities available to test out and develop their human-being skills. Ideally such opportunities are in line with their maturation and state of readiness. People's social circumstances can restrict their access to opportunities, for instance poverty. Furthermore, children can be fortunate or unfortunate in having parents, significant others and peer groups that open up rather than restrict learning opportunities. Children and adults also need to assume personal responsibility for developing their skills in seeking out information and in creating opportunities.

Lastly, *anxiety and confidence* are important factors influencing how well human-being skills are learned. Children grow up having both helpful and harmful experiences for developing self-esteem. Those who are fortunate acquire a level of anxiety that both protects against actual dangers and also motivates them toward realistic achievements. Those less fortunate may acquire debilitating anxieties through role modelling, provision of faulty consequences, poor instruction, and through missing information and misinformation. Even parents who communicate carefully can bruise children's fragile self-esteem. Far worse are parents who communicate aggressively in the first place and then become even more defensive and aggressive if challenged. Deficient behaviours resulting from as well as manifesting anxiety include unwillingness to take realistic risks, tense and nervous rather than relaxed learning, insufficient persistence when faced with problems, and a heightened tendency to say and do the wrong things. Performing new and seemingly strange skills poorly may heighten anxiety still further and make future skills learning even more difficult. However, people who are helped or who help themselves to acquire anxiety management skills can learn human-being skills more easily than those without such skills.

Maintenance: Keeping living skilfully and/or unskilfully

How do people keep functioning at sub-normal, normal and supra-normal levels? In relation to mind skills and communication/action skills, all people have two pasts. The first past refers to how they acquired good and poor skills initially, with the second past being how they have maintained or altered their skills once acquired. Many skills were acquired when people were relatively powerless as children, so the first past is more 'What others have done to me.' However, the second past, when people were older, is more a matter of 'What I kept and keep doing to myself.' This section focuses on why many people choose to continue behaving less skilfully than is desirable, often at great cost to their own and others' happiness and fulfilment. A tragedy of contemporary life is that, despite huge scientific advances, there have not been correspondingly large advances in how skilfully people live. Instead, many people continue to create serious levels of avoidable suffering and think and communicate far below their potential.

Inadequate mind skills

A contributing factor to maintaining poor mind and communication/ action skills is that many people do not possess a clear concept of mind and think insufficiently about how they think and act in skills terms. Furthermore, people may settle for less than they are capable of because they possess inadequate visions of what their true nature is and of what being fully human entails.

Continuing to create poor mind skills in each of the areas depicted in Box 3.2, 'Seven central mind skills', maintains living at a lower level of humanness than possible. For example, people remaining insufficiently aware of their feelings and sensations continue having a poor base for guiding and improving their lives. Regarding rules, people may continue to place perfectionist demands upon themselves, others and their environment rather than think in preferential terms.

People mainly tend to perceive of themselves as rational human beings. The more insecure they feel, the more they are likely to have rigid perceptions about what sort of person they are. Instead of having what Rogers termed openness to experiencing, both inner and outer, they are likely to react defensively by denying and distorting information that differs from their self-pictures (Raskin and Rogers, 2000).

Much thinking takes place in the form of self-talk. If people keep repeating anxiety- and anger-engendering thoughts to themselves, this habit sustains negative feelings and increases the probability of insufficiently skilful communications and actions. In addition, negative visual images may be repetitively rehearsed.

Regarding creating explanations, people may possess insufficient awareness of their personal responsibility for making the most of their own and others' lives by cultivating happiness and lessening suffering (Nelson-Jones, 1984). Furthermore, tendencies to blame others for misfortunes are widespread. People who do not acknowledge their contributions to creating their suffering are in poor positions to do anything about it. People can also create unrealistically negative expectations about the possibility of change that, in turn, interfere with making a real effort to change. Such expectations include: 'I've tried before' and 'My partner will never change'.

Fear of goodness

A simplistic 'good guy/bad guy' distinction is unrealistic because virtually all human beings show some warmth and compassion. Nevertheless, assuming that all people possess an inner core of goodness or a cluster of instincts of varying levels of strength towards affirming their own and others' human life, the questions then become: 'Why is it so hard for many people to express this inner core of goodness fully?' and 'Why do so many people fear actually being as contrasted with seeming to be good?' For most, the inward journey towards true human sympathy involves a conflict between heeding quiet inner voices and overcoming fears. The journey is one of renouncing less essential thoughts to come closer to the more essential values of being fully human. The following discussion illustrates some fears blocking people from showing their humanity.

One of the main fears stems from shattering the illusion of being nice. When people glimpse their potential for genuine goodness, if they are honest with themselves, they also glimpse how far short they fall of fulfilling this potential. To put this in Jungian terms, they are confronted with the darker side of their shadow. Another illusion that people may need to give up is that of being special. Compassion entails seeing other human beings as essentially the same as oneself. Becoming more sensitive to the plight of others can provide further psychological challenges. In Western culture, especially for males, becoming more in touch with tender feelings towards other human beings is sometimes associated with being soft and vulnerable. Such fears may generate further fears such as those concerned with being feminine, being taken advantage of, and being different. In addition, people may fear being overwhelmed by acknowledging the true extent of misery in the world. This fear can be somewhat mitigated by acknowledging the extent of happiness and of the overcoming of suffering too.

If the suffering of other human beings is more clearly acknowledged and experienced, the next question is 'What am I going to do about it?' Fears connected with answering this question include fears about having sufficient inner strength and equanimity to make a contribution in others' lives without drowning in their suffering, and fears connected with giving time, concern and money for cultivating others' rather than one's own happiness. In addition, people can worry about not being appreciated by others.

Negative external influences

The negative factors that originally contributed to people learning to function poorly may continue. For instance, people may still suffer from absence of the kind of supportive relationships that will help them become better and more skilled persons. They may continue to be exposed to significant others demonstrating poor mind and communication/action skills and limited human sympathy and commitment to mental cultivation. Role models for supra-normal functioning are still rare in our culture. In addition, people may fail to be rewarded for constructive thoughts and actions and succeed in being rewarded for the wrong reasons.

People may still suffer from receiving inadequate or no instruction in mind skills and communication/action skills. In addition, they may continue with missing or incorrect information about how to live effectively and may lack suitable opportunities in their personal and work environments to develop their skills and potential. The persistence of the above negative external influences may make it more difficult to change for the better and easier to change for the worse. However, the most important factor in resisting and surmounting these influences is how skilful people are at creating and using their minds.

Some dehumanizing contexts

People acquire and maintain skilful and unskilful behaviours in contexts that extend beyond their immediate personal relationships. Before chronicling some contextual pressures and cultural pathology that contribute to the struggle to be fully human, some of the benefits of living in the Western world at this period of time are briefly mentioned. Many of these benefits are quantifiable facts, though the challenge is to transform them into quality of life for oneself, others and the human species.

Nowadays, people are living much longer, physically healthier and wealthier lives than at any period in human history. There is easily sufficient wealth in Western countries to provide food, shelter, education and basic health care for all citizens, even though this does not always happen. A combination of improved living standards and better health care have markedly reduced the amount of serious disease and considerably increased life expectancy. Furthermore, for over 50 years, there have been no major world wars and the prospects of major European powers fighting one another appears increasingly remote. If anything, there has been a spread of democracy and a weakening of the likelihood of totalitarian regimes re-emerging.

An aspect of some of the dehumanizing contexts reviewed here is that they represent negative sides of positive developments. For instance, technological change and increased material wealth create benefits, yet have the potential to make it harder for people to be fully human as well. Another aspect of the dehumanizing contexts is that they are in a continuous state of flux, which can have positive as well as negative consequences. As emphasized by the Buddha, change and impermanence are integral parts of the human condition and of the contexts in which human beings live.

Restrictive worldviews

Many worldviews exist that can help people to become and stay out of touch with their own and one another's humanity. One example is that of a crude economic worldview that sees everyone's motivation as the need to increase material wealth. Greed is good and life is a jungle in which the strong prevail over the weak. Research evidence exists suggesting that when people believe that selfishness is the true motivation of human beings, they may be less inclined to help others and more inclined to take advantage of them (Sober and Wilson, 1998). Myths forming part of the economic worldview include the idea that greater wealth automatically brings increased personal happiness and the success of countries in fulfilling their citizens' needs can be measured solely by gross national product.

Religious worldviews, especially if dogmatically applied and/or misunderstood, can also restrict people's capacity for human sympathy and mental cultivation. Viewing people as living in a state of sin and needing the help of a supernatural power to provide salvation can have the negative consequences of insufficiently acknowledging human beings' social instincts and their ability to solve problems without some form of divine intervention. Fundamentalist religious worldviews are expanding throughout the world (Argyle, 2002). Fundamentalism traditionally means believing literally in what is written in the Bible or in some other sacred book (Beit-Hallahmi and Argyle, 1997). Such belief in literal truths – for instance, that God made the world in six days and that evolution does not take place – can restrict people's capacity to think for themselves and to assess existing and emerging evidence rationally. Religious beliefs can also be highly divisive when taken to extremes, for example religious differences hugely contribute to the troubles between Catholics and Protestants in Northern Ireland, Hindus and Muslims in India, and Palestinians and Jews in the Middle East. Furthermore, some religious traditions' strict distinctions between believers and non-believers or infidels have the unwelcome effect of restricting human sympathy to like-minded people.

Nationalism is another worldview limiting human sympathy and mental cultivation. Instead of identifying with the human species, many people unthinkingly see the values and way of life of their own countries as superior to that of others. Nationalism entails believing myths about cultural superiority. Other restrictive attitudes include racism – of whatever kind, sexism – most often men are superior to women, heterosexism – most often homosexuals are inferior to heterosexuals, and ageism – increasingly, in the Western world, older people are less valued than younger people.

Popular psychology, aided and abetted by advertising, the media and self-help books, can also provide a set of mental blinkers about what it means to be fully human. The thrust of popular psychology is on fostering conventional values of individualism, romantic love, being popular, making money, showing off one's success to others, having fun, and seeming to behave and look young as long as possible.

Capitalism and consumerism

The success of capitalism has helped to humanize most people in the West by freeing them from subsistence existences and providing them with a reasonable level of basic economic security. In the nineteenth century, the alienation of labourers from their work stimulated the rise of Marxism (Fromm, 1961). Today, many people still feel *dehumanized by the processes of production*; for example blue-collar workers doing repetitive tasks on car assembly lines. In addition, the pressures on chief executive officers and managers to create shareholder value increasingly lead to people being viewed as units of production to be hired, fired, downsized or relocated as perceived economic realities dictate. Business is 'war without bullets' and the psychological suffering caused by the ruthless competition of the marketplace can be huge. Despite having increasing wealth, many people feel more insecure because of the very real threat of losing their jobs and the career and personal dislocation that this can entail. Furthermore, in the struggle to survive and succeed in organizations, people can feel pressure to market themselves as commodities, play 'the company game', and sometimes to cut ethical corners.

Another result of capitalism is that often people judge themselves and others more by the size of their bank balances and perceived status rather than by the size of their hearts. Capitalism can lead to an excessive emphasis on acquisition, hoarding and competing. Even rich people can suffer by comparing themselves to even richer people, feeling that they need to accumulate more, and being insecure about not making money quickly enough or about losing it.

Now, at the start of the twenty-first century, people can be even more alienated from their humanity because not only are they dehumanized by the processes of production, but they are also *dehumanized by the processes of consumption* – a so-called 'double whammy'. Consumerism is rampant in Western societies and the situation is probably growing worse. *Homo sapiens* is now also *Homo consumens*. Instead of people being freed to enjoy the fruits of greater wealth, under an illusion of freedom they are encouraged to enslave themselves to a never-ending process of creating and consuming wealth. Businesses need to sell the goods they produce, so from a tender age potential consumers are urged by clever advertising to buy, buy, buy. For example, Greer (1999) observes that magazines, encouraged by the beauty industry, target young girls to start building up early their habits of consuming beauty products.

Consumers are encouraged to live up to and beyond their incomes in a compulsive search for artificially induced happiness. Perceived needs for new purchases expand to fill the income and credit available for them. Thus free-market economies have helped many step out of physical suffering through not having basic necessities of life and step into psychological suffering connected with the effects of possessing false values that emphasize selfishness, short-range hedonism, and thinking one never has enough material possessions or wealth. Many add to their suffering by falling badly into debt.

Consumerism can have an insidious effect on family life. Family members of all ages can feel under pressure to 'keep up with the Joneses' rather than to be content with what they have. Parents can experience stress in trying to provide material goods for their consumer children, who are already the targets of advertising campaigns. In addition, material goods can be seen as substitutes for genuine love both by givers and receivers.

Pockets of poverty within wealthy countries can be another effect of unrestrained capitalism. People can resent funds being diverted to public services, such as schools and hospitals for the less privileged, thus risking a cycle of deprivation. Excessive taxation can interfere with entrepreneurial activity that increases a country's wealth, but a balance needs to be struck with having sufficient public funds to help poorer people experience more of their humanity by developing the requisite skills so that they can partici- pate actively in society. In addition, there is the broader issue of assisting people in the developing world out of their poverty traps. Unfortunately the Third World's situation is worsened by factors including backward attitudes to birth control and to preventing AIDS – particularly in the Catholic Church – rampant corruption among many of these countries' so-called elite, and restrictive tariff barriers on the part of the world's richer nations.

Rate of technological change

As well as offering many benefits, the staggering rate of technological change is another potentially dehumanizing factor. The gap caused by scientific advances outstripping current levels of human wisdom continues to grow. For example, the attacks on New York's World Trade Center on 11 September 2001 showed the dangers of modern technology being allied to primitive interpretations of religious beliefs. In future, with the threat of nuclear, chemical and biological terrorism, there may be far more serious incidents. Already, many people in the Western world feel more insecure because of the risks of terrorist attacks and the perceived threat of personal annihilation. One of the challenges to such people is to learn to address the causes of their increased anxiety, some of which may lie in the insufficient levels of mental cultivation of themselves and their leaders.

Another cause of insecurity can be that of failure to keep up with change. Human beings can feel obsolescent in a continually changing environment, where the old ways may no longer be seen as the best ways. The rate of change can have insidious effects on families and on how valued older people feel. In traditional societies, the elders were usually perceived as the source of wisdom and knowledge about how the world worked, which is no longer so true in the modern world. In families, sometimes parents struggle to keep up with their children's grasp of and interest in the new technology, such as the Internet. The rate of change also contributes to instability in the workforce, for example in many industries computerization has led to lay-offs.

Mechanistic approach to education

Another dehumanizing context is the mechanistic approach adopted in many educational institutions. The scientific approach to knowledge and education is absolutely vital to advancing the human race. Nevertheless, it needs to be smart science that realizes its limitations and fosters creativity. At the front of his book *Freedom to Learn*, Rogers quotes Einstein's observation: 'It is in fact nothing short of a miracle that the modern methods of instruction have not yet entirely strangled the holy curiosity of inquiry; for this delicate little plant, aside from stimulation, stands mainly in need of freedom; without this it goes to wrack and ruin without fail' (Rogers, 1969). Modern methods of instruction reflect modern academic values such as excessively breaking down knowledge into small parts, the tyranny of the narrow research study, undervaluing the subjective and theoretical, undervaluing applied as contrasted with 'pure' approaches to generating knowledge, and emphasizing quantity rather than quality and originality of output.

It is hard for students to learn to be self-directed and creative and to think broadly and deeply when often their professors and lecturers single-mindedly pursue narrow interests. Furthermore, self-referent education is undervalued. For example, in psychology, great value is placed on students studying cognitive processes, but little value is placed on staff and students using the considerable body of knowledge that already exists about how people can skilfuly and/or unskilfully develop and cultivate their minds.

Individualism and isolation

Many factors contribute to people feeling isolated and lonely. The movement from predominantly agricultural to urban life has broken up communities and families. People's feelings of isolation can be heightened by the anonymity of living in big cities. In addition, factors such as personal ambition for career advancement and the uncertainties and pressures of the market economy can motivate people to move locations and then lose direct contact with existing networks. In countries like America and Australia, the distances involved in career moves can be very large, thus further increasing the breakdown of ties to parents and extended families.

Pressures from the media and popular psychology to search for individual self-actualization may be increasing the dissatisfaction people feel with their existing partner, marital and family arrangements. In addition, marital and family instability has been heightened by such factors as the decline in observing religious teachings, women's increasing economic independence and unwillingness to stay in loveless marriages, and the higher expectations that people of both sexes have for marriage and partner relationships. Furthermore, in materialist societies, people can feel under great pressure to make money, spend long hours at work and face job insecurity. When part of dual career couples, they can experience conflicts of work and personal interests. The past was far from perfect, but there are many pressures in contemporary life that appear to make it harder to sustain intimacy over a long period of time. In addition, unlike in the East where taking care of one's parents is still given very high priority, in the West children's responsibilities to their parents are often taken less seriously, thus increasing the likelihood of people feeling isolated and abandoned in their old age.

In families, technology also can put pressures on people to avoid communicating with one another and to pursue individual agendas. For instance, the television set dominates the living room in many homes. Sometimes, further fragmentation of family communication results from individuals watching television on their personal sets. In addition, although computers and the Internet have the potential to bring people in families together, they can also divide when family members spend excessive time in such activities as working on them, playing computer games, and participating in Internet chat rooms.

Pressure to conform

In Chapter 4 the mid-point on the five-point human sympathy scale was described as 'Reciprocal' and that on the mental cultivation scale as 'Adapted'. When writing about the characteristics of self-actualizing people, Maslow saw their values as differing from 'the pervasive psychopathology of the average' (Maslow, 1970, p. 177). The word psychopathology may appear too strong, but the sad truth is that the levels of human-being skills of the vast majority of people fall far below their potential. It is a minority of people who attain the enhanced and committed levels of human sympathy and the superior and enlightened levels of mental cultivation. Swimming in a sea of the commonplace, people feel under huge pressures to conform to normal standards of behaviour and levels of human-being skills.

Pressures to conform come from families, partners, peers, social groups and the pervasive influence of the media, to mention but some avenues. Such pressures can help people to behave skilfully, unskilfully or a mixture of the two. Here the focus is on the negative effects of pressures to conform that can encourage the bad and inhibit the good. Popular or mass Western culture often appears to legitimize levels of greed, aversion and ignorance. On the surface people can be encouraged to behave differently, but much of the time they are bombarded with messages indicating that it is acceptable to be greedy, materialistic, aggressive and narrow minded. For example, some of the role models of popular television programmes, such as soap operas, can contribute to viewers thinking and communicating poorly rather than helping them to become more skilful human beings.

Human sympathy and mental cultivation are frequently met with ambivalence, if not downright hostility. Derogatory words and phrases used to describe those concerned with helping others include 'do-gooders', 'bleeding hearts', 'interfering bastards', 'softies', and 'suckers'. Such people may be viewed as effeminate – if male, tender-minded rather than tough-minded, and as encouraging dependency. The motivation of those actively helping others can be disparaged as 'making themselves feel good', 'wanting to prove that they are superior', 'needing to control others', 'wanting something in return', and 'compensating for personal inadequacies'. Furthermore, if people talk too much about their efforts to help others, such disclosures can be perceived as boasting, being 'holier than thou', or being boring. In addition to or instead of direct messages, people disclosing good deeds may receive subtle messages to desist, for instance by others pretending not to hear, changing the subject, and using distancing vocal and body messages. Probably there is a level of human sympathy with which the average person is comfortable. Exceeding that level and then talking about it can threaten many people, possibly because they feel confronted with their own limitations without wishing to admit them.

Sense of meaninglessness

Numerous human beings in the modern world suffer from a sense of meaninglessness and feel that life is empty and futile. Nowadays, many people have little contact with nature and lack a sense of being grounded in the land and its seasons. Human beings are also less guided than in bygone times by traditional values and religion. They live under threat of nuclear annihilation and environmental degradation. Furthermore, such factors as consumerism, the rapid rate of technical change, and the intrusive effects of the media can contribute to people feeling that they are living in an artificial society. In addition, there is a tendency towards cynicism and denigrating those in leadership positions so that it becomes hard to find people worthy of respect. As indicated above, people who do good deeds may find themselves being disparaged instead of praised.

A sense of meaninglessness sometimes leads to people finding superficial answers, for instance either in conformity, doing what others want them to do, or in fundamentalist religions or totalitarianism, doing what others want them to do. The relative lack of old certainties provides a potentially dehumanizing context and, in some ways, can make it harder to grow up and exist than in more settled times. Nevertheless, within the widespread sense of meaninglessness there are challenges to individuals, societies and the human species to discover their personal and collective meanings, to rediscover fundamental human values and to live skilfully according to them.

PART TWO

CULTIVATING BEING FULLY HUMAN

SIX Overview of Cognitive Humanistic Therapy

Chapter 1 mentioned that psychotherapy can address the needs for two different kinds of healing. As depicted in Figure 6.1, cognitive humanistic therapy consists of two, somewhat overlapping, components: adaptation CHT and mental cultivation CHT. Adaptation CHT aims to assist moderately to slightly sub-normal and normal clients to attain the mind and communication/action skills whereby they can function comfortably and well in their societies. Such adaptation assumes that the societies are not pathological beyond the norm for Western countries.

Mental cultivation CHT aims to assist clients and others to attain higher levels of functioning or of supra-normalcy. In varying degrees, it entails clients, self-therapists and others in transcending the values and norms of their societies by thinking and behaving much more skilfully. Paradoxically mental cultivation CHT develops the mind to awaken and strengthen the heart. Such therapy trains the mind to access, activate and implement in action the positive inner core of one's being. Important goals include achieving genuine human sympathy and developing skills for cultivating happiness and eliminating suffering for others as well as for oneself.

The following are some further points by way of introducing the practice of cognitive humanistic therapy. First the therapist, client and personal practitioner skills described in this second part of the book owe much to the contributions of existing therapeutic approaches and religious traditions. Adaptation CHT, in particular, has its origins in the cognitive behavioural and humanistic psychotherapies. Mental cultivation CHT draws especially on the cognitive behavioural psychotherapies and the Christian and Buddhist religious traditions. Second, the practice of cognitive humanistic therapy has not been developed in relation to severe mental disorder as described in the American Psychiatric Association's *Diagnostic and Statistical Manual of Mental Disorders* (2000). Third, solving human problems requires a multifaceted and multidisciplinary approach. As shown in the review of dehumanizing contexts in Chapter 5, the problems of individuals reflect problems in broader society and *vice versa*. Disciplines like biology and biochemistry, anthropology, sociology,

Figure 6.1 Overview of cognitive humanistic therapy

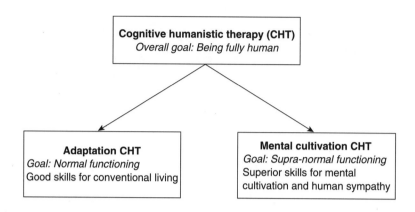

social psychology, political science, economics and theology each have a role to play in understanding and addressing human problems.

Along with some perennial ones, human problems continually change and evolve. Some problems that have already existed in the second millennium will become much more pressing in the third, for example searching for existential meaning. As technological advances continue to outstrip human development, the challenge of creating not just richer but better human beings becomes increasingly important. Indeed, the survival of the human race may depend on human success in synergistically creating better people and better societies. Attaining supra-normal functioning has been insufficiently addressed in the psychotherapy and counselling literature. This state of affairs needs to be changed. Developing and articulating CHT is but a small step in what needs to be a much larger attempt within the helping professions to create psychotherapy and training approaches that raise the bar for normalcy while at the same time encouraging higher levels of supra-normal functioning.

Therapeutic goals

The goals of adaptation CHT can include providing emotional support, managing specific problem situations better, managing problems, and improving poor skills that sustain problems. In many instances, CHT aims to attain all four goals with the same client. Adaptation CHT is appropriate for the kinds of problems that form much of the case loads of psychotherapists and counsellors. For example, presenting concerns involving feelings and physical reactions include being depressed, anxious, confused, stressed, tense and dealing with illnesses such as heart attacks or cancer. Possibly most clients come to psychotherapists because of relationship difficulties including shyness, difficulty showing affection, difficulty managing anger, and conflicts between partners. Many clients also come with work-related presenting concerns including procrastination, public speaking anxiety, problems relating to colleagues and customers, inappropriate risk-taking behaviour, dealing with negative performance appraisals, stresses attached to managerial, supervisory and sales roles, and sexual harassment.

There are at least two important ways that goals may be stated for adaptation CHT presenting concerns. One way is to state them as overall or outcome goals. For example, the overall or outcome goal for a client who seriously procrastinates over work or study assignments is to do this much less so. Therapist and client could work together to define how to measure the outcome of procrastinating less. Another way is to state them as process or skills goals. For example, 'What are the mind skills and the communication/action skills that the client needs to improve to start work/study assignments more quickly?' These two ways of stating goals are both important. Overall or outcome goals indicate where clients want to go, whereas process or skills goals indicate how clients can attain their overall goals both now and in future.

Invariably, developing clients' mind skills forms an important part of adaptation CHT. Mental cultivation CHT aims to take this process further. Some reasonably well-functioning clients want to develop their minds so that they can be even more successful in the conventional terms of status, promotions and money. The goal here is greater mental efficiency for personal gain rather than any inner transformation focused on the wider good.

However, the main purpose of mental cultivation CHT is to help those clients and others who want to take the inner journey towards becoming more in touch with their innate goodness and, thus, become more fully human. Drawing on Eastern and Western traditions, qualities of the good person include equanimity, autonomy, mental purification, honesty both with self and others, inner strength, goodwill or lovingkindness, sympathetic joy, gratitude, compassion, wisdom, generosity and service (Adler, 1998; Dalai Lama, 2002; Fromm, 1976; Maslow, 1970; Salzberg, 1995; Thitavanno, 2002; Walsh, 2000).

Mentally cultivated people are able to maintain a balanced or middle way between cultivating positive and curbing negative aspects of themselves and between attachment and detachment. Being mentally cultivated is not an ego-less state of being, but rather one in which the individual's ego or self remains strong and intact, yet capable of a compassionate identification with the human species. Mental cultivation CHT seeks inner transformation by reshaping, deepening and humanizing the self and its ego processes.

Process of therapy

All major approaches to the practice of psychotherapy and counselling have the idea of process or progression built into them. A psychotherapy process model is one that explicitly rather than implicitly articulates the stages of the therapy process. Adaptation CHT is structured around the skilled client model that is described more fully in the next chapter (Nelson-Jones, 2002a, 2002b). Suffice it for now to say that the skilled client model has three major stages – relating, understanding and changing – each of which is divided into three phases. The model provides a framework or set of guidelines for therapist choices. The skilled client model is useful not only for managing or solving problems but also for addressing underlying problematic skills.

An early version of a process model was that of Carl Jung, who cited four stages of analytical therapy: confession, elucidation, education and transformation (Jung, 1966). However, for the most part, the major theorists have refrained from stating the practice of their therapeutic approaches in clearly numbered stages. Nevertheless models of the psychotherapy and counselling process abound (for instance, Carkhuff, 1987; Corey and Corey, 1998; Egan, 2002). An important point about these psychotherapy and counselling process models is that, in the main, they apply the concept of learning and using skills to psychotherapists and counsellors rather than to clients. These models are problem-management models that may insufficiently address assisting clients to improve their skills for preventing and managing future similar problems.

If we are to have skilled psychotherapists and counsellors, why not have skilled clients too? It is inconsistent to teach and learn about psychotherapy skills and then insufficiently acknowledge that thinking about clients and their problems in skills terms can be equally useful. In the final analysis the purpose of using psychotherapy skills is to enable clients to become more skilled in their own right. Whether explicitly acknowledged or not, arguably all positive changes from psychotherapy involve clients in learning and using better skills. Psychotherapists and counsellors are only skilled to the extent that they can be successful in skilling clients, hence the desirability of a skilled client model.

The dividing line between adaptation therapy and mental cultivation therapy is not clear cut. Adaptation therapy can be used to address and disentangle some of the prior emotional baggage that may get in the way of mental cultivation therapy. Furthermore, during adaptation therapy, therapist and client need not just focus on curbing negative qualities, but can incorporate a focus on cultivating positive qualities as well. Paying attention to qualities like compassion and generosity can form part of adaptation therapy. In addition, mental cultivation therapy can lead out of adaptation therapy for those clients interested in growing even more in touch with their innate goodness, further cultivating their minds, developing higher levels of human sympathy, and being more actively compassionate in how they relate to the world.

Alternatively, mental cultivation CHT may be more of a therapeutic approach on its own. Clients need to be reasonably strong and skilled people to start with. If this is not the case, therapists can tactfully suggest that they focus on improving targeted conventional human-being skills either before or alongside working on more advanced skills. Within the framework of the skilled client model, mental cultivation CHT for those already functioning well can include providing safe atmospheres in which clients can acknowledge and experience their yearnings to be better human beings. Therapists can assist clients in acknowledging and identifying areas for possessing supra-normal human-being skills in which they need to improve. Therapists can also teach clients about the concept of human sympathy and mental cultivation. Furthermore therapists can assist clients to use their minds to disencumber inner blocks to getting in touch with the positive core of their being and also to curb their negative emotions. In addition, therapists can assist clients as they learn and implement mind skills and communication/action skills to be more fully human.

Personal practice always forms part of both adaptation therapy and mental cultivation therapy. Ideally mental cultivation therapy should be initiated by working with wise, humane and skilled therapists, but this state of affairs may happen more in the future than now. With the current prevailing focus of psychotherapy and of practitioner training on normal or adaptive functioning, many of those wishing to cultivate themselves mentally and to demonstrate high levels of human sympathy may have to achieve these ends largely on their own. Sometimes mentors, who although not accredited as psychotherapists nonetheless embody and model supra-normal human-being skills, can assist personal efforts at becoming more fully human. Such superior human beings may come from the helping services, or from religious or non-religious backgrounds. Personal practice is discussed briefly towards the end of this chapter and then reviewed more fully as part of the book's final chapter.

The therapeutic relationship

Therapeutic relationships are the human connections between psychotherapists and clients both in their direct dealings and in one another's heads. Within the overall relationship between psychotherapist and client, there are a number of dimensions or strands. The public or observable relationship consists of all the communications relevant to any particular therapist-client relationship. For example, clients may have had telephone, answering-machine or e-mail contact with therapists before meeting face-to-face. In addition, therapists may have handed out brochures or other pre-psychotherapy information. During psychotherapy sessions, both therapist and client send and receive numerous verbal, vocal and bodily communications. In addition, therapists may provide clients with handouts and worksheets, assist clients using whiteboard or notepads, and sometimes make up cassettes and/or videotapes. After psychotherapy, there may be further face-to face contact and/or phone, letter and e-mail contact.

In addition to the public relationship, CHT relationships also take place in both participants' minds. Clients start forming impressions of therapists by processing any pre-psychotherapy information such as telephone contacts and letters confirming appointments. Similarly, therapists start forming impressions of clients both from any contact they have had and, sometimes, from records provided by third parties. During psychotherapy sessions both participants relate to one another in their minds. For example, the client decides how far to trust the therapist and how much to reveal, when and in what ways. Furthermore, both participants are constantly forming and reforming mental conceptions of one another. Between sessions too therapists and clients mentally relate in the thoughts and fantasies they have about one another and in regard to agreed upon tasks to be undertaken between sessions.

In CHT the mental relationships that clients have with therapists after psychotherapy are crucial. The goal of psychotherapy is self-helping in which former clients use the insights, knowledge and skills gained from therapy to live more effectively and be more fully human. At first, therapists may continue to be present as conscious 'voices in the head' that guide how clients think and act. However, as time goes by, therapist influence is likely to be more subconscious as clients become more skilled and comfortable with the task of self-help.

An important aspect of the CHT relationship is that it is conducted in simple, everyday language. In CHT, therapists think about their clients in the same language as they conduct the actual psychotherapy conversation. Therapists actively try to influence the language in which clients talk to themselves so that it becomes helpful rather than harmful. The approach educates clients to converse with themselves creatively. Furthermore, therapists collaborate with clients to ensure that they understand how to talk to themselves once psychotherapy ends so that they can continue to maintain their skills. Useful elements of the therapist's language are exported to and then hopefully imported by clients so that they can become and remain more self-aware and increasingly self-reliant.

One way of thinking of CHT relationships is to see them as consisting of two relationships, namely, the relationship from the therapist's perspective and the relationship from the client's perspective. The following are ten characteristics from the client's perspective of effective CHT relationships and indeed of virtually all good psychotherapy relationships. Some of the characteristics are more appropriate at different stages of therapy or with certain clients, whereas others seem desirable throughout the therapeutic process.

The first three characteristics are *acceptance, affirmation* and *attention*. Regarding acceptance, clients need to perceive their therapists as non-judgmental, open-minded and as prizing them as persons, despite any problems and feelings of unworthiness they exhibit. Clients should experience therapists as compassionate and able to reach beneath their surface distress and to accept lovingly the underlying core of their humanity. Regarding affirmation, clients who hear themselves sharing aloud their thoughts and feelings in an accepting emotional climate feel affirmed and validated. Regarding attention, possibly for the first occasion in their lives, clients have sufficient 'air time' from an impartial third party to focus exclusively on them and their concerns.

Emotional relief, encouragement and support, and *facilitation of self-understanding* are also very important for clients. Talking to therapists about their problems can provide clients with emotional release. Often clients who are highly distressed have no one to whom they can turn. They need to be able to 'get it off their chests', vent their problems, and unload them outside the context of family and friends. Furthermore, many clients lack confidence and appreciate therapists who support them and give them more courage to face life and to risk change. Especially early in therapy, vulnerable clients may experience some dependence on their therapists as a legitimate part of a growth-promoting process. Clients also benefit from therapists who can provide safe emotional climates and help them move forward in disclosing, exploring, experiencing and understanding themselves. On many occasions, the realizations that are most useful to clients are those arrived at on their own.

Gaining new perspectives and *learning skills* are two further effective relationship characteristics from the client's viewpoint. Many new perspectives come from within clients, but they can also gain new perspectives that expand understanding from their therapists. Sometimes changes in perceptions come from therapists who challenge clients when they are inconsistent. Clients may also find therapist feedback useful; for example, when assessing and coaching clients in specific communication skills. In addition, acquiring some new or improved skills for dealing with problems is an important source of gain from CHT relationships. Clients like to feel that they have learned some tangible skills for managing problems and becoming more fully human that are useful both now and in future.

The final two characteristics are those of *shared humanity* and a *unique relationship*. Clients want to share psychotherapy relationships with warm, appropriately involved and caring human beings. Therapists should be tactfully honest and where necessary firm, yet remain sensitive to how much self-disclosing, challenging and feedback clients prefer to handle at any given moment. Clients also appreciate being treated as unique individuals. Most clients prefer warm and friendly person-to-person human relationships within professional boundaries. Nevertheless, to some extent, each therapy relationship should be creatively tailor-made to the client – for instance, by fine tuning the balance between facilitating and training or by appropriately adjusting the relationship to take into account clients' differing interpersonal styles (Lazarus, 1993).

A collaborative working relationship in which both client and therapist actively participate, even if in different ways, is essential to implementing the skilled client model. When in personal contact, both therapist and client work as a team in each stage and phase of the model. For example, in the understanding stage, therapists help clients to assess their problems. However, as clients hold almost all the information about their past and current thoughts, feelings and experiences, it is essential that clients actively participate in the joint search for greater understanding. In this way therapists and clients can work closely together to arrive at insightful shared definitions of clients' problems by stating the mind skills and communication/action skills they need to improve. In the changing stage, clients actively collaborate with their therapists to develop skills in ways that work for them and are not just imposed from outside.

Throughout CHT, clients should feel free to raise concerns and provide feedback about the therapeutic relationship and what they are doing in therapy. Furthermore, the same applies to therapists, though always they need to be careful about client sensitivities. In the skilled client model clients and therapists create their own unique relationships to further the process of attaining mutually shared goals.

Whereas in the adaptation CHT the therapist might be termed a client-centred coach, in mental cultivation CHT the therapist is also a wise guide or mentor assisting clients in the inner journey of accessing and implementing their innate goodness. The assumption is that clients are better and wiser than they know. However, they require empathic and knowledgeable help so that they can listen to their biological nature more deeply and also curb negative and cultivate positive aspects of their minds. Since therapists and clients are on the same inner journey, it is important that therapists model the human sympathy and compassionate actions that clients seek to make contact with and elicit from themselves. The ultimate emphasis is on personal practice with clients learning to relate to themselves so that they become their own wise guides or mentors.

Applications of cognitive humanistic therapy

Cognitive humanistic therapy has applications in different modes or ways of therapeutic work including psychotherapy and counselling, personal practice, supervision, and training.

Psychotherapy and counselling assume that clients are working with properly trained and skilled practitioners. Psychotherapy may be brief (say up to six sessions), medium term (say up to twenty sessions), or long term (more than twenty sessions). Most often, it is likely to be brief or medium term rather than long term. Although individual therapy is this book's main focus, adaptation CHT might also be conducted with couples, families and small groups of around eight participants.

Mental cultivation CHT is likely to be on an individual basis, though this need not always be the case. Young adults may be good candidates for mental cultivation CHT so long as they are reasonably emotionally stable and think and communicate/act at an above-average level of skilfulness. Many of those most suited to mental cultivation CHT may be clients and others, like Jung's analytic therapy patients, who are in the afternoon of their lives. Such people may have additional time, energy and motivation for this kind of therapy at a time when job and/or child rearing are less central preoccupations.

As CHT has a major emphasis on imparting, using and maintaining human-being skills, *personal practice* is always extremely important. Personal practice refers to a range of activities performed by clients and others independently of therapists. The term personal practice is preferred to the term self-help for two main reasons. First, the word 'practice' more accurately reflects what is involved in working on one's own than does the word 'help'. Second, especially in mental cultivation therapy, the outcome of personal practice is to help others as well as oneself, which is not implied in self-help.

One aspect of personal practice is that of performing homework assignments during psychotherapy. Another use of personal practice is that of applying the skills learned in psychotherapy once regular contact with the therapist ends. Take the example in adaptation CHT of working with a client anxious about being more assertive at work. During therapy, the therapist can encourage the client to practise the targeted mind skills and communication/action skills in a series of progressively difficult homework assignments. Furthermore, the therapist can pay attention to assisting the client to consolidate these targeted skills as self-help skills for afterwards. Then, when regular therapy sessions end, the former client becomes her or his own personal coach for using and maintaining the targeted assertion at work skills on her or his own.

Another aspect of personal practice can be that of self-therapy, which entails former clients systematically working with themselves as if they were their own therapists. Self-therapy that focuses on either CHT's adaptation or mental cultivation components is also relevant to psychotherapists and counsellors, whether they be students, trainers or practitioners.

With clients who are focusing on the mental cultivation component of CHT, personal practice can be used during and after formal psychotherapy in much the same way as in adaptation CHT. However, mental cultivation CHT may lend itself more readily than adaptation CHT to personal practice independent of psychotherapists. One reason for this is that those concerned with developing mental cultivation and human sympathy are already likely to possess reasonably good mind and communication/action skills and to be well motivated to improve themselves.

Starting with Chapter 8, the remaining chapters of this book are all relevant to mental cultivation CHT. Each of these chapters ends with a group of practices that can be used, as appropriate, either in conjunction with psychotherapy or in personal practice, supervision and in cognitive humanistic training groups. Likewise the world's major religions have a long and rich tradition of practices or activities that people can use either on their own or with mentors to awaken and develop their hearts and minds (Walsh, 1999).

Personal practice goes beyond spending quiet time doing specific practices to integrating higher level human-being skills into daily life. As such, personal practice involves regular inner dialoguing, or conducting mental conversations, in which clients and personal practitioners working independently of therapists endeavour to cultivate and implement humanistic consciences. As part of this process they need to develop and articulate visions or self-concepts of themselves as genuinely humane persons and then have the courage and skills to keep acting on them. This struggle will entail overcoming numerous temptations to fall back into previously conditioned unskilful patterns of behaviour.

Supervision is part of the initial training of psychotherapists and counsellors and can continue throughout their professional careers. With regard to adaptation CHT, supervisors and supervisees are likely to keep the focus of supervision on clients' problems. However, a valuable part of supervision can also be to assist supervisees in assessing their levels of human sympathy and mental cultivation. Then, if both parties are sufficiently motivated, they can explore how supervisees can become more skilful on these dimensions. As part of this process, supervisors may find themselves assessing their own levels of human sympathy and mental cultivation. Such material is probably best explored with their own supervisors or with colleagues rather than with those they supervise.

Cognitive humanistic *training* is another application of CHT. Participants in such training may be groups of psychotherapy clients or students and others outside of therapeutic settings. Training in human-being skills, such as different kinds of communication skills – for instance listening skills and assertion skills, is similar in nature to that already conducted by cognitive behavioural therapists and trainers. All these skills involve mental processes as well as outer communication/actions. Regarding training participants in groups to think more effectively, the cognitive humanistic focus on mind skills can allow for mental processes to be addressed more comprehensively and flexibly than if the focus is only on one area of thinking, such as on altering either irrational beliefs or inaccurate perceptions.

Cognitive humanistic training can also focus on the higher level skills of human sympathy and mental cultivation. Such training courses could form part of the pre-service training or continuing professional development of helping service workers. In addition, psychologically grounded training courses focusing on human sympathy and mental cultivation may be attractive to people whose religious commitments challenge them to become more fully human. There is also a need to develop higher level human-being skills training courses for use in schools, higher education settings and voluntary agencies. The practices provided at the end of the human-being skills chapters in this book are intended for use in training courses as well as for psychotherapy and personal practice.

SEVEN   The Skilled Client Model

Adaptation CHT and mental cultivation CHT can both be approached within the framework of the skilled client psychotherapy and counselling process model or, more briefly, the skilled client model. Therapists using the skilled client model are practitioner-researchers who, within the context of accepting, affirming and collaborative working relationships, assist clients to improve specific mind skills and communication/action skills in order to manage current and future problems more effectively and to become more fully human. Improving clients' skills can entail releasing skills already in their repertoires, lessening poor skills, and initiating and/or improving good skills. Box 7.1 shows the stages and phases of the skilled client model.

Box 7.1: The skilled client model

Stage 1: Relating
Main task: Form a collaborative working relationship

Phase 1: Pre-therapy contact
Communicating with and providing information for clients prior to the first session.

Phase 2: Starting the initial session
Meeting, greeting and seating, making opening remarks, and encouraging clients to tell why they have come.

Phase 3: Facilitating client disclosure
Allowing clients space to reveal more about themselves and their problem(s) from their own perspective.

Stage 2: Understanding
Main task: Assess and agree on a shared definition of the client's problem(s)

Phase 1: Reconnaissance
As necessary, conducting a broad review to identify the client's main problems and to collect information to understand her/him better.

Phase 2: Detecting and deciding
Collecting specific evidence to test ideas about possible poor skills and then reviewing all available information to suggest which skills might require improving.

Phase 3: Agreeing on a shared definition of the client's problem(s)
Arriving at a preliminary definition of the client's problem(s) including, where appropriate, specifying mind skills and communication/action skills for improvement.

Stage 3: Changing
Main task: Achieve client change and the maintenance of change

Phase 1: Intervening
Helping clients to develop and implement strategies for managing current problems and improving relevant mind skills and communication/action skills for now and later.

Phase 2: Terminating
Assisting clients to consolidate their skills for use afterwards and to plan how to maintain them when therapy ends.

Phase 3: Personal coaching
Former clients, acting as personal coaches, keep using their skills, monitor their progress, retrieve lapses and, where possible, integrate their improved skills into their daily living.

Using the skilled client model

There are numerous considerations in applying the skilled client model in a humane and effective way. A more detailed discussion of these issues may be found elsewhere (Nelson-Jones, 2002a). Therapists need to use the model flexibly. For instance, recently bereaved partners may require sensitive supportive listening with, possibly, some practical suggestions for getting through the day rather than any mention of poor skills. Another example is that of clients, badly emotionally undernourished by negative early experiences, who require therapists to bear sensitive witness to their previous and current suffering and to help them gain the courage to face what has happened and move beyond it. In sum, therapists should always tailor their application of the skilled client model to the circumstances, level of vulnerability, diverse contexts, learning styles and problems of individual clients.

The fact that the skilled client model is presented in a series of three stages, each of which has three phases, may imply a degree of tidiness inappropriate to the often more messy and unpredictable practice of psychotherapy and counselling. Often stages and phases overlap and therapists should not be surprised to find themselves moving backwards and forwards between them. In addition, sometimes in a single session, therapist and client can focus on more than one aspect of a complex problem.

Therapists need to use good judgement in whether and how they introduce the concept of skills. With some clients, especially in very brief therapy, it may be wise to assist them to become more skilled without emphasizing the term 'skills'. In general, the longer therapy lasts, the more reason there is for helping clients to see themselves as acquiring and maintaining skills. Furthermore, therapists may become better in the training aspects of therapy when they clearly view themselves as using client-centred coaching to impart applied skills.

A brief overview is now provided of each stage and phase of the skilled client model from both the therapist's and from the client's perspectives. Then the skilled client model is illustrated with a case study focused on the final phase of the understanding stage and the first phase of the changing stage.

Stage 1: Relating

The main goal of the relating stage is for the therapist and the client to start establishing a good collaborative working relationship. Other goals are to find out why clients have come for therapy and to gain an initial understanding of their problem or problems.

Phase 1: Pre-therapy contact

The therapist in the process

Psychotherapy really begins from the moment the client first hears about the therapist. Therapists can gain or lose clients from how they advertise, the quality of information they offer about their services, how easy they are to get hold of, the kind of messages they leave on their answering machine, how friendly they sound on the phone, and whether and how they answer e-mail enquiries.

If therapists work for an agency, how the office staff behave towards potential and first-time clients is very important. Warmth, tact and quiet efficiency all convey positive messages towards clients, some of whom may be feeling highly vulnerable. Comfortable and tasteful furnishings in reception areas can also be reassuring.

Arriving early gives therapists time to relax, get the room ready, and if using recording equipment, to ensure that it works. They can check the client's name and any pertinent details about him or her. If possible, therapists should do all their preparation in private. Then, when they meet clients, they can devote their full attention to them.

The client in the process

Clients have different preconceptions about therapy. These ideas are of varying degrees of accuracy and some of the ways in which they are formed are mentioned above. Some clients may have had good, bad or indifferent experiences with other therapists prior to coming. Clients' expectations may also be shaped by whether they were referred either by previous clients or by referral sources who said positive things when making the referral. Sometimes clients come for therapy reluctantly because they have been made or told to do so. Clients' pre-therapy expectations are also shaped by factors like culture, social class, financial status, age and gender.

Most often clients have a limited idea of what to expect in therapy and what their role is likely to be. Clients consider coming to therapy with varying degrees of trepidation. It can be a huge step for some clients to seek therapy. Reasons for this include their reluctance to face up to difficult issues, to make intimate disclosures, and to break barriers about talking to third parties about family and other problems. Some potential clients will find it too difficult to come. Others may only come as a result of overcoming their fears and desperately wanting to ease their suffering.

Phase 2: Starting the initial session

The therapist in the process

Therapists need to develop good skills at meeting, greeting and seating clients. They can provide warm and friendly, but not effusive, welcomes to clients. Where clients are in reception areas, therapists can go over to meet them, call them by name and introduce themselves. Most therapists are relatively sparing about small talk. A little of it may humanize the process. Too much risks diverting attention from the client's agendas. Therapists show clients into the therapy room and indicate where they should sit.

When both parties are seated therapists can make an opening statement that indicates the time boundaries of the session by saying something like 'We have about 45 minutes together' and then give the client permission to talk. Sometimes therapists may need to fulfil agency requirements to collect basic information before giving permissions to talk. Furthermore, therapists may need to ask the clients if they can record the session. Examples of permissions to talk are 'Please tell me why you've come', 'Where would you like to start', 'You've been referred by ___ . Now how do you see your situation?'

Therapists should try to create an emotional climate of warmth, respect and interest in which clients can feel reasonably safe in sharing their inner worlds and wounds. They use active listening skills to help clients experience that their thoughts and feelings are being received and understood sensitively and accurately. At some stage therapists may make a further statement that describes to the client the structure of the initial session and how they work within the skilled client model. Therapists should be prepared to answer questions, but avoid long-winded replies. Some questions are really seeking reassurance and a counsellor's manner of responding can help calm unnecessary fears.

The client in the process

From the moment they set eyes on their therapists, clients start summing them up. Therapists' vocal and bodily communication may speak just as loudly as their verbal communication. Therapists may feel anxious, but clients probably feel far more threatened by the situation. They are on unfamiliar territory, uncertain of how to behave, and know that they are likely to be asked to reveal personal information to someone whom they do not know.

Questions running through clients' minds include: 'Can I trust this therapist?', 'How confidential is the session?', 'How much am I prepared to reveal?', 'Will this person like me?', 'Will we be on the same wavelength?' and 'Can this person help me?' Clients come to therapy bringing varying degrees of wounds and unfinished business from past relationships. It may take them some time to view therapists as individuals in their own rights who differ from people who have inflicted past hurts and rejections.

Phase 3: Facilitating client disclosure

The therapist in the process

A decision therapists have to make is when to curtail giving clients space to share their internal worlds on their terms and to change to being more active in collecting information. Where time permits, the author generally prefers to encourage clients to keep talking for the first 10 to 15 minutes rather than assume much direction near the beginning of the session. The main purpose of the early part of initial therapy sessions is to build good relationships with clients. Helping clients to feel accurately understood as they share their inner worlds is a good way of achieving this objective.

In addition, it can be good for clients to become used to the idea of participating actively in sessions and not just responding to the therapist all the time. Another reason is that therapists never know where clients are going to take them and by becoming too focused too soon they may stay on the surface rather than accessing material that is more important to clients. Furthermore, as clients reveal themselves on their own terms, therapists can start making useful hypotheses about what are their problems, their strengths, and their self-defeating thoughts and communications/actions.

During this process of client disclosure, therapists require good relationship-enhancement skills such as active listening, summarizing and sparingly asking questions, for instance encouraging clients to elaborate. When necessary, therapists can provide brief explanations of the stages of the helping process.

In the skilled client model, it is advisable for therapists to take notes discreetly in the initial session(s). They can explain that they take notes to remember relevant information for when they later suggest ways of viewing their problems differently. Memory is fallible. When attempting to agree on shared definitions of their problems, it is very helpful for therapists to do this from actual material that clients have provided, including quoting back pertinent statements that they have made. Clients vary in the degree to which they are emotionally accessible and willing to disclose. Assuming clients have come to therapy of their own accord and that the therapist is both confident and tactful when explaining the purpose of note taking, most clients do not mind it.

The client in the process

Clients possess varying levels of ambivalence about disclosing problems and talking about their lives. Many clients, at the same time as being willing and eager to talk about themselves, will economize on how much they reveal. Varying levels of client and therapist anxiety are ever present throughout the therapy process and can distort the amount and nature of disclosure. Although it is not always the case, during the initial session many clients' anxiety about the therapy process is at its highest. Some rationing or avoidance of disclosure is deliberate. On other occasions, as clients explore and experience themselves more, they get in touch with and reveal material of which they were previously unaware. Clients can be inconsistent in what they reveal. To maintain a safe emotional climate, sometimes it is best just quietly to notice this inconsistency rather than bring it to their attention. The time for greater consistency may be later rather than now.

Stage 2: Understanding

The main goal of the understanding stage is for therapists to collaborate with clients to clarify and assess their problem(s) so that they can agree on shared initial definitions of how clients might change. Therapists, with the assistance of clients, move from describing and clarifying problem(s) in everyday terms to assessing and analysing how clients sustain their difficulties. Throughout, therapists respect clients as intelligent co-workers who are by the end of this stage entitled to a reasoned initial analysis of their problem(s). Depending on the complexity of problems and, sometimes, the verbosity of clients, the understanding stage may take place over more than one session. Furthermore this stage can include activities that clients undertake between sessions.

Phase 1: Reconnaissance

The therapist in the process

Even when, on the surface, clients' problems seem reasonably clear cut, it may be beneficial to conduct a broader reconnaissance. Together, therapist and client may identify further problems. In addition, they may uncover information relevant to understanding clients' presenting concerns. In stage two of the skilled client model, therapists perform a more active role than in stage one. While maintaining a relationship orientation, therapists adopt more of a task orientation as they assist clients to review various areas of their functioning. Some therapists will also use biographical information or life-history questionnaires that they ask clients to fill out either prior to or after the first session.

When conducting a reconnaissance, therapists tactfully move the focus of the interview from area to area. A reconnaissance varies in length and depth according to what seems appropriate for each individual client. The areas that therapists and clients cover are influenced by the contexts in which they meet, the clients' presenting concerns, and anything clients have previously revealed about themselves.

Some of the reconnaissance may refer to clients' childhood and adolescence: for example, their early family experiences, schooling, relationships with parents and significant others, problems experienced when growing up, traumatic incidents, view of themselves and anything else that the client considers relevant. The reconnaissance can also review how clients function in their intimate and friendship relationships, what are their living arrangements, how they get on at work or in study, any health issues, and issues related to diversity such as culture and biological sex. Additional areas include information about their previous experience of therapy, any medication they are taking, any unusual current stress, and what clients perceive as their strengths. Further questioning can establish their favourite hobbies and pastimes, their short-, medium- and long-term goals, their central values and philosophy of life, and anything else that clients want to share.

Therapist skills for conducting a reconnaissance include helping clients to see that its purpose is to help them to understand themselves better and that it is not just for the therapist's benefit. Therapists should ask questions in ways that avoid making clients feel interrogated, for example by interspersing empathic responses with questions. Furthermore, therapists can make the process personal by letting clients know that they are interested in their experiencing and perceptions of events. The reconnaissance is an exploration of clients' subjective worlds as well as of external facts. Where possible, therapists should keep the interview moving because they can come back to areas requiring more detailed consideration later. In addition, therapists should continue to look for evidence concerning clients' main problems and what poor mind skills and poor communication/action skills sustain them.

The client in the process

A few cautions are in order regarding the possible negative impact of a reconnaissance on clients. Clients need to perceive that the reconnaissance is of some potential benefit to them. Consequently its scope needs to be tailored to clients' purposes and problems. Clients who come to therapy with fairly specific concerns are only likely to respond positively to questions in or around the area of their concerns. Where clients' problems are multiple, complex or long-standing, there is more of a case for a thorough reconnaissance. Clients also may have areas they are reluctant to discuss in detail, if at all, and such wishes require respect.

Often clients are willing collaborators in sensitively conducted attempts to understand themselves and their problems more fully. They appreciate the time, space and concern provided for reviewing their lives and problems. Many clients have been starved of opportunities to be the focus of attention. When helped to review different aspects of their lives aloud, they feel affirmed and can gain useful insights. In the initial session clients may feel more understood by therapists who both facilitate their disclosure and review different aspects of their lives than by therapists who facilitate their disclosure alone.

Phase 2: Detecting and deciding

The therapist in the process

By now therapists have already assembled a number of ideas about clients, their problems, their strengths and potential poor skills. How therapists handle this next phase can depend on the complexity of clients' problems. For example, if clients come with specific problems, say improving public speaking skills, therapists can perform more detailed analyses of any feelings, physical reactions, thoughts, and communications/actions that can help them to make more accurate hypotheses about how clients are sustaining such difficulties.

In a more complex case, such as that of George presented later, the authors prefer to offer an overall definition of his problem rather than a detailed definition of any part of it. This overall definition consists of the main mind skills and the main communication/action skills the client needs to improve. In some ways providing an overall definition is made easier by characteristic poor mind skills tending to carry across a range of situations. This should come as no surprise, because Ellis manages to detect irrational beliefs and Beck manages to identify inadequately reality-tested perceptions in all of their clients.

Therapists may still collect more information to test ideas about possible poor mind skills and poor communication/action skills. When this process is over, they should pull together their conclusions for presenting to clients. Therapists can ask clients to give them a few minutes to look over their notes and any other information so that they can offer specific suggestions to them about where they might fruitfully work in future. Earlier, when making notes, the author may highlight any information that may be of later importance, for example by writing and encircling a 'T' by any thoughts that appear to be of particular relevance for subsequently identifying poor mind skills. Later these thoughts can be quickly spotted to provide evidence for, decide on and to illustrate potential poor skills.

The client in the process

Clients can be very co-operative in providing additional information that helps them to understand specific problems more clearly. For instance, in the example of improving a client's public speaking skills, therapists may want to ask follow-up questions that elicit thoughts and feelings before, during and after giving a talk. Clients can also help the therapist to understand how their distress varies across different public speaking situations. Furthermore, therapists can ask clients to show them their actual verbal, vocal and bodily communication when, say, starting a speech.

The author finds that clients do not become upset if he politely asks them to give him some time to pull together the information that he has collected so that he can make some specific suggestions about how they might improve their lives. What is damaging is a confusing and ill-considered assessment of their problems, not one that is carefully constructed from what they have told the therapist.

Phase 3: Agreeing on a shared definition of the client's problem(s)

The therapist in the process

Prospective skilled clients require some idea of where they have been going wrong. After making preliminary assessments, therapists attempt to agree with clients on shared definitions of the mind skills and the communication/action skills that clients need to improve. Therapists offer suggestions for discussion with clients. Furthermore they illustrate how they have come to their conclusions with material that clients have provided earlier.

Good therapist suggestions of skills that clients might improve follow logically from information revealed to date. If the groundwork has already been laid in the earlier parts of the session there should be no surprises. Therapists work with clients as appropriate to explain, modify or even discard suggestions with which clients are unhappy. It is vitally important that clients not only own their problems but agree on where best to improve their skills because they are the ones who need to work hard to change.

Often the author conducts therapy sessions with a small whiteboard between the rear ends of the therapist's and client's chairs, so that each person can turn to it when wanted. It is probably best to avoid using the whiteboard before agreeing on a shared definition in the initial session. Premature use of the whiteboard can slow the assessment process down and may divert it by getting into too much detail about a specific area too soon.

Using visual as well as verbal presentation to define clients' problems has many advantages. As in teaching, visual as well as verbal communication can stimulate interest. In addition, clients' memories are fallible and by the time therapists move onto the next topic clients may have started forgetting what has just happened unless there is a visual record of it. Furthermore, therapists can use the whiteboard to modify suggestions of poor skills in line with client feedback. By the time that therapists finish, clients can see a good overview not only of their problems, but of goals for change. Once agreement is reached on the skills clients need to improve, both parties can record this as a basis for their future work. However, as psychotherapy progresses, therapists need to be flexible about modifying shared definitions of problems and the skills that clients need to improve.

The client in the process

Most often clients come for therapy because they are stuck. Their existing ways of defining problems and their coping strategies are not working for them. They sustain their difficulties by under-utilizing their strengths as well as by perpetuating their weaknesses. Many clients genuinely appreciate therapists who take the trouble to break their problems down and show them how they can improve in easily understood language. Clients need to be active participants in the process. They should be helped to understand how important it is for them to question anything that seems unclear. In addition, clients should feel free to seek modifications of, or abandonment of, any of the therapist's suggestions concerning skills requiring improvement.

Clients like to be invited to contribute feedback. Furthermore, they want any suggestions of skills for improvement to be worded in language with which they are comfortable. They appreciate illustrations of how therapists have arrived at their suggestions based on material they have shared before. In short, clients like being treated as intelligent collaborators in the process of creating shared definitions of how they can change for the better. Often clients who see their problems broken down experience feelings of relief. They experience glimpses of hope that problems that up until now have seemed overwhelming can be managed both now and in future.

Stage 3: Changing

The main goals of the changing stage are first for therapists to collaborate with clients to achieve change and then for clients to maintain that change on their own after therapy ends.

Phase 1: Intervening

The therapist in the process

Therapists intervene as user-friendly coaches as clients develop self-helping skills and strategies. To intervene effectively therapists require good relationship skills and good training skills. Skilled therapists strike appropriate balances between relationship and task orientations; less skilled helpers err in either direction.

Therapists work much of the time with the three training methods of 'tell', 'show' and 'do'. 'Tell' entails giving clients clear instructions concerning the skills they wish to develop. 'Show' means providing demonstrations of how to implement skills. 'Do' means arranging for clients to perform structured activities and homework tasks.

Within collaborative working relationships, therapists deliver specific mind skills and communication/action skill interventions drawn from cognitive behavioural and humanistic sources to help clients manage problems and improve specific skills (Cormier and Nurius, 2002 Nelson-Jones, 2002a). In instances where therapists find it difficult to deliver interventions systematically, they weave them into the fabric of the therapy process. Whenever appropriate, therapists assist clients to acknowledge that they are learning and using skills. Frequently clients are asked to fill out 'take away' sheets in which they record skills-focused work done on the whiteboard during sessions. In addition, homework assignments form a regular part of therapy. Instructions for assignments are written down in order that clients are clear what they have agreed to do.

The client in the process

The intervening stage focuses on assisting clients to manage current problems and to acquire mind skills and communication/action skills as self-helping skills. Clients are learners whose therapists act as user-friendly coaches as they change from their old self-defeating ways to using new and better skills. Clients actively collaborate during therapy, for instance in setting session agendas, sharing their thoughts and feelings, participating in in-session activities to build their knowledge and skills, and keeping their own records of work covered during therapy.

Clients also negotiate and carry out appropriate homework assignments. Some such assignments prepare for the next session: for instance, listing their demanding rules in a specific manner so that time can be saved when this topic is addressed during therapy. Other assignments involve implementing skills learned during previous sessions: for example, learning to challenge demanding thinking and replace it with rational statements or trying to improve their verbal, vocal and bodily communication in a specific situation.

Phase 2: Terminating

The therapist in the process

Most often either therapists or clients bring up the topic of ending before the final session. This allows both parties to work through the various task and relationship issues connected with ending the contact. A useful option with some clients is to fade contact by spacing out the final few sessions. Certain clients may appreciate the opportunity for booster sessions, say one, two, three or even six months later.

The skilled client model seeks to avoid the 'train and hope' approach. Therapists encourage transfer and maintenance of skills by such means as developing clients' personal coaching abilities, working with real-life situations during therapy, and using between-session time productively to perform homework assignments and to rehearse and practice skills. Often therapists make up short take away cassettes focused on the use of specific skills in specific situations – for instance, the use of coping self-talk to handle anxiety when waiting to deliver a public speech.

In addition, therapists work with clients to anticipate difficulties and setbacks with implementing and maintaining their skills once therapy ends. Then together they develop and rehearse coping strategies to prevent and manage lapses and relapses. Sometimes clients require help identifying people to support their efforts to maintain skills. Therapists can also provide information about further opportunities to build skills.

The client in the process

Clients terminate therapy for many reasons, some negative, some neutral and some positive. Negative reasons include feeling unhappy with therapists and their way of working and failure to make significant progress. Neutral reasons include clients or therapists moving to another location or either party only being available for a fixed number of sessions. In the skilled client model, positive reasons for terminating therapy are that clients have evidence that they can manage with their current problems better and possess some skills to prevent and/or successfully cope with future similar problems.

Clients can ensure that termination is handled as beneficially as possible for them. For example, they can actively participate in discussions about how they can consolidate and maintain their skills once therapy ends. Some dependency may arise in the earlier parts of therapy when clients may feel especially vulnerable, but the consistent message they receive during therapy is that they have the resources within themselves to become happier and more effective human beings.

Phase 3: Personal coaching

This is presented as a single section rather than divided into two parts since it relates to what clients do on their own once therapy ends. The purpose of skilling clients is so that they become more skilled individuals independent of their therapists. Throughout the skilled client model, the emphasis has been on giving clients the skills to help themselves and, where relevant, others too. Therapists try to help them understand how to apply the skills so clearly that they carry them around in their heads afterwards and coach themselves in them.

Clients can view the time after therapy as a challenge to maintain and, where possible, to improve their skills. When necessary, clients can revise their skills by referring back to any notes and any records of skill-building activities made during therapy. Furthermore, clients can listen to cassettes made during therapy to reinforce their understanding and application of targeted skills. In addition, clients can apply strategies discussed during therapy to help them to overcome setbacks and to retrieve lapses.

Clients can also involve other people to support them in their self-helping. Before therapy ends they may have worked with their therapists to identify people and resources for assisting them afterwards. After termination, clients can request booster sessions and keep in touch with therapists by phone or e-mail to monitor their progress, handle crises, and become even more skilled.

Nevertheless, in the final analysis, it is up to clients to keep practising their skills and coaching themselves. The skilled client model assumes that there is no such thing as cure. Often, after termination, clients have to work hard to contain their poor skills and maintain their good skills. Sometimes using good skills provides obvious rewards, in which case it is comfortable to continue using them. On other occasions clients may perceive losses as well as gains when using good skills. One strategy for former clients tempted to go back to their old ways is to perform a cost-benefit analysis of why they should keep using their improved skills.

Case study: George

The following case study illustrates the final phase of the understanding stage and the first phase of the changing stage of the skilled client model.

George, aged 52, had been unemployed for six months after being fired from his position of managing director of a communications company. He was obsessed with getting back into the workforce and had become extremely depressed at his lack of success. He had discussed his depression with his doctor, who put him on anti-depressant medication that he felt terrible about taking. As part of his termination package, George was given the opportunity to use a well-respected outplacement company for senior executives, where he had been seeing a consultant to assist with his job search programme and to provide support and encouragement. The outplacement company hired the author on a sessional basis to work with clients whose job search problems went beyond the ordinary. While George felt some anxiety about seeing a counselling psychologist, he was prepared to give it a go and to reserve judgement.

Stage 2: Understanding

Phase 3: Agreeing on a shared definition of the client's problem(s)

About two-thirds of the way through the first session the therapist told George that he was now ready to offer some suggestions for how he might become happier on the whiteboard. The therapist wanted this to be a two-way process and invited comments as he was making suggestions so that George would be satisfied with the way they were stated. Therapist and client agreed that there were three main inter-related areas requiring attention: his depression, his job seeking impasse and his marital difficulties.

Table 7.1 shows the shared definition of mind skills and communication/action skills that George might improve to become happier and more effective. Note that each key mind skill is illustrated with examples that George provided earlier on in the session. Other than his job-seeking skills, George is also provided with an indication how to improve each of the targeted communication/action skills.

George participated actively in this process of identifying skills that he might improve. He thought he had the job-seeking skills, but was just too depressed to use them properly. At the end of the session client and therapist each wrote down the mutually agreed definition for their records.

Table 7.1   Shared definition of George's problem in skills terms

Mind skills I need to improve	Communication/action skills I need to improve
Creating rules 'I must be successful' 'I must have approval' 'I must feel guilty' 'I must not get depressed' 'I must provide financial support for Jill' 'I must not take a break/enjoy myself'	*Job seeking skills* *Assertion skills* (verbal, voice, body) • especially when Jill disparages me *Friendship skills* • spending more time on own with friends • disclosing my feelings more
Creating perceptions • myself 'I'm a failure, worthless, inadequate' 'I'm always letting Jill (wife) down' • others Inclined to put some people on pedestals 'Jill is highly dependent/vulnerable' 'Jill is powerful/tyrannical'	*Pleasant activities skills* • taking a vacation • playing sports with friends *Managing sleep skills* • sleeping too much in day and then not sleeping well at night.
Creating explanations 'I'm totally responsible for Jill and for her feelings' 'My feedback hurts Jill, she is never contributing to hurting herself'	
Creating expectations 'The future is hopeless' 'I'm unable to influence my future positively.'	

Stage 3: Changing

Phase 1: Intervening

When George came back for the second session, he was looking brighter and said that he had bottomed out. He had done some homework examining his thought processes. He now realised that he didn't want a job and found it scary to think that he was losing his work ethic. As therapy progressed, the prime focus was on learning to handle Jill's disparagement of him better both inside his mind and when dealing with her. Between the second and third therapy session, George had stood up to Jill and had taken a week's out-of-town holiday.

The therapist and George unearthed a self-defeating communication pattern that he described with the following imagery: 'The drier the (emotional) desert, the more I am looking for water (affection, love and unconditional acceptance).' He went on to reflect that 'Deserts are full of cacti, spiky plants, scorpions, no wonder it's a bloody unpleasant place.' With the therapist's assistance, George conducted a cost-benefit analysis on whether he wanted to stay in his marriage and decided that he did, partly because it made good economic sense. He explored, challenged and restated demanding rules about needing approval, feeling guilty and having to provide a high level of income and status.

George used skills of challenging perceptions about himself. For example, he made a list of over 100 people who valued him. Furthermore he listed his skills and strengths. He also tested the reality of his perception that Jill would provide him with emotional nourishment, an unrealistic perception that drove him to keep unsuccessfully looking for the approval he was never likely to get from her. Despite her deep unhappiness, Jill did not want to seek professional help.

George assumed more responsibility for acting independently in the relationship. Instead of discussing his job-search efforts with Jill daily and then being put down, he kept what he was doing more to himself. When Jill disparaged him, he developed better skills for either not responding or responding neutrally and not letting himself become hooked into responding aggressively.

The major focus of the therapy was on assertion skills for dealing with Jill. However, among other things, time was also spent on looking at sleep skills and the therapist lent George a cassette on the behavioural treatment of sleep problems. There was also a focus on engaging in more pleasant activities. George took a 320-item *Pleasant Events Schedule* (Lewinsohn, Munoz, Youngren and Zeiss, 1986) and listened to a cassette by Dr Peter Lewinsohn emphasizing the importance of depressed people engaging in more pleasant activities. There was never any great emphasis on improving George's job-seeking skills, since his depression was being sustained by poor skills elsewhere.

George received fourteen 50-minute sessions of therapy over an eight-month period, with sessions being more frequent at the start than at the end. In the first four months of therapy his mood and energy level gradually and intermittently improved and by the ninth session he was feeling noticeably happier. Despite occasionally having blue patches, by the fourteenth and final session George's energy level was hugely improved and he was actively pursuing a number of work-related pursuits as well as coping far better at home. He considered that he could get by on his own now, especially because he now understood how he had become so depressed in the first place and possessed the insight and skills to avoid this happening again.

EIGHT Calming and Disillusioning the Mind

The book's remaining chapters represent a selective integration of strands of psychotherapeutic and religious thought – in particular Buddhism and Christianity – with cognitive humanistic psychotherapy and personal practice. The approach taken here to religious concepts is agnostic and, as such, does not assume any adherence to Buddhism or Christianity. However, although grounded in applied psychology, the following chapters assume that a simple division between the problems addressed by psychotherapy and the eternal moral, ethical and existential issues addressed by the world's major religious traditions is misleading and detrimental. Buddhist and Christian psychology might be much stronger than at present for being able to integrate theoretical and practical ideas from psychotherapy. Similarly psychotherapy can fruitfully learn from the psychological insights, compassion, wisdom and humanity of the Buddha and Jesus Christ. In particular, when extending the boundaries of psycho-therapy from adaptation therapy to mental cultivation therapy, religious insights have much to offer.

The human-being skills required for adaptation and mental cultivation overlap. To simplify matters the following practical discussion focuses only on some of the main areas and skills. The underlying idea of this part of the book is to provide readers with a road map for navigating how to become better human beings. Those who are familiar with Buddhism can probably anticipate that the upcoming chapters address some central Buddhist areas for curbing unskilful and cultivating skilful actions and mental states. With sometimes differing emphases, the same areas are also stressed in Christianity and the world's other major religious traditions.

The review of human-being skills in the following chapters seeks to avoid falling into the traps of a number of simplistic dualities. Cultivating being fully human entails curbing negative qualities and unskilful behav-iour and cultivating positive qualities and skilful behaviour. However, curbing poor skills is also a positive quality to be cultivated, although the language of curbing negatives and cultivating positives obscures this fact. Another duality is that between communication/action skills and mind skills. In reality, the two are closely interwoven: for instance, specific human-being skills such as showing gratitude contain an interplay of mind skills and communication/action skills components. A further duality is that between mind and heart or between reason and love. Those who strive to improve either their clients or themselves in the skills described in this and the coming chapters will implicitly, if not explicitly, be cultivating the fusion of reason and love.

Calming and centring the mind

Eastern religions have long realized the importance of learning to calm and concentrate the mind. Buddhist mind training has three goals: to know the mind, to shape the mind, and to liberate the mind (Nyanaponika, 1962). Buddhists sometimes use the analogy of the monkey mind to describe the agitated way in which an undisciplined mind jumps from topic to topic and sensation to sensation. Buddhist meditation is usually divided into two main areas: *anapanasati* or mindfulness of breathing and *vipassana* or insight into seeing clearly the nature of reality until one can get rid of defilements and attachments to everything (Thitavanno, 2002). Tranquility is one objective of breathing meditation. Strengthening the ability to concentrate and focus without being easily distracted is another objective. Tranquillity and improved concentration provided by proficiency in breathing and meditation lay the foundations for *vipassana* or insight meditation, which entails more advanced practices for knowing, shaping and liberating the mind. A central feature of *vipassana* meditation is systematically and dispassionately observing the moment-to-moment arising and passing of bodily sensations, thoughts and consciousness itself (Goldstein, 1994; Hart, 1987).

Western cognitive behavioural psychotherapy has realized the value of calming the mind for becoming more relaxed. For example, mental relaxation in which the subject imagines a restful scene can be an intervention either in its own right or in conjunction with progressive muscular relaxation. However, Western psychotherapy has been slow to recognize the value of calming and concentrating the mind in order to help it to become a sharper tool for addressing problems and becoming more fully human. Just as in Buddhist practice, CHT therapy clients and personal practitioners can learn to calm and concentrate their minds both as ends in themselves and also as preludes to therapeutic work for knowing, shaping and liberating their minds.

An obvious reason for learning to calm and concentrate the mind is that it provides an antidote to the stresses of modern life. The pace of contemporary life can be so hectic that people feel can feel slaves to time – doing things on time, getting there on time, and fitting as much as possible into a given period of time. Making the mind more tranquil can alleviate some of this stress. Furthermore, when feeling calmer and less stressed, it is likely that one's mind will become clearer and better able to focus on what is really important for one's own and others' happiness and fulfilment.

Another important reason for learning to calm and concentrate the mind is that of assuming more personal responsibility for influencing the course of one's life. Much of the time most people live their lives from outside to inside rather than from inside to outside. It is very easy to fall into the trap of allowing oneself to be constantly reacting to external stimuli rather than proactively shaping what one does. Humans need to get in touch with their own centre or with what Rogers called their organismic valuing process so that they have an appropriately internal locus of control (Rogers, 1959). Calming down can be part of the process of 'centring down', which in turn allows individuals greater choice about how they influence their lives. This does not mean that people need be insensitive to external stimuli; rather, they are able to process them in a personal way rather than to be blindly under their influence.

To become fully human people require the capacity to lead rich inner lives as well as authentic and effective outer lives. With the hurry-sickness, consumerism and competitiveness that are so prevalent in Western societies, many people sacrifice their inner lives in the pursuit of external goals. The skills of contemplation and reflection can become lost, especially when people come to fear solitude as well. Contemplation and reflection require a mental change of gear from busily responding to external circumstances to listening quietly and carefully to one's own inner voices and mental processing. Thus Western therapists, clients and self-therapists can benefit from learning basic skills derived from Eastern religions regarding how to develop more tranquil, contemplative and inwardly focused states of mind.

Mindfulness of breathing

Mindfulness of breathing provides a gateway to a calmer, more concentrated and inwardly focused state of mind. Focusing attention on breathing is possibly the most universal of meditative or contemplative practices in the world. It is also the starting point of Buddhist mind training (Hart, 1987; Kornfield, 1993; Nyanaponika, 1962; Thitavanno, 1995, 2002).

Breathing is fundamental to life, which cannot exist without the dual aspect of breathing in and breathing out. The word 'mindfulness' means attention. Mindfulness of breathing means paying attention to and being highly aware of or conscious of the processes of one's breathing. As people become more practised in breathing meditation, they bring about an increase in the intensity and quality of their attention. They may notice subtle differences in the alertness and clarity of their attention. Furthermore, they may be able to concentrate their attention on the flow of their breathing for progressively longer periods of time. In addition, they can bring about a calming, equalizing and softening of the rhythm of their breathing.

Those wishing to practise mindfulness of breathing should find a quiet place, away from distracting noises and disturbing sounds. They should decide in advance how long they wish to practise in any session, with ten or twenty minutes being sufficient at first. In Eastern countries, the lotus posture with fully crossed legs is most commonly adopted for breathing meditation. Westerners, who are generally not trained to sit in the lotus posture when young, may experience difficulty and pain in trying to get into and maintain this position. From personal experience on a meditation retreat, the author knows that sitting with both legs tucked back to one side can also be difficult and painful to maintain. Westerners engaging in mindfulness-of-breathing practices and not wanting to use the lotus posture can sit upright in a relatively comfortable chair with their legs slightly apart and feet placed firmly on the floor.

The hands of those meditating on breathing are usually cupped on their laps, most commonly with the left hand being placed palm up below the right, which is also palm up – however Japanese Zen practitioners usually put their right hand below their left one (Dalai Lama, 2002). Alternatively, those practising mindfulness of breathing can place their hands face down on their knees. When attending to their breathing, people may close their eyes to prevent the mind being distracted by what is seen. Some people, however, when focusing on breathing for extended periods of time, prefer to keep their eyes slightly open to avoid drowsiness. One option here is to then focus on the tip of one's nose and attempt to be oblivious to all other things.

The main task in mindfulness of breathing is to concentrate on the natural flow of the breath – breathing in, breathing out, breathing in, breathing out and so on – to establish concentrated awareness. The nose is the starting point of the in-breath, the chest the middle, and the abdomen the end. While breathing out, the reverse is the case. Those engaging in mindfulness of breathing can follow the process of their breaths through these stages of breathing in and breathing out. Either after or instead of doing this, people can establish a check point, with the nose-tip being most recommended, and fix their attention there where the breaths are sure to pass in and out. One variation on mindfulness of breathing is to accompany each out-breath with gently and sub-vocally saying 'calm' to oneself. Another variation is to accompany successive in-breaths by quietly and sub-vocally counting from one to nine, then down to one, then up again to nine, and so on.

When starting to learn mindfulness of breathing, and even when more experienced in it, people's minds meander into extraneous thoughts or fantasies, be they past, present or future. On such occasions, people should gently bring their minds back to focusing on their next breath. They should not worry if they repeatedly have to bring themselves back to being aware of their breathing. Analogies that are sometimes used for training in mindfulness of breathing are those of training a puppy or a calf. At the end of a mindfulness-of-breathing session, those who have closed their eyes should gently reopen them.

Some people may find mindfulness-of-breathing activities useful in their own right. In CHT, an important use of mindfulness-of-breathing techniques can be as a bridge *into* personal practice sessions. A less frequent use and one dependent on personal preference can also be as a bridge *out of* personal practice sessions. In addition, mindfulness of breathing can be used as a self-help strategy. For example, Roger Walsh, a professor of psychiatry and author of a book on religious practices called *Essential Spirituality*, finds that some calming breaths can be a wonderful way to start each hour and that doing this makes an enormous difference to the quality of his day (Walsh, 1999). Sometimes, at the start of book-writing sessions, the author uses brief mindfulness-of-breathing periods to become calmer and more inwardly focused. Others may use mindfulness of breathing as a way of coping with stressful situations or tuning out of annoying environmental circumstances. The Buddhist meditation teacher Nyanaponika Thera has observed that: 'By simply observing our breath, we can easily and unnoticed by others withdraw into ourselves if we wish to shut ourselves off from disturbing impressions, empty talk in large company, or from any other annoyance' (Nyanaponika, 1962, p. 62).

Disillusioning the Mind

The term illusion means a misapprehension of a true state of affairs. The following discussion examines some ways in which therapists, clients and personal practitioners can possess restrictive illusions or misapprehensions regarding the nature of themselves and their minds that create suffering rather than liberation. The three illusions reviewed here are the illusion of an independent self, the illusion of permanence, and the illusion of mental efficiency.

The illusion of an independent self

The concept of 'self' or 'ego' is prominent in Western psychotherapeutic and popular thought. However, there is a danger that people think about themselves far too rigidly. Once given names, people can become embodied selves who live and talk as though they have independent personalities. However, the question remains 'to what degree are people deluding themselves when they think of themselves as having an independent self?'

Few humans attain a real awareness of the extent to which what they view as a largely autonomous or independent 'self' is dependent on their past and current conditioning. Radical behavioural psychologists go so far as to say that individuals are solely products of evolutionary-based needs combined with their conditioning and that any notion of personal agency is inaccurate and illusory (Skinner, 1953; 1969). Without going this far, conditioning by families, peer groups, societies, cultures, the media is nevertheless so pervasive and insidious that it can be a real struggle to identify when it happened in the past and is happening now. It is impossible for individuals to become fully mentally free whilst remaining unawares of the extent to which their thoughts, feelings and communications/actions are the result of rewarding consequences received either directly or indirectly by observing others receiving them. Under the illusion of independence, they experience great difficulty in knowing what they truly think, feel and what they want to do.

The Buddhist concept of dependent origination provides a striking challenge to the notion of an independent self. One way of looking at dependent origination is in terms of causation (Batchelor, 1997; Dalai Lama, 2001, 2002). For example a flower arises dependently since it is the result of causes and conditions, for instance a seed, appropriate soil, the act of planting, watering and so on. Similarly individuals also emerge from the unprecedented and unrepeatable matrix of biological, family and cultural causes and conditions that have formed each one of them.

Another way of looking at dependent origination is in terms of how a phenomenon depends on its parts, for instance the way a flower depends on its petals, stamen and pistil. Human beings are also dependent on their diverse and interacting parts. In Buddhism there is no essential or substantial self that exists independently of each person's unique configuration of causes, conditions and interactive cluster of processes. The Dalai Lama observes: 'All persons and things are dependent upon their causes and upon their parts and cannot exist independently of them ... Because all phenomena are dependent arisings, they have a nature of emptiness' (Dalai Lama, 2002, p. 164). A major purpose of the concept of dependent origination is to reduce human beings' self-centredness and their consequent need for attachment and craving.

The challenge to the idea of an independent self can go even further when people realize the extent to which they are dependent on others for so many things, including the making of all their material possessions. American psychiatrist Howard Cutler gives the example of how many people were involved in making his shirt. Such people included the farmer who grew the cotton, the sales person who sold the farmer the tractor to plough the field, the people who made the tractor, the miners who mined the metal for the tractor, and each of the different people involved in the process of turning the cloth into a shirt (Dalai Lama and Cutler, 1998). Another example that challenges the notion of an independent self is that, with rapid technological improvements outstripping human wisdom, the security of each one of us may be more interconnected than we heretofore realized.

Albert Ellis's advocacy of unconditional self-acceptance (USA) provides a further useful insight into the dangers of a simplistic notion of an independent self (Ellis, 2001). It is erroneous to think of an independent self that automatically subsumes its various parts. All too often, when individuals perform and evaluate specific actions, they wrongly place their 'egos' on the line. Ellis seeks to stop clients and others from giving their selves or egos too much of a life of their own – their central view of themselves as persons insufficiently acknowledging its interdependence with its parts. He contrasts unconditional self-acceptance (USA) with non-acceptance and conditional self-acceptance (CSA). Non-acceptance, which is rare, involves individuals in rating their whole selves negatively for everything that they do 'badly'. Conditional self-acceptance entails individuals accepting themselves when they have done well and won the approval of others and rating their whole selves negatively when they do badly. An example is that of an individual who does poorly in a test and then thinks that this makes her or him a rotten person. Unconditional self-acceptance entails individuals in always accepting themselves as persons, but evaluating their performances – how they do in specific areas of their life – as good or bad depending on whether they help or hinder them in leading happy or effective lives. Ellis is making a clear distinction between the value of oneself as a person and functional evaluations of one's specific actions. His message is that individuals should be very careful about how they define their 'self' so as to avoid engaging in counter-productive self-rating.

The point of the above discussion is to assist readers in realizing the dangers of adopting simplistic and inflexible ideas of individuals possessing independent selves. Therapists, clients and others may unknowingly be failing to realize the extent of their conditioning, the causes that created and continue to create them as human beings, the way their different parts interact, their degree of dependence on others, and how their notion of themselves can become too over-generalized. As such, in varying degrees, they can create the illusion of an independent self that restricts both freedom of choice and their ability to rise above excessive self-centredness.

The illusion of permanence

Another illusion that can interfere with mental liberation is that of insufficiently realizing the impermanent nature of human existence and of the outside world. Every moment, the cells of which the body is composed arise and pass away. Every moment, the contents of the mind keep changing. Buddhist *vipassana* or insight meditation aims to help people increasingly realize the arising and passing of all their thoughts and sensations. Instead of allowing themselves to become attached to any one of them, those meditating are encouraged to settle into the meditative process and simply observe and become attuned to the transitory nature of all mental phenomena. American meditation teacher Joseph Goldstein writes: 'The emphasis in the meditation process is very much on undistracted awareness: not thinking about things, not analyzing, not getting lost in the story, but just seeing the nature of what is happening in the mind' (Goldstein, 1994, p. 100).

The purpose of insight meditation is to help people attain a deeper understanding of the nature of reality. Buddhists consider that by being more deeply aware that everything is impermanent and changing people become less prone to cravings and attachments which are the cause of human suffering. However, one does not have to be a Buddhist to realize that human life and everything to which humans are connected, such as their families, friends, work situations, and physical environments are continually changing and decaying. Becoming excessively attached to impermanent phenomena can interfere with one's freedom to react creatively to the changing nature of reality. An example is that of some parents who are reluctant to acknowledge adequately that their teen-age children are growing up and are wanting more mature and less dependent relationships. A further instance is that of business people who fail to adapt to changing environmental circumstances because they are too attached to their old ways of doing business. Unless business people adapt, they risk losing market share and ultimately their businesses.

Inability to accept the fact of one's death or existential finitude is one of the main factors contributing to the illusion of permanence. The 'self' is impermanent as well as interdependent. It is part of the human condition to undergo old age, sickness, death, and leaving behind all one's loved ones and possessions. American existential therapists Irvin Yalom and Rollo May stress that death anxiety, the fear of ceasing to be, can be both conscious and unconscious (May and Yalom, 2000; Yalom, 1980). From early in their lives children are extremely preoccupied with death. Strong death anxiety is likely to be repressed. To cope with the terror of potential non-being, people erect denial-based defences against death anxiety. One defence is that of specialness. While at a conscious level, most people accept that their lives are finite, deep down they can develop irrational beliefs about their own immortality and inviolability. Another defence is that of belief in an ultimate rescuer – however bad things may get, the individual is not alone in an indifferent universe and some omnipresent observer will come to the rescue. Though not mentioned by Yalom and May another defence may be that provided by religious beliefs in an afterlife, be it a Christian heaven, Buddhist rebirths, or an Islamic paradise.

Shedding the illusion of personal permanence and gaining increased awareness of death can lead to heightened appreciation of life. As Viktor Frankl, the founder of logotherapy, pointed out death does not rob life of its meaning. If people were immortal they might put off doing things indefinitely. Death belongs to life and gives it meaning (Frankl, 1955, 1975). Consequently individuals with an inadequate grasp of their finiteness are unable to assume full responsibility for the shaping or authorship of their lives.

The Buddha regularly exhorted 'Make haste in doing good.' The Dalai Lama enjoins Buddhist practitioners to contemplate their own impermanence so that, by doing so, they can increase their resolve to engage in practices that will bring about their spiritual liberation (Dalai Lama and Cutler, 1998). For Buddhists, practices that increase mindfulness of death prevent them from being careless and doing evil in life and stimulate them in making haste in doing good. To heighten awareness of impermanence, one of the main Buddhist chantings for meditation practice focuses on the Recollection of Death (Thitavanno, 2002, p. 54):

Living is impermanent,
death is permanent,
surely we shall die,
my life has death as the end.
My living is not permanent,
my death is for certain.

Buddhist meditation practices sometimes include nine Cemetery Contemplations graphically describing the dead human body in various stages of decomposition (Nyanaponika, 1962).

The illusion of mental efficiency

The following discussion does not focus on academic intelligence, but rather on the use of mental processes in conducting one's daily life and in becoming fully human. In the Western world, a simple distinction is often made between those people that have mental disorders and the remainder who think of themselves as being mentally efficient. However people are not brought up in environments where systematic mind training in how to deal with applied situations in their lives forms part of their education. Furthermore, mental cultivation is not a widespread goal in Western cultures. Consequently, it is easy to compound illusions of an independent self and of permanence with the illusion of mental efficiency.

In the second half of the twentieth century, there was a cognitive revolution in psychotherapy and counselling (for example, Beck, 1988; Ellis, 2001). Increasingly it has been clarified that how well people function when faced with problems in their lives is heavily influenced by how efficiently they think. Cognitive and cognitive behavioural therapists assist their clients to think about specific aspects of their thinking so that they can change them for the better. To date the most influential psychotherapeutic approaches to helping clients change how they think have been the rational emotive behaviour therapy (REBT) approach of Albert Ellis and the cognitive therapy (CT) approach of Aaron Beck. Both Ellis and Beck recognize the importance of such knowledge becoming more widespread in the community and have written self-help books for this purpose. Nevertheless, there is still a huge gap between the degree of applied knowledge in how the mind works that members of the general public possess and that of psychologically trained helping service professionals. Furthermore, even helping service professionals skilled at working with clients' minds may become rather less skilful when it comes to possessing insight into and improving their own mental processes.

An important reason why so many people are under the illusion of mental efficiency is because they remain unaware of the knowledge and skills required for being any different. Even if some people acquire an intellectual awareness of such knowledge and skills, they may still resist applying it to themselves because it threatens their existing illusions of independence and efficiency. Although a simplification, mental efficiency for being a successful human being is presented here as comprising four main components: possessing an adequate conceptual framework; being able to access feelings; understanding the interrelationships between feelings, physical reactions, thoughts and communications/actions; and, where necessary, improving one's mental processes.

The first component is that of possessing an adequate conceptual framework. Conceptual frameworks provide languages and sets of concepts in which clients, therapists and lay people can understand and think about themselves, others and the world. So far theoretical frameworks for psychotherapy and counselling have been developed more to address subnormal functioning than to improve normal functioning. Furthermore, in varying degrees, the frameworks mainly help therapists to understand clients rather than helping clients to understand themselves. Theorizing has been more therapist centred than client centred, let alone ordinary people centred. However an important criterion of good psychotherapy theory is that it should be comprehensible to clients so that they can use it for self-help both during and after therapy.

In the cognitive and cognitive behavioural approaches there is some attempt to teach clients a conceptual framework for understanding how they sustain their problems, but this is much less the case in the psychoanalytic and humanistic approaches. Furthermore, even the existing cognitive and cognitive behavioural conceptual frameworks are insufficiently comprehensive: for instance, in failing to incorporate a clearly articulated concept of mind and of mental cultivation. Thus the illusion of mental efficiency has been sustained by the relative failure of psychologists, psychiatrists and others in the helping professions to develop comprehensive conceptual frameworks for what it takes to be a successful human being. Nonetheless, when formulating more broadly based conceptual frameworks, existing psychotherapeutic approaches possess many useful insights and approaches in how to become more mentally efficient. This book, with its emphasis on mind, mind skills and mental cultivation, attempts to use some of this existing therapeutic knowledge and merge it with nontheistic religious ideals and insights.

The second component of being mentally efficient is that of being able to access feelings. People differ in their skills of truly accessing and listening to their feelings, physical reactions and underlying instinctual remnants. The illusion of an independent self helps to sustain this aspect of mental inefficiency in most humans who fail to realize the extent to which the feelings and thoughts that they attribute to originating from their 'selves' are in fact products of past and present causes and conditioning. To be fully alive and in touch with what the French call their *élan vital*, people need the ability to disencumber themselves of feelings and thoughts that are ill-digested hand-me-downs of the ways in which others taught them to feel and think. Both negative or unpleasant and positive or pleasant emotions can be the consequences of unskilful past conditioning, though negative feelings are more likely to predominate.

Humans vary in how well they have learned the skills of being able to listen to their true feelings and the wants and longings of their underlying animal nature. Everyone needs to engage in an ongoing process of paying close attention to feelings. For those sufficiently knowledgeable, personal practice can provide a valuable forum for doing this. Earlier in this chapter, mention was made of mindfulness of breathing and also of learning to become mindful of the flow of the contents of the mind. Such contemplative methods can be modified so that individuals observe and explore their feelings and physical sensations in order to get in touch with deeper, and sometimes higher or purer, levels of feeling. Good skills at accessing one's finer feelings are fundamental to the ability to fuse heart and head, reason and love.

The third component of mental efficiency involves understanding the interrelationships between feelings/physical reactions, thoughts and communications/actions. Most people, at the same time as harbouring the illusion that they possess independent or autonomous 'selves', inadequately realize how much they can influence how they feel, physically react, communicate and act through how they think. Albert Ellis (Ellis, 2000, 2001) has an Activating event-Beliefs-Consequences or ABC theory, which in its most simple form states that the consequences (C) of an activating event (A) are heavily influenced by the individual's beliefs (B), which may be either rational, irrational or a mixture of both. Consequences (C) include how people feel and act as a result of the activating event and their beliefs about it.

The author's preference is to think in terms of a Situations-Thoughts-Consequences or STC framework because, in addition to beliefs or rules, people have other kinds of thoughts, for instance perceptions and expectations. Furthermore, T can stand for thinking or mind skills, for instance skills of creating rules, perceptions and expectations. Let's take the situation (S) of Kate, who has made what she considers a generous donation to a school in a Third World country to fund six scholarships for poor students. Kate's thought at (T) is 'The school should be more open in showing me appreciation'. The consequences (C1) of Kate's situation (S) and her thought about her situation (T1) are that she feels sorry for herself rather than for the poor students and that she will probably not renew the scholarships next year.

Were Kate to possess good mind skills, she would be able to examine the reality of her perception that the school was not showing her adequate appreciation and challenge her rule about needing to be overtly appreciated for what she was giving. This might result in Kate creating some different thoughts about her situation (T2) that would have the consequences of making it easier for her to feel better about herself and to continue funding the scholarships next year (C2). Without their realizing it, people's mental efficiency can be severely curtailed if they do not possess much insight into how their thinking influences their feelings and behaviour.

The fourth component of mental efficiency is that of improving one's mental processes. Individuals require the skills of knowing how to improve their mind skills. They also require a vision of and a commitment to mental cultivation. Basically, there are six main steps in altering or improving mind skills. First, individuals need to become aware of, or identify, the mind skill or mind skills in need of improvement. The STC framework described above can be a helpful tool for detecting mental inefficiencies. Second, they can gain further useful information by assessing and monitoring how they currently think in targeted areas. Third, they can learn to challenge poor ways of thinking about situations and problems; for example, they can search for evidence that confirms or negates the way they currently think. Fourth, they can form statements and self-talk that incorporates more balanced and realistic ways of thinking. Fifth, they can do homework assignments and practise improved mind skills in real life, including changing the way they act to accord with their improved thinking. Sixth, they can evaluate their progress in implementing their improved mind skills and modify the way they think accordingly.

This discussion challenging the illusion of mental efficiency should not be taken too simplistically. Many individuals do think about their lives and problems reasonably efficiently and some are very insightful and skilful. However, the vast majority of people are using their minds at levels well below their potential. Furthermore, many of those who are functioning well could benefit themselves, others and the human species by becoming even more mentally cultivated and skilful.

Introduction to Practices

This chapter and the following chapters address material that is either generally not covered in psychotherapy books or is addressed in them with a different emphasis, so practices or activities are provided at the end of each chapter. The word 'practice' is used in preference to the word activity since being more fully human can entail practising how to live more skilfully for the rest of one's life. As appropriate, these practices can be used as part of CHT therapy, personal practice, supervision and training. There are three main sources that have influenced the content of the practices. One source is the writing of leading writers about psychotherapy, in particular Albert Ellis and Aaron Beck. The second source is that of religious literature incorporating specific exercises, with special reference to mind-training practices. On the assumption that many readers are relatively unfamiliar with the religious literature, as contrasted with the psychotherapy literature, some sources are cited here. These religious sources include Batchelor (1997); Chodren (1990); Dalai Lama (1999, 2000, 2001, 2002); Dalai Lama and Cutler (1998); Goldstein (1994); Hart (1987); Hodge (1999); Kornfield (1993); Nyanaponika (1962); Salzberg (1995); Thitavanno (1995, 2002); and Walsh (1999). In the interests of practicality and readability no sources are cited in the text of any practice. The third source for the content of the practices is that of personal input from the author.

Practices

Practice 8.1: Mindfulness of breathing

Part A: Developing mindfulness of breathing

Find a suitable place, free from distractions, where you can practise developing mindfulness of breathing. Select a time that suits your schedule where, for at least the next five to seven days, you can develop your mindfulness-of-breathing skills. Now go back and re-read the section in this chapter on mindfulness of breathing and, when ready, start conducting your mindfulness-of-breathing practice sessions. Remember that the major goal of mindfulness of breathing is to develop here-and-now attention to your breathing processes and that any resulting relaxation is a by-product of this goal.

Part B: Using mindfulness of breathing as a self-help skill

In the section on mindfulness of breathing, three examples were provided of using brief periods of mindfulness of breathing as a self-help skill: at the start of every hour, when wanting to become more inwardly focused as a writer, and for coping with stressful situations. Think of occasions in your everyday life when you could employ mindfulness-of-breathing skills; when appropriate practise using your skills in these situations, and then evaluate the consequences.

Practice 8.2: Challenging the illusion of an independent self

1. What do you think was the contribution of each of the following causes and conditions in creating what you currently view as your 'self'?

    * your biological and genetic inheritance;
    * your family or families of origin;
    * your formal education;
    * your friendships at various stages in your life;
    * your participation in groups;
    * your experience of intimate relationships;
    * your experiences in the world of work;
    * significant events in your life;
    * your culture, race, social class, biological sex, gender-role conditioning, sexual and affectionate orientation, and religion or philosophy;
    * the historical, political, economic and technological contexts in which you have lived and now live;
    * anything else not mentioned above.

2. What do you think are the main causes and conditions that maintain what you currently view as your 'self'?
3. Do you have a tendency to put your ego on the line by rating your whole self as a person when you think, feel or communicate/act poorly or well in specific ways? Remember the earlier example of an individual doing poorly on a test and then thinking that she or he was a rotten person. Provide one or more examples from your own life.
4. What are some of the dangers from maintaining the illusion of an independent 'self' and failing to recognize the interdependence of one's 'self'.

Practice 8.3: Challenging the illusion of permanence

Part A: Impermanence of mind

Engage in mindfulness of breathing until you feel calm and centred. Then switch to insight meditation in which you attend to the arising and passing of the contents of your mind, whether they relate to feelings, inner physical sensations, sensations from outside, images, fantasies, or thoughts. Do not try to hold on to any of them or deliberately make associations. Without struggling or forcing your mind, be as aware as you can of its contents at any given moment. Avoid a judging mind; instead just quietly and calmly accept the flow of your mental experiencing as you settle into a state of quietly attending to and observing the shifting content of your mind.

You may do this practice for brief periods, say 10 minutes or so, over a period of days. Buddhists consider that both breathing and insight meditation require ongoing regular practice for major benefits.

Part B: Impermanence of body

The following are some practices that may increase death awareness:

- *Physical signs of aging.* Write out a list of any physical signs of aging that you can recognize in yourself now – for instance, greying hair, scaly skin, aching bones, increasing deafness and so forth. What is your attitude towards these signs of your impermanence?
- *Writing your obituary.* How long do you expect to live? Write an obituary for yourself if you continue living the way you are now. How does this make you feel about your impermanence and about the wisdom of the choices that you are currently making about living? Should you be making more haste in doing good?
- *Visualizing your dying and death.* Take yourself on a guided fantasy through the process of your dying, death, funeral and the final disposing of your body. Imagine 'when', 'where', 'how', 'who' in each instance.

Part C: Impermanence of environment

Think about the continuously changing nature of each of the following environments associated with your life. These changes may be momentary, daily, monthly, yearly or over much longer periods of time:

- your natural environment;
- your relationship environment;
- the technological environment;
- the socio-political environment;
- any other environment that you consider relevant.

Practice 8.4: Challenging the illusion of mental efficiency

1. Do you possess an adequate conceptual framework for conducting your life and for becoming more fully human? Give reasons for your answer and, where appropriate, identify gaps in your existing knowledge.
2. How skilled are you at accessing your true feelings and the wants and longings of your animal nature? Give reasons for your answer and identify any problems you may have in listening to your finer as well as to your baser feelings.
3. How skilled are you at understanding the interrelationships between your thoughts, feelings/physical reactions, and communications/ actions? Do you ever consciously try to analyse these connections, possibly using something like the ABC or STC frameworks as an aid to your exploration?
4. If you were to identify a mind skill that required changing, how would you go about improving and maintaining improved performance in it?
5. Refer back to Box 4.2, Levels of Mental Cultivation. What do you consider to be your current level of mental cultivation? Give reasons for your answer.

NINE   Awakening the Heart

This chapter continues exploring unskilful illusions that can interfere with people becoming fully human by focusing on two illusions that can harden people's hearts against their fellow humans. One illusion is that of human differentness or failing to acknowledge that all humans share the same specieshood. Another illusion is that of human badness, what Maslow called the 'bad animal' view of human nature (Maslow, 1970, 1971). Such illusions need to be challenged and replaced with more balanced and accurate assumptions. Two of the cornerstones of humanism, be it either the strict secular version or as part of religious traditions, are that all human beings belong to the same species and that they have an innate potential for goodness that provides the basis for developing humanistic consciences.

On the surface it may seem easy to believe that all humans are the same and that they have the potential for good. However, many people would consciously disagree with either or both of these perceptions. Others might seem to agree, but in varying degrees their behaviour indicates that they disagree. Subconsciously many people have great resistance to the realities of human sameness and potential for good because of what acceptance of these two truths means. For example, they would then need to discard illusions of superiority and beliefs that it is right to take advantage of fellow humans. Instead, they would need to accept responsibility for opening their hearts to others, understanding them and striving to bring out the best in them. This is much more easily said than done.

The illusion of human differentness

Today the challenge to humankind is to acknowledge the characteristics people share as part of the same human family, while cherishing life-affirming forms of diversity. Darwin clearly saw humans as a distinct species. He wrote: 'Nevertheless all the races agree in so many unimportant details of structure and in so many mental peculiarities, that these can be accounted for only by inheritance from a common progenitor: and a progenitor thus characterized would probably deserve to rank as man' (Darwin, 1998a,

p. 631). Furthermore in his book *The Expression of the Emotions in Man and Animals*, first published in 1872, Darwin observed that the chief expressions of humans are the same throughout the world (Darwin, 1998b). That Darwin was essentially correct about universal human facial expressions has been confirmed by extensive research evidence (Ekman, 1998). However, despite being a uniform species, Darwin considered that the degree to which individual humans identified and felt alienated from one another was guided by the laws of natural and sexual selection.

Creating alienation from the human species

From the moment of birth people are bombarded with messages that reinforce their sense of an independent self. Many of these messages are useful in helping the growing young person develop an identity and skills for navigating the world. However, without necessarily intending this outcome, many of these messages teach people a false sense of difference from one another and from the human species. Either explicit or implicit in many of these teachings is that, because of differences in certain characteristics, people are in varying degrees superior or inferior to other humans. Such perceived differences may be worsened when combined with individual and group pathology. Existential isolation or a degree of separateness from other humans is inherent in the human condition. Therefore, it is not the fact of separation but the degree of perceived separation from other humans that characterizes the illusion of human differentness. In moderation, all of the areas of identification and alienation discussed below can be realistic. It is only in immoderation that they become illusory and potentially dangerous.

Perhaps excessive egocentricity is the most obvious way in which people can fail to identify closely with their fellow humans. People can become crippled, stunted and diminished by adverse life circumstances and all too readily perceive others as threats rather than sources of affection and friendship. The distinction between 'me' and 'not me' can become far too rigid and punitive and provide little opportunity for the degree of identification on which genuine human sympathy is based.

Human beings are social animals and there are many ways in which distinctions between 'us' and 'them' can serve to sustain illusions of difference and superiority. Families and kinship networks, if functioning well, can provide individuals with emotional nurturing and skills for identifying with the human community. However, in many instances, a barrier comes down between families and the outside world in which the humanity of other family members is acknowledged, but 'outsiders' are treated as less important and human. The extent of nepotism that takes place in some countries is a clear example of treating non-family members as second-class citizens and sometimes worse than that.

Perceived differences in humanity can also be based on social class, educational attainment, income and wealth. The British class system, although weakening, provides a good illustration of a state of affairs where some people's humanity is more valued than others. Wealth and money snobbery, either in conjunction with or independent of social class, is another way in which the humanness of those less financially success-ful can be discounted. In addition, despite sometimes admitting the problem at an intellectual level, tolerance of world poverty in which numerous people go to sleep hungry is a glaring money-related example of failing to acknowledge a common humanity at an emotional and action level.

Nationalism provides a further example of how individuals can deny their common humanity with others. Even in times of peace, citizens of countries can believe myths about the superiority of characteristics of their own nation and, by default, relative adversaries can subscribe to collective illusions in which they demonize and de-humanize one another as 'the enemy' (Beck, 1999). Two outcomes of this process are that it can dissolve inhibitions about violence and can create closed-mindedness in which the enemy is crudely framed by focusing on, distorting and exag-gerating their negative qualities.

Nationalism and illusions of cultural – and sometimes racial – superi-ority can go hand in hand. Illusions of cultural superiority are wide-spread and not confined to the Western world. For example, numerous Chinese, Japanese and Thais consciously and subconsciously think that they possess cultures superior to others. Racism is one of the most per-nicious ways in which individuals can deny and disparage the worth of other humans. American civil rights leader Martin Luther King saw racism as a philosophy based on contempt for life and a despicable expression of man's inhumanity to man (King, 1967). Nazi Germany, with its myth of Aryan superiority, was an obvious case of merging nation-alism with racism.

There are a number of other ways in which people insufficiently acknowledge their specieshood. Sexism in which one sex, usually men, think of themselves as different and superior to the other sex, usually women, is widespread in the world, perhaps especially in Muslim coun-tries. Heterosexism, in which the needs for human warmth and intimacy of gay and lesbian people are devalued, is another instance of creating an illusion of differentness where there exists an urgent need to affirm a com-mon humanity. Despite everyone going through the cycle of birth, aging and death, ageism, which in the Western world usually means insuffi-ciently acknowledging and celebrating the humanity of older people, also can be a component of the illusion of differentness. Furthermore, people can feel alienated from those with varying forms of physical disability or deficiencies in the structure and functioning of some body parts. Another important component of the illusion of differentness can be that based on religion or philosophy, be it Christian, Hindu, Muslim, Buddhist or some secular belief system. The core of any truly religious teaching should be that all humans share a universal specieshood and common humanity that transcends differences, including religious ones.

Frequently people are so imbued with their illusions of differentness that they consider them to be natural rather than learned. Furthermore, often assumptions that deny universal common humanity operate subconsciously, which makes it much harder for people to challenge them. Sometimes negative potentials remain quiescent under benign circumstances, but become activated under conditions of threat or when manipulated. For example, when individuals become very angry they may resort to more primitive forms of black-and-white thinking in which they loose sight of the humanity of perceived adversaries. In addition, illusions of differentness based on such factors as nationality, race and religion are capable of being activated and fanned when it serves the interests of unscrupulous leaders.

Creating identification with the human species

Rising above the illusion of differentness resulting from one's conditioning and acknowledging a common humanity goes much further than just paying lip service to it. It requires a radical challenge to identify oneself a part of the whole human species rather than a superficial mental joining with humanity just when it suits one. Relinquishing the illusion of differentness entails a huge shift in almost everyone's personal perspectives and worldviews. It should be seen in terms of the process of becoming more mentally cultivated rather than something that either happens or does not. Individuals start at varying stages along the process. Furthermore, their internal barriers to acknowledging the underlying fact of universal sameness can occur in any combination of the areas of potential alienation just reviewed.

Rather than address overcoming the separate components of the illusion of differentness, the focus here is on affirming basic characteristics that all human beings share in common. Some of these characteristics are common to non-human species as well; nevertheless the fact remains that they are common to all human beings. Furthermore, although individual differences among human beings exist across all characteristics, this does not negate their universality. All human beings have the same life cycle of birth, aging and death as all other humans. They are subject to sickness and the uncertainties of fate, including not knowing precisely when they are going to die. Except in rare circumstances, all human beings have the same bodies – head, arms, trunk of body, legs, central nervous system and so on. Furthermore, they have the same senses – sight, sound, smell, taste and touch. In addition, they have the same main facial expressions: for example, happiness, sadness, fear and anger. All human beings have the same biological functions – eating, drinking, disposing of waste, reproducing. They also have the same needs for physical safety, food, shelter and warmth as all other humans.

All human beings share the instincts and instinct remnants including the potential for human sympathy as well as for being aggressive. They share the same capacity to experience a range of feelings and physical reactions, both pleasant and unpleasant. They also have the same capacity to experience suffering and happiness as other humans. They have the same needs for love, belonging and human warmth. They have the same mind, which is capable of storing, generating and processing information. They have the same ability to have thoughts, images, fantasies and nocturnal dreams. All human beings seek to find meaning in their lives. More than any other species, human beings possess the capacity for symbolic mental processing and have the potential to control their thoughts.

The above is just a partial list of ways to challenge the illusion of differentness. Ellis (2001) uses the term 'unconditional other-acceptance' and stresses that people deserve unconditional acceptance and respect whether or not they behave competently or morally just because they are alive, human and unique individuals. Unconditional other-acceptance (UOA) is a valuable insight, but it still has implicit in it the duality between self and others. In addition, there needs to be a concept of universal other-identification (UOI), which espouses universal sameness and dissolves much of the duality between self and others. Awakening the heart is much more possible when the duality between self and others is diminished. For virtually everyone, relinquishing the illusion of differentness and achieving universal other-identification is a lifelong struggle.

The illusion of human badness

How people view human nature illustrates the state of their heart and mind and also shapes their actions. Two extreme viewpoints regarding human nature follow – one 'bad-animal' viewpoint and the other a 'good-animal' viewpoint, to use Maslow's terms. The first view is that humans are treacherous, irrational, incapable of judgement, base, stupid, lazy, cowardly, weak and bestial. This 'bad-animal' view of human nature was held by Adolf Hitler, whose actions made a significant negative impact on the lives of millions of people (Waite, 1977). The second view is that the true nature of the human mind is pure; that love, compassion and forgiveness are deeply rooted in human nature and that negative emotions are ultimately based on ignorance. This 'good-animal' view of human nature is held by the current Dalai Lama who has remained committed to non-violence despite his own exile and the Chinese occupation of Tibet (Dalai Lama, 2000).

Few people are as cynical and negative about their fellow humans as was Hitler. Nevertheless many people consciously or subconsciously hold predominantly 'bad-animal' views of human nature that harden their hearts towards their fellow humans, thus increasing the meanness of their actions towards them, which in turn creates further negativity. Such 'bad-animal' views of human nature need to be challenged to arrive at a more balanced set of perceptions. Challenging the illusion of human badness does not mean denying that human beings throughout history have shown themselves capable of being highly aggressive and destructive. Rather it means looking at why many people feel the need to perceive their fellow human beings so negatively and making the case for innate goodness. Increased recognition of the innate nature of humankind's better qualities provides fertile soil for awakening the heart.

Maintaining the illusion of human badness

Many factors seek to maintain the illusion of badness. The illusion of difference can heighten the illusion of badness in that once human beings see others as different from themselves it is much easier to judge them negatively. A jungle outlook is sustained by misunderstanding Darwin's evolutionary theory. As illustrated in Chapter 2, Darwin thought that human beings had developed both intellectual and moral faculties, the latter being based on their social instincts (Darwin, 1998a). Darwin's evolutionary theory contained no simplistic survival of the fittest explanation of human nature, although human sympathy was reserved only for members of one's own group. The unsophisticated economic view of human interaction, in which individuals are always trying to maximize their selfish ends, also helps sustain the illusion of human badness.

Religious worldviews that emphasize or misinterpret the original sinfulness of humankind sustain the illusion of human badness. These worldviews can be even harder on human beings when they distinguish between believers and non-believers, the former being candidates for salvation while the latter are doomed to damnation. For instance, even more so than the Bible, the Koran, as a book of warning to non-believers, is explicit about the horrible things that will befall them if they do not follow the path of Islam. They also contain positive visions of human potential, but the idea in religions such as Christianity and Islam that human beings require divine intervention for redemption arguably supports the notion that human nature is more bad than good.

Some psychotherapy theorists have been less than flattering about human nature. For instance, Freud and, to a lesser extent, Jung viewed human civilization as a thin veneer that covered baser instincts. Maslow, however, thought that psychological theorizing was overly based on examples of crippled people and sought to redress the balance by looking at the ways psychologically superior human specimens lived (Maslow, 1970). Adler, Fromm and Rogers are some other prominent psychotherapy theorists who pointed out positive aspects of humankind. If anything, the leading cognitive behaviour therapy theorists have focused more on explaining the origins of irrationality and negative emotions rather than the origins of humankind's finer thoughts, feelings and behaviours. Two prominent psychotherapeutic viewpoints that are still common are that humans are either primarily driven by predominantly darker unconscious forces, as in psychoanalysis, or are mainly the victims of their environmental conditioning, as in behaviourism.

The history of the human race is characterized by numerous examples of inhumanity. Furthermore, every day people are confronted by negative behaviour in their daily lives, in their homes, on the streets and at work. Newspapers and magazines appear more ready to feature bad than good news. The images provided by television news outlets, such as CNN, also emphasize areas of the world in which there is conflict and killing. In addition, frequently the content of popular 'action' films and TV programmes is violent. There are numerous factors assisting people to maintain and justify the illusion of human badness.

A case for humankind's innate goodness

Human goodness consists of a mixture of the characteristics of human sympathy and mental cultivation suggested in Chapter 4. In making a case for human goodness, no attempt is made to deny that humans have the potential to be aggressive and destructive. However, human nature is often sold short. What is sought is a balanced viewpoint that more fully acknowledges the potential for goodness, compassion and human sympathy as integral parts of humankind's biological make-up. The following are some reasons why humans might be viewed as having an innate, and often unrealized, potential for goodness.

1. Darwin's evolutionary perspective indicates that social instincts, important among which are sympathy and love, had survival value from the viewpoint of the human species (Darwin, 1998a). Co-operation was involved in sexual activity, the rearing of offspring and in play. In addition, co-operation was involved in warning calls against predators, and in group hunting, group defense and attacks on predators. Darwin considered that what he termed the moral qualities, founded on the social instincts, could be developed by habit, reasoning powers and instruction. Thus, developing a humanistic conscience can be viewed as biologically rooted in humankind's evolutionary history.

2. Human beings need to give and receive love and affection. Frustrating this need can lead to emotional starvation, human diminution and, if people are exceptionally unlucky, to irreversible stunting of their ability to become truly loving persons. The fact that the frustration of positive qualities can lead to emotional problems suggests that these positive qualities are inherent in humankind's biological make-up. The need both to care and be cared for is biologically rooted. Infants and young people vary in resiliency, but no reputable child psychologist or psychiatrist suggests that starving them of affection is good for their emotional development. Children require warm, stable and loving environments in which they are respected as independent human beings. Both hostile and indifferent environments in which, for whatever reasons, parents and other significant care-givers fail to provide adequate nurture and love create emotional trauma, pain and suffering. Furthermore, people who are emotionally disadvantaged when young may still possess low self-esteem and poor human-being skills when grown up, thus making it difficult for them to give and receive affection.

    Adults are probably happiest when they can give and receive love and affection. For most adults, true happiness comes from transcending their existential separateness to care for and be cared for in a primary relationship. In studies of life satisfaction in Britain and America, marriage and family life were rated highly (Argyle, 1987). In short, people valued close relationships in which they could fulfil their biologically grounded need not just to receive, but also to give love and affection.

3. Naturalistic observations and studies of children do not seem to suggest a 'bad-animal' interpretation of human nature (Maslow, 1970; Argyle, 1991). Children can be selfish and aggressive, but they are also capable of being co-operative and caring to one another. Helping and sharing are two important types of childhood co-operation. Helping in this context refers to behaviours intended to relieve another child's state of need or distress. Helping may take the form of

touching, comforting and forms of concrete help. Empathy and helping behaviour are observed at a very early age in children, so it is probable that they represent nature rather than nurture. Sharing can involve such items as toys, food and money. Taking turns with another child in using toys is an example of sharing. Mothers who are warm, sensitive and responsive rather than anxious or tense with their children are more likely to have children who feel secure in their attachment to them. The same is probably true for paternal relationships with children. Such fortunate children, in turn, are likely to be more co-operative and socially competent with other children than those feeling more insecure in their maternal and paternal relationships.

4. The ideals common to the world's religious traditions point to a measure of agreement about some purer or higher aspects of the human potential. Walsh reviewed exercises from seven of the world's major religions to cultivate seven practices or areas of living. The seven religions were Judaism, Christianity, Islam, Hinduism, Buddhism, Taoism and Confucianism. The seven practices were the cultivation of kindness, love, joy, peace, vision, wisdom and generosity. Walsh found that each religious tradition provided both the seven perennial practices and an array of exercises to implement them (Walsh, 1999). These religions seek to cultivate universal qualities arguably inherent in human nature.

5. Anthropological research into primitive cultures suggests a wide range amongst them from high levels of co-operation to much hostility and aggression (Argyle, 1991; Mead, 1937). Maslow, in his 1939 research into the Northern Blackfoot Indians, despite consciously looking for evidence of aggression, found extremely little of it (Maslow, 1970). He concluded that much of the aggression found within cultures might be attributed to either the frustration of, or threats to, basic needs. Anthropological findings point to the possibility of humans living co-operatively within identifiable groups. However, to date, the issue of inter-group aggression is more intractable.

6. In a study of values conducted in twenty countries including Australia, Brazil, Germany, Israel, Japan and mainland China, Schwartz (1992) identified eleven major value types. Schwartz considered that these value types have evolutionary significance because not only do they represent the needs of individuals as biological organisms, but are crucial to the survival and welfare needs of groups. At least two of the value types, benevolence and universality, can be viewed as representing the innate goodness of humans. The motivational goal of benevolence is the preservation and enhancement of the welfare of people with whom one is in personal contact. The motivational goal of universalism is understanding, appreciation, tolerance, and protection for the welfare of *all* people and for nature.

7. Evidence from psychotherapy suggests that numerous clients have previously experienced a mixture of unsatisfactory relationships and inadequate training in human-being skills that has contributed to them developing and maintaining their problems. In the context of good therapeutic relationships and when relevant to their problems, clients almost invariably choose to become more loving and co-operative and less hostile and destructive. In short, during the process of successful therapy clients often become more skilful at uncovering and enacting the positive aspects of their human nature.

8. Apart from a simple 'bad-animal' explanation, negative human behaviour is sometimes explained in terms of the frustration-aggression hypothesis – human beings behave badly when their basic needs are frustrated. The frustration-aggression hypothesis is also too simple. The position adopted in this book is that human beings have a range of instincts and instinct remnants. What differentiates whether they show the brighter rather than the darker side of their nature is mainly their level of human-being skills, including their ability to cope with frustrating and dehumanizing environmental contexts. Human beings who behave badly are in varying degrees ignorant and unskilful rather than inherently evil. There are many factors, some of which are totally outside of their control, which can interfere with people learning and maintaining good human-being skills. Therefore simple 'bad-animal' explanations are inappropriate when people fail to think and behave skilfully.

9. Human beings often experience difficulty in getting in touch with their finer and more tender feelings. Maslow observes that people fear their higher as well as their lower potentials (Maslow, 1970, 1971). This does not mean that such affectionate feelings are not part of their biological make-up, but some of these feelings may be weak or what Maslow termed 'instinct remnants'. The concept of repression applies to innate goodness as well as to sex and aggression. The human species unconscious contains social instincts, the derivatives of which may become repressed. Furthermore, the personal unconscious and subconscious of individual humans contain positive impulses that often go unnoticed and unheeded. Many people require assistance in making contact with and cultivating their underlying humanity.

10. Individuals can come under considerable social psychological pressure not to show the kinder and more compassionate side of their human nature. Chapter 5 mentioned how the level of human-being skills of most people falls far below their potential. Consequently those helping or wanting to help can face pressures to conform and not stand out. Though many admire behaviour that serves the interests

of others, many other people are ambivalent, if not hostile towards it. Some individuals may feel inhibited from either doing good deeds or talking about the good deeds that they actually do because they fear a backlash of derogatory comments and disparagement about their motivation. Both inhibition and silence contribute to 'bad-animal' perceptions of humankind.

10. Negative emotions like continued hatred and resentment can be bad for physical health. For instance, they are associated with hypertension, heart attacks and even cancer. There is no evidence that happiness is associated with poor physical health. Probably happy people are more resilient to falling victim to physical illness and quicker to recover than those who are angry and hostile. If anything, good physical health is associated with a 'good-animal' rather than a 'bad-animal' view of human nature.

11. Most people's everyday experience contains many examples of goodwill, co-operation and kindness. Nonetheless, people often possess the poor mind skill of perceiving more easily what is wrong than what is right. Furthermore, if they disproportionately focus on other people's negative behaviour they risk eliciting even more negative behaviour from them. People can counteract their tendencies towards selectively perceiving human badness and celebrate humanity by looking for universal goodness in themselves, in those with whom they interact daily – including those whom they find difficult, and in the wider world.

12. Around the world, popular culture represented in songs, movies and TV programmes extols virtues like loving another and looking after those whom one loves. In a movie with worldwide appeal like *Titanic*, it would be unthinkable for the romantic lead Jack to value his own life above that of Rose. Furthermore, most often heroes in action and war movies and TV programmes are people who are loyal, steadfast and look after others. The ability of audiences throughout the world to identify with people exemplifying virtuous and loving behaviour indicates that such qualities resonate with their underlying animal nature.

13. Just as human history has a chamber of horrors, like Hitler, Stalin and Pol Pot, it has a chamber of inspirational people like Mahatma 'great soul' Gandhi, Martin Luther King, Mother Teresa and the current Dalai Lama who, despite deprivations and hostility, have had the strength to keep loving and working for the betterment of others. Martin Luther King lived under the daily threat of white terrorism, was nearly fatally stabbed at a book signing, his home was bombed at least twice, and yet he continued to struggle to free people from racism. King, whose greatness included rising above hatred to

remain a loving human being, wrote: 'If only to save myself from bitterness, I have attempted to see my personal ordeals as an opportunity to transfigure myself and heal the people involved in the tragic situation which now obtains. I have lived these last few years with the conviction that unearned suffering is redemptive' (King, 1963, p. 155). People should not make the mistake of judging human nature by its worst specimens while ignoring or discounting the thoughts, feelings and actions of its finest specimens. Furthermore, throughout the world there have been and are many people whose good deeds, without attaining great public acclaim, provide inspiration to others.

Striving for balance

Therapists, clients and all other people require a realistic and balanced view of human nature. Such a view seeks to go beyond superficial assessments based on external actions to understand the causes and conditions that create skilful and unskilful thoughts and behaviours. Especially when feeling threatened, people can easily slip into thinking the worst about human nature. They need constantly to remind themselves of the fact of universal sameness and that, like all other humans, they possess immense potential for good and life-affirming actions as well as for aggressive and destructive ones. When tempted to think badly about humankind, people can strive for more balanced perceptions. Two ways of achieving this end are to acknowledge the powerful forces at work that sustain the illusion of human badness and to remind oneself of the considerable evidence for innate goodness, some of which was briefly reviewed above.

The following are some reasons why negative assumptions about humankind require challenging and correcting. First, they are wrong and not based on a careful and thorough assessment of the evidence. Second, they devalue other human beings by ignoring or discounting their finer qualities. Third, negative assumptions about human nature are self-devaluing because all human beings are part of the same species and share the same basic nature. Fourth, they risk perpetuating negative behaviour because thinking of other people in negative terms can provide justifications for behaving negatively towards them which often leads to tit-for-tat escalation, including wars. Fifth, negative assumptions about humankind can close rather than awaken people's hearts and, in so doing, interfere with behaving positively towards others. As in good marriages, there is much to be said for searching for positive explanations of other people's behaviour and, where necessary, being prepared to give them the benefit of the doubt (Beck, 1988). Therapists, clients and others may need to look deeply into how they feel, think and behave to discover if their assumptions about human nature are as balanced and loving as they might initially like to believe.

Practices

Practice 9.1: Contemplating universal sameness

Put yourself into a contemplative frame of mind, possibly by using mindfulness of breathing as a means to becoming calmer and more centred. Either read or say aloud the following material as often as is necessary to allow the message of universal sameness to really sink in both mentally and emotionally. As you may need to keep reminding yourself of the obvious truth of universal sameness, in future repeat this contemplative practice as often as appropriate.

- I have the same cycle of birth, aging and death as all human beings.
- I have the same body – head, arms, trunk of body, legs, central nervous system – as all human beings.
- I have the same senses – sight, smell, sound, taste and touch – as all human beings.
- I have the same main facial expressions as all human beings.
- I have the same biological functions – eating, drinking, disposing waste, reproducing – as all human beings.
- I have the same needs for physical safety, food, shelter and warmth as all human beings.
- I have the same instincts and instinct remnants, feelings and physical reactions as all human beings.
- I am subject to sickness and fate as are all human beings.
- I have the same capacity to experience suffering and happiness as all human beings.
- I have the same needs for love, belonging and human warmth as all human beings.
- I have the same mind, which is capable of storing, generating and processing information, as all human beings.
- I have the same ability to have thoughts, images and nocturnal dreams as all human beings.
- I need to find meaning in my life like all human beings.
- In sum, I am essentially the same as all human beings.

You may add other areas of universal sameness that have meaning for you.

Practice 9.2: Contemplating human nature

1. To what extent do you think that how positively or negatively people view human nature influences the degree to which they open or close their hearts towards their fellow human beings? Give reasons for your answer.
2. To what degree do you think human nature is bad? Give reasons for your answer.

3. When making a case for humankind's innate goodness, what do you think about each of the following challenges to the illusion of badness:

- evolutionary evidence about social instincts;
- the human need to give and receive affection;
- evidence of co-operation in children;
- agreement in the world's religious traditions on virtues to be cultivated;
- anthropological evidence about co-operative cultures;
- cross-cultural values of benevolence and universalism;
- positive choices made by psychotherapy clients;
- level of human-being skills explanation of goodness or badness of behaviour;
- repression of innate goodness;
- social pressures inhibiting good deeds and talking about them;
- negative emotions being bad for physical health;
- daily evidence of goodwill, co-operation and kindness;
- worldwide emphasis in popular culture on good qualities;
- inspirational examples of superior human beings?

4. Are there other challenges to the illusion of human badness that you consider important? Please specify them.
5. All things considered, what is your current assessment of the goodness, badness, or mixture of goodness and badness of human nature? How will this assessment of human nature influence how you feel, think about and relate to others?

TEN   Curbing Anger and Aversion

Curbing anger or hostility and aversion or dislike is a problem not just for clients but for therapists in their own lives and for people in general. Dealing with destructive emotions and communications requires a two-pronged approach: curbing the bad and cultivating the good. In addition to curbing unskilful mental states and communications associated with anger and aversion, another approach to lessening their power is to cultivate skilful ones. Hence the following chapters on cultivating goodwill, sympathetic joy, gratitude, compassion, generosity, helping and service are highly relevant to anger and aversion. However, clients, therapists and others should beware of what might be termed the psychological bypass – focusing mainly on higher and more elevated forms of personal functioning and bypassing or inadequately dealing with the family of origin residues and other agendas that can interfere with being more compassionate and generous. Those clients and others wishing to exhibit higher levels of human sympathy over a period of time almost invariably need to address how they may be creating and sustaining destructive anger and aversion.

There is a danger of casting aggression and anger in too negative a light and getting people out of touch with a vital life force and source of energy. Aggression and anger are part of human beings' evolutionary heritage and can have distinct benefits. Anger can be a guide to a clearer definition of oneself. Lerner (1985, p. 93) sees some women as afraid to acknowledge their anger because, to do so, 'would expose our differences, make the other person feel uncomfortable, and leave us standing alone'. Probably, however, everyone can use anger to become more expert at knowing who they are and what they want. In addition, anger can be a signal that something is wrong and requires attention. Such anger should be a cue for people to examine their own thoughts, feelings and actions and not just those of others. Anger can also be a motivator that leads to more honest and compassionate communication and actions: for example, confronting festering issues in relationships and trying to right social injustices.

In some situations expressing angry feelings may serve positive functions, especially if the displays are assertive rather than aggressive. For example, showing anger can serve as a call for attention if someone fails to receive milder messages. Displaying anger can also be used to curb or control unwanted behaviours, although it is preferable if people can change how they act willingly. A controversial issue is the use of anger as a cathartic purge so that, afterwards, people calm down and become more rational. When people's level of emotional arousal increases beyond a certain point, their capacity for balanced thinking significantly decreases. In relationships, improved emotional climates do not always follow from angry outbursts because, frequently, recipients of angry messages close their ears and retaliate. Hence 'letting it all hang out' by aggressively ventilating anger can make matters worse rather than better, though this is not always the case.

Anger and aversion can have serious negative consequences for clients and others. Relationships whether they are between partners, family members, work colleagues or nations, can become soured and sometimes irretrievably destroyed by unskilful angry thoughts, feelings and communications. Relationship conflicts can become much harder to manage once partners angrily blame one another rather than calmly addressing their genuine differences. Instead of co-operating, angry individuals can become far too competitive and psychologically, and sometimes physically, attack one another. Furthermore, anger can turn into ongoing resentment and hatred, as in the case of aggrieved partners who feel that they have been hugely disadvantaged by their ex-spouses and their lawyers in unfair and long-term financially crippling divorce settlements. Inasmuch as anger is symptomatic of personal pain and suffering, failure to deal with it adequately maintains this suffering and interferes with positive feelings of self-esteem and happiness. Furthermore, anger and resentment are important contributors to health problems, in particular to cardiovascular disease.

Becoming less prone to anger and aversion

People can develop the inner strength to address the real problems in their lives with minds free from the agitated distractions of anger, hatred and aversion. Few may attain the levels of mental cultivation exhibited by people like Gandhi, Martin Luther King and the current Dalai Lama, but virtually everyone can fruitfully work on further internally disarming themselves (Dalai Lama, 1999). One approach to internal disarmament is to deal constructively with negative thoughts and emotions that arise in specific situations, which is the emphasis of this chapter's next section on assisting clients to deal with anger problems. A further approach is for individuals consistently to try to calm their minds through the practice of mindfulness of breathing. Yet another approach, which is the emphasis in this discussion, is to examine and, where necessary, train the mind to counteract the assumptions and illusions that contribute to vulnerability to anger and aversion.

The illusion of an independent self can lead to a false sense of pride and a tendency to judge others negatively. To a large extent life is a lottery and the good and poor human-being skills individuals acquire and maintain are related to the causes and conditions of their parental upbringing, socio-economic status, gender and culture among other considerations. The illusion of an independent self interferes with individuals having the humility to recognize how they and others have been dependent and may continue to be dependent on circumstances that have been largely out of their control. Rather than rigidly seeing themselves and others as independent entities, another approach is to see people as highly dependent on the causes and conditions that have influenced and continue to influence their development. Anger and aversion are created by people's tendencies to judge too readily their own and others' behaviour. Individuals are less likely to adopt pathologically judgmental modes when they train their minds so that they remain aware of the extent to which they and others are creatures of circumstances as well as of their own making.

The illusion of an independent self can also leave individuals vulnerable to anger and aversion when they fail to distinguish between judgements of a person's parts and of their whole worth as persons. This can happen in two ways. Individuals can be quick to take offence when they put their egos on the line and take critical comments about specific aspects of their behaviour as criticisms about their whole 'independent' selves. Their ability to evaluate the feedback can become clouded by their anger at the perceived slights to them as persons. Instead of remaining calm and centred, they allow their self-esteem to be unduly influenced by others' behaviour. Moving in the reverse direction, individuals can also add fuel to their anger and aversion by going beyond judging others' specific behaviours negatively to negatively framing others' 'independent' selves as bad. Individuals need to train themselves to be very careful about how they define and construct their own and others' selves, so as to avoid angering themselves unnecessarily.

There are many ways in which shedding some of the illusion of permanence can assist people to become less prone to anger and aversion. People can train themselves to observe their anger and become aware of how transient it often can be. Such insights can prevent them from acting in the heat of anger. Furthermore, individuals can train themselves to attain greater insight into the transitoriness of many anger-arousing situations and then, with this changed perspective, they can refrain from self-defeating actions. Related to the transient nature of such situations, people who are aware that change is built into life's fabric are less likely to be threatened by it and are less likely to react with anger and frustration when it occurs. Individuals can also gain greater insight into the impermanence of themselves and of others. Realizing the fragility and transient nature of existence can act as a brake on anger and aversion towards others.

Shedding the illusion of mental efficiency can also help reduce proneness to anger and aversion. For example, possessing a conceptual framework that sees people as having a mixture of good and poor human-being skills can make it harder to pass global judgements on them as good or poor persons, the latter justifying anger and aversion. One of the most important ways in which people can become more mentally efficient is to learn to assume responsibility for creating and influencing their feelings. In relation to anger and aversion, this involves individuals training their minds to understand and act on the understanding of how they create their anger much of the time. Once they accept responsibility for angering themselves, people can then use the mind skills described earlier in this chapter to think more efficiently to prevent and lessen their proneness to destructive anger and aversion. They can acquire much greater *response-ability* – the capacity to choose how to respond constructively to real and perceived provocations.

Becoming less prone to anger involves an increasing shift from hard heartedness to human heartedness. The illusion of differentness sustains much anger and is a root cause of aversion. Instead of attaining universal other-identification (UOI) in the numerous ways described in the previous chapter, individuals can see themselves consciously and subconsciously as different from, and hence often superior to and less blameworthy than, various of their fellow human beings. People holding restrictive worldviews, such as nationalism, racism and religious bigotry, can be prejudiced against and stigmatize whole groups of people. Such aversions can lower their thresholds for and legitimize destructive displays of anger. Individuals can become less prone to anger and aversion by systematically training their minds to challenge, dispute and replace any thoughts or feelings that create alienation rather than identification with others as being part of the same human species.

The illusion of human badness can provide considerable justification for anger and aversion. If life is a jungle, individuals are justified in doing whatever they can to seek their own advantage. Getting angry with and trampling on those standing in the way is a logical extension of a bad-animal view of human nature. For some individuals, a bad-animal view of human nature applies to everyone. For others, it may be restricted to those outside their sphere of identification and to those with whom their relationships have deteriorated to such a point that they can think nothing good about them. Needless to say, a bad-animal view of human nature can be a self-fulfilling prophecy in that angry and aggressive actions towards others stimulate 'tit-for-tat' retaliation. People are much less likely to be prone to anger if they can train their minds to take balanced views of the underlying nature of their fellow human beings and, where reasonable, give them the benefit of the doubt. Furthermore, they are more likely to move beyond anger to forgiveness if they become capable of seeing the good or potential for good in others.

Dealing with anger and aversion

The following are some approaches for dealing with anger and aversion. The major emphasis here is on their application in psychotherapy using the skilled client model, but such approaches can be adapted to personal practice. The discussion here assumes that clients have not had severely emotionally deprived backgrounds, in which case longer term psycho-therapeutic work may be indicated. As with any emotion, there are three areas in which therapists can help clients to become more skilful: experiencing anger, expressing anger and managing anger. These three areas are interwoven in the following discussion.

In their review of empirically supported treatments applied to anger management, Deffenbacher and his colleagues pointed to four main group-ings of promising cognitive behavioural interventions: relaxation-based, cognitive, social skills, and combined. They concluded that 'Whereas there is emerging empirical support for the absolute effectiveness of several anger-reduction strategies, there is little or no evidence supporting the rela-tive efficacy of one over another' (Deffenbacher, Oetting and DiGiuseppe, 2002, p. 271). Here cognitive interventions come under the heading of improving clients' mind skills, whereas social skills and relaxation-based interventions come under the heading of improving clients' communication/ action skills. It is important to develop strong collaborative working rela-tionships with clients as they explore what may be difficult areas for them, develop insight and motivation, and work for change.

Improving clients' mind skills

Leading cognitive behavioural therapists Albert Ellis and Aaron Beck have both written books specifically focusing on anger (Ellis, 1977; Beck, 1988, 1999). Angry feelings are invariably accompanied by angry thoughts. Therefore focusing on clients' ability to think about and control their thinking provides many useful insights and approaches to assisting angry clients. This is a huge area and the following discussion is at best illustrative. Furthermore, at times the mind skills overlap and interrelate. In addition, poor mind skills often represent exaggerations of good mind skills. For example, though rules about one's own and others' competence are realistic, it is when they turn into rules about being perfect that they become demanding and potentially anger-engendering. The following review is focused on assisting clients to improve four mind skills relevant to anger: namely, improving their rules, perceptions, self-talk and explanations.

Improving clients' rules

There are many ways in which clients with anger problems can sustain their difficulties because they continue to create demanding rather than preferential rules. Some clients' rules may make it difficult for them to acknowledge and experience their angry feelings: for instance, 'Christians/Buddhists should feel loving and compassionate', 'Our relationship must never have conflict', 'Women should not become angry' and 'I must not have wishes of my own'. Clients may also have difficulty expressing angry feelings assertively because of these and other rules: for instance, 'I must always be nice', 'I must have approval' or 'I must not hurt others'. Instead, the anger may 'come out sideways', for instance in passive-aggression and gossiping, without the real issues being addressed.

Clients can also generate anger by being judgmental about themselves, others and their environments. For instance, they may get angry with themselves when they fail to live up to unrealistic standards: 'I must do this job right first time'. Sometimes clients' anger is a by-product of demanding rules that cause them to feel stressed and tired: for instance, 'I must get to the top' or 'I must never waste time'. Perhaps much more common is to go around judging others' shortcomings in living up to one's standards in some ways. Examples of anger generating rules in intimate relationships include 'A wife/husband must always ...' and 'My partner must not in any way attempt to restrict my freedom'. Demanding rules held by clients who are bosses and supervisors in work settings often centre around the theme of perfectionism and can lead to unjustified anger when their employees' performance falls short of this standard. Some clients place anger-engendering demanding rules on their environments: for example, 'Life must always be fair' or 'Unforeseen external circumstances must never interfere with what I want to do.'

Therapists working to improve clients' skills of creating rules can assist them to detect demanding rules, dispute demanding rules, and create preferential rules (Ellis, 2001; Ellis and Dryden, 1997). For instance, rigid and demanding rules that may create destructive anger are often characterized by use of the words 'must' 'ought' and 'should'. Clients can also be helped to backtrack from inappropriate angry feelings and self-defeating communications/actions to the demanding rules that may be contributing to or driving them.

Once identified, therapists can assist clients to use reason, logic and facts to support, negate or amend their rules. Questions that therapists can ask clients and teach clients to ask themselves can be grouped under two main headings: functional disputing and empirical disputing. Typical functional disputing questions are 'Is getting angry helping you?' and 'How is continuing to think (or behave, or feel) this way affecting your life?' Typical empirical disputing questions are 'Where is the evidence for your demanding rule?' and 'Where is it written?' For example, 'Where is the evidence that women should not get angry?' For some angry clients a further useful question stemming from the Buddhist religious tradition is 'To what are you inappropriately attached?' Such attachments can include false pride and overly needing others' approval.

A useful way of reducing the hold of demanding rules is to restate them succinctly into preferential rules. Clients' disputations or challenges can be too many and varied to remember easily. Together therapist and client can create a revised rule easy to record, remember and recall. In creating revised rules, it is particularly important that clients develop skills of expressing preferences rather than demands. An example is 'I'd PREFER to do very well but I don't HAVE TO' (Sichel and Ellis, 1984). Clients can also replace rules about mastery and perfection with rules incorporating competence, coping and 'doing as well as I can under the circumstances'. Furthermore, clients' rules can be appropriately flexible and amenable to change and updating. However, because such flexibility is based on inner strength, they can still hold firmly to well-thought-through core beliefs and values. The following is an example of a partner in an intimate relationship who has been helped to restate an anger-engendering demanding rule as a preferential rule.

Demanding rule. 'I must always get my revenge.'
Preferential rule. 'My interests are not best served by thinking in terms of revenge. Instead I can work out more appropriate strategies for gaining my preferences and keeping our relationship intact.'

Working with clients' anger-engendering rules addresses issues of aversion as well. Demanding anger-engendering rules can lead clients to dislike or hate others who infringe these rules. Such people may be viewed as not only behaving poorly but as being bad persons.

Improving clients' perceptions

A Chinese proverb states 'two thirds of what we see is behind our eyes.' The truth in this proverb is highly relevant to how clients create and sustain their anger. Beck's cognitive therapy is built around the idea that clients can have systematic biases in how they interpret information. Angry clients are prone to jump to conclusions in which they frequently misinterpret others' behaviour and intentions far too negatively. If this process is allowed to go unchecked, clients can develop 'negative cognitive sets' about significant others in which they interpret virtually everything that they do or say in negative ways (Beck, 1988, 1999). Clients' misinterpretations and faulty perceptions can significantly contribute to aversion, dislike and hatred.

Therapists can work to improve the ways angry clients create perceptions in four main ways: helping them to acknowledge their anger, to identify automatic perceptions, to test their reality, and where necessary to form more accurate perceptions. Therapists may need to assist some clients in getting in touch with and acknowledging the full extent of their anger. Clients can require help in perceiving that they are angry persons. For various reasons, clients may deny and distort their anger. Examples of short-term advantages of doing this include not having to deal openly with anger in a relationship or maintaining one's self-picture as a loving partner/ parent and so on. Helping clients to perceive their anger more accurately may require sensitive listening to catch glimpses of anger and then giving clients permission to experience and disclose the extent of how angry they are.

Some clients may require assistance in perceiving how angry they are before it becomes too late. Therapists can assist clients to develop skills of tracking their level of anger arousal. For instance, becoming aware of their level of angry feelings when they are 20 per cent angry may make it easier for them to be rational than when they are 50 per cent angry. At some stage clients' level of arousal may become so high, say 85 per cent to 100 per cent, that it is impossible for them to become rational until they calm down. As part of perceiving more accurately the processes whereby their anger may become destructive, clients can be helped to identify trigger situations in which they feel vulnerable. Many clients may be using anger as a defense to conceal and so avoid dealing with feelings of vulnerability and hurt.

Automatic perceptions can take the form of words, images or both and occur very rapidly and usually at the fringe of awareness. For example, Charlie says to his wife Fiona 'I've decided that we need a new car'. Fiona's automatic perception or interpretation is 'Charlie doesn't respect my judgement'. As a result of this perception Fiona feels hurt, becomes angry and communicates aggressively 'I don't see why we need a new car. What's wrong with the one we've got?' Ways in which therapists can help clients elicit anger-engendering automatic perceptions include asking them what was going through their minds during upsetting situations and encouraging them to monitor their perceptions in homework assignments. Clients can also be requested to identify any 'hot' perceptions that may be driving their anger.

Therapists can emphasize to angry clients the importance of testing the reality of their perceptions rather than continuing to jump to conclusions. Generally the two most important questions for checking the accuracy of perceptions are 'Where's the evidence?' and 'Are there other ways of perceiving the situation?' For example, Fiona could be asked to state or write out 'evidence that supports my automatic perception' and 'evidence that does not support my automatic perception'. Clients can become less hostile if they can find evidence that does not support their hot perceptions. Clients can also be encouraged to generate and evaluate alternative ways of perceiving situations. For example, alternative perceptions for Fiona include 'Instead of reading his mind, I could ask Charlie why he thinks we need a new car' and 'Charlie is trying to make me happy by suggesting that we get a new car'.

After identifying their automatic perceptions and testing their reality, therapists can assist clients in how to state more accurate perceptions. Based on the supporting and negating answers to 'Where's the evidence?' therapists can ask clients to state a more balanced perception and then, if necessary, help them to improve on it. In instances where clients generate alternative perceptions, therapists can ask them to select the perception that best fits the available facts. In Fiona's case this might be 'Instead of reading his mind, I could ask Charlie why he thinks we need a new car.'

Therapists can train clients in how to form more rational responses to angry automatic perceptions. Box 10.1 provides an example of a client providing a counteracting rational response for herself (Beck, 1988, p. 264). Finding a rational response can help clients see their automatic perceptions as interpretations rather than as 'the truth'.

Box 10.1: Example of forming a rational response

The situation

Wendy was phoned by her husband Hal to say he was tied up at the office.

Emotional reaction: Anger.

Automatic perception: 'Its not fair – I have to work too. If he wanted to, he could be home on time.'

Rational response: 'His job is different. Many of his customers come in after work.'

Improving clients' self-talk

Another term for self-talk is self-instruction. Therapists can train clients who have problems with anger and aversion to talk to themselves better in two important ways: improving their calming self-talk and improving their coaching self-talk. Clients can develop skills of calming their minds before, during and after specific problem situations so that they can better handle unwanted feelings such as harmful anxiety or becoming excessively angry. When calm, clients are likely to become more centred and focused and thus better able to think through or talk through how best to communicate or act in anger-engendering situations. As with using their mindfulness-of-breathing skills, clients' use of calming self-talk helps them to clear a psychological space for getting in touch with their feelings and for thinking more sharply and deeply. Therapists can train clients who are prone to angry outbursts in trigger situations in calming self-talk statements, of which examples are provided in Box 10.2.

Box 10.2: Examples of calming self-talk statements

'Keep calm'	'Cool it'
'Slow down'	'Count to ten'
'Relax'	'Be careful'
'Take it easy'	'Don't overreact'
'Take a deep breath'	'Don't let my pride get in the way'
'Breathe slowly and regularly'	'I can choose not to get hooked'
'I can manage'	'Problem solve'

Coaching self-talk is central to the skilled client model, which assumes that clients are best trained in skills to the point where they can competently coach themselves in the skills targeted in therapy after it ends. In coaching self-talk, clients learn to instruct themselves through the sequences of choices involved in using both mind skills and communication/ action skills. For instance, clients can use coaching self-talk to identify, challenge and restate anger inducing rules, perceptions and explanations. Coaching self-talk is also involved as clients learn to implement the verbal, vocal and body messages required for communicating more effectively in specific situations in which they are at risk of self-defeating anger displays. In addition to instructing themselves in therapy sessions as they rehearse targeted communication skills, clients can use visualized rehearsal outside of therapy to prepare themselves for enacting their changed behaviour in real-life situations. Furthermore, clients can learn to coach themselves in action skills for managing anger that do not require communication with others, for instance muscular relaxation.

Improving clients' explanations

Implicit in the skilled client model is the explanation that, because clients are contributing to sustaining their problems, they can be the agents of change by improving their skills. The issue of improving clients' explanations of the causes of their anger can be approached either indirectly, by getting them to work on related mind and communication skills, or directly, by specifically targeting the mind skill of creating explanations. Angry clients are often loath to admit their role in creating and sustaining problems, so such work requires tact within the context of good therapeutic relationships.

Probably blaming is the most common way that people anger themselves by creating faulty explanations. Blaming can freeze clients in rigid positions that interfere with the flexibility needed to find constructive and creative solutions to problems and conflicts. Though clients can blame themselves, most often they externalize the cause of their problems and anger outside of themselves. For instance, clients can think 'This problem is all your fault' and 'Look how angry you have made me'. In relationships, partners can get into destructive patterns of mutual blaming in which they hurl propaganda at one another and fail to address and solve their problems. Thus blaming can be a powerful contributor to creating and sustaining aversion and dislike.

When therapists work to improve clients' mind skill of creating explanations, they can encourage them to become more mindful of the risks and negative consequences of blaming. Let's take the example of therapists working with clients who become unreasonably angry in close relationships. Therapists can help such clients ask themselves the following questions:

- 'What are the real problems?
- 'How have I contributed to their creation?'
- 'How am I contributing to their maintenance?'
- 'What is the outcome I would really like for myself and for our relationship?'
- 'What can I think and do to achieve that outcome?'

When therapists assist angry clients to improve their skills of explaining cause, they help them to stop thinking from 'outside to inside' (others are responsible for my problems and angry feelings) and start thinking more from 'inside to outside' (I am responsible for doing something about my problems and angry feelings). For instance, clients who previously may have thought 'I won't make any effort unless the other person does first' may now have the mental strength and flexibility to address problems about which they feel angry co-operatively rather than competitively.

Improving clients' communication/action skills

Improving clients' assertion skills

As a starting point, therapists working with clients who communicate poorly when angry can consider describing the threefold distinction between non-assertive, aggressive and assertive communication (Alberti and Emmons, 2001). Each of these three ways of communication incorporates vocal and bodily communication as well as words. When communicating non-assertively, clients are passive, compliant, submissive and inhibited. When communicating aggressively, clients are self-enhancing at the expense of others. For instance, they can be threatening, quarrelsome and unnecessarily hostile. When communicating assertively, clients feel and show respect for themselves and for others. They manage to control potentially negative angry feelings, their verbal, vocal and body messages are clear and appropriately firm, and their actions back up what they say. Assertion can be compassionate. Another starting point related to communicating assertively is for therapists to get clients to ask themselves questions like 'Am I handling this situation compassionately?' and 'What is a compassionate way to communicate?'

Therapists can use instructing, demonstrating and coaching skills to assist clients to express anger assertively. Clients may be contributing to their aversive feelings towards others through bottling up their anger towards them. Therapists can work with clients to decide what might be appropriate verbal, vocal and body messages for communicating anger. Clients should try to own their angry feelings rather than blame other people: for example, saying 'I feel angry …' rather than 'You make me feel angry …' In addition, it can be helpful if clients provide specific feedback to others about why they feel angry. Skilful expressions of anger can take the form of invitations or challenges that can lead to honest discussions rather than to fruitless fighting.

When people relate to one another over a period of time, they build up patterns of communication and behaviour. Where appropriate, therapists can help angry clients to request changes in other people's behaviour and hence lessen the risks of creating and maintaining aversion towards them. Behaviour change requests can have the goals of encouraging others

- to do something that they are not already doing;
- to do something that they are already doing either more/and or better; and
- lessening or stopping an unwanted behaviour.

Where possible, clients who assertively request behaviour changes should emphasize the positive by stating what they want rather than what they do not want. In addition, they can remember that others are more likely to maintain their changed behaviour if they reward them, for instance by thanking them. Defensiveness is a common initial reaction to behaviour change requests. It does not necessarily indicate either that clients have asserted themselves poorly or that they may not ultimately be successful. Even if unsuccessful, they can only be responsible for their own communication. The expectation that others will always do what clients want is unrealistic and can only contribute to their denigrating themselves when they do not.

Therapists can help clients who need to persist in their assertions to see that they have a number of options. For instance, they may pause after the negative response and then calmly yet firmly repeat their behaviour change request. Alternatively, they can reflect the other person's feelings before repeating their request.

Person A: When you play a compact disc so loud, I can't concentrate on studying for my test tomorrow. Please turn the volume down.
Person B: Why the hell are you complaining?
Person A: I realise you're angry at my request, but I badly need to concentrate on studying and would be grateful if you could turn the CD player down.
Person B: (*still not too pleased*) OK.

Another option is to use more 'muscle'. For instance, clients may both use a firmer voice and also strengthen their verbal message by saying 'I'm serious, please turn the CD player down'. A further option is to try to negotiate a mutually acceptable solution – for instance, negotiating times when the Person A can study in peace and Person B can play the CD player loudly.

Angry clients can also require skills for assertively retrieving the negative consequences of their behaviour. Therapists can train them in skills of apologizing and taking corrective action. Clients capable of acknowledging hurtful behaviour when pointed out and willing to change may defuse situations and make it easier for others to do likewise. Making genuine apologies is a vital assertion skill for repairing relationships. A good apology restores balance by acknowledging that the client has broken a norm or relationship rule: for example, 'I'm sorry that I was so rude about (specify) last night.' Sometimes, clients can make amends by their actions instead of or as well as their words: for instance, by an unsolicited gift. They can also mend fences by offering some sort of compensation or restitution: for example, 'Please let me know if there is anything I can do to make it up to you?'

Therapists may also need to help clients to improve their skills of accepting others' apologies, forgiving them and moving on. For example, clients can learn to make the simple statement 'I accept your apology'. Martin Luther King (1963) observed that forgiving does not entail ignoring what has happened but entails choosing not to allow it to remain as an insuperable barrier in a relationship. Sometimes another person may not have the inner strength to make a verbal apology, but will take corrective action. Here the best policy for clients may still be to forgive and move on in the relationship. However, by whomsoever they are made, insincere apologies and corrective actions risk contributing to further hurt, anger and aversion.

Improving clients' relaxation skills

The author has not used training in relaxation skills with angry clients, but their successful use in anger management research studies indicates that they are a useful treatment option (Deffenbacher, Oetting and DiGiuseppe, 2002). Deffenbacher and his colleagues (for example, Deffenbacher *et al.*, 1996) have developed a cognitive-relaxation coping skills (CRCS) approach to managing anger. Therapists can train clients in progressive muscular relaxation and in the four relaxation coping skills of:

- relaxation imagery, in which they visualize a specific personal relaxation image;
- cue-controlled relaxation involving calming self-talk in which they slowly repeat a word or phrase such as 'relax', which has been paired with relaxation;
- relaxation without tension, focusing upon and releasing muscle tension generally or in specific muscle groups without tensing muscles; and
- breathing cued relaxation, relaxing after each of three to five slow deep breaths.

Once trained in these skills, clients can visualize anger arousing situations and they can practise using their cognitive-relaxation coping skills. The scenes that clients visualize can cover situations that arise before, during and after angering. They should be encouraged to practise both relaxation and using cognitive-relaxation coping skills as homework. Clients suffering from high blood pressure and hypertension are good candidates for relaxation procedures that address both their anger and physical problems.

Clients can also be encouraged to engage in physical activities, for example swimming, jogging, working out in the gym, that may have the effect of reducing stress, releasing aggressions and 'clearing out the cobwebs'. For some clients, time spent in beautiful natural surroundings can be deeply relaxing. One of the great advantages of engaging in physical activities and spending time with nature is that doing so relaxes the mind as well as the body.

Improving clients' mind skills and communication/action skills

Most often therapists using the skilled client model focus on improving both clients' mind skills and their communication/action skills. When therapists select interventions either in their heads or in writing they can make out treatment profiles that identify the interventions that they intend using for each targeted skill. Box 10.3 shows the result of the author working with a client to break down her anger problem, translate it into skills terms, and the interventions required to address each poor skill.

Box 10.3: Example of skilled client model treatment profile for an angry client

Andrea Davidson, 38, was a very bright and able lawyer who came to therapy because she had been forced by the other partners to leave the firm of lawyers where she worked because of her atrocious relationships with the support staff. At then time of the first session, after a difficult job search period, Andrea was about to start work with a new firm of lawyers and sought therapy to prevent a repeat of the previous disastrous episode. Married and with two teen age daughters, Andrea was a hard-driving perfectionist who did not suffer fools gladly and wanted her work done promptly and with no mistakes. Andrea told the therapist that she had always been

---

competitive and that the culture of her previous firm was very competitive too.

   Previously Andrea had experienced stress-related health problems, during which periods she had taken relaxant medication at night. At the end of her time at her former firm Andrea felt very upset, her concentration was diminished, sometimes her hands shook, her sleep was disturbed and she lost weight. After the initial assessment session, Andrea had a further three therapy sessions between which she practised her improved skills in her new firm. Andrea, who was an extremely well motivated and co-operative client, regarded therapy and her 'on the job' homework assignments as going through a reorientation period.

Treatment profile for Andrea

Poor skills *Mind skills to improve*	Proposed intervention
Creating rules	
'I must be perfect' 'Others must not make mistakes'	Training in detecting, disputing and replacing demanding rules
Creating perceptions	
Perceiving weaknesses and not strengths	Training in reality-testing perceptions
Creating self-talk	
Anger-engendering self-talk Absence of self-talk to guide skilled communication	Training in calming and coaching self-talk
Creating explanations	
Excessive blaming	Training in explaining cause accurately and in assuming responsibility for her thinking and communication

---

Communication skills to improve

Showing interest in others' skills

Listening/showing understanding	Training in communication skills of treating support staff and other lawyers as persons
Disclosing human side of self	
Indicating availability for feedback	

Giving instructions skills

Cold manner	Training in giving instructions and answering queries clearly and politely
Staff afraid to request clarification	

Expressing appreciation skills

Always critical	Training in showing appreciation and in providing encouragement

---

Practices

Practice 10.1: Becoming less prone to anger and aversion

As appropriate, this practice may be performed as part of either therapy or personal practice.

1. Assess the extent to which either the client is or you are

   - prone to anger;
   - prone to aversion.

2. To what extent and in what ways either does the client or do you consider that insufficiently practising calming her/his/your mind through mindfulness of breathing contributes to her/his/your proneness to anger and aversion?
3. To what extent and in what ways either does the client or do you consider that each of the following illusions contributes to her/his/your proneness to anger and aversion:

- illusion of an independent self;
- illusion of permanence;
- illusion of mental efficiency;
- illusion of human differentness;
- illusion of human badness?

4. Develop a plan to challenge and correct any of the above areas in which either he or she is or you are insufficiently skilled.

Practice 10.2: Dealing with a specific anger situation in therapy and self-therapy

Part A: Therapy

One person acts as therapist and the other as client. The therapist assists the client to identify a specific situation in which they either have exhibited or are at risk of exhibiting destructive anger. Using the skilled client model described in Chapter 7, the therapist works with the client to agree on a shared definition of her/his anger problem in skills terms. Therapist and client should start by identifying one mind skill to improve and one action skill to improve and then, if necessary, build on this. Next, therapist and client discuss interventions for improving the client's skills (see Box 10.3 for an example).

Afterwards, if appropriate, reverse roles.

Part B: Self-therapy

Acting as a self-therapist, identify a specific situation in which you have exhibited or are at risk of exhibiting destructive anger. Using the skilled human being model described in Chapter 15, work with yourself to define your anger problem in skills terms. Start by identifying one mind skill to improve and one action skill to improve and then, if necessary, build on this. Next identify and implement strategies for improving your skills.

Practice 10.3: Dealing with anger in personal practice

The following are just some of the ways that you can deal with anger in personal practice.

Part A: Assuming responsibility for self-defeating anger

For as long as it is necessary to get the message to really sink in repeat to yourself either or both of the following self-talk statements.

Statement 1
'To a large extent, I am responsible for distressing myself and others by creating and maintaining self-defeating angry feelings and behaviour.'

Statement 2
'By learning to think more skilfully and to communicate/act more skilfully I can greatly diminish the extent to which I disturb myself and others by my self-defeating angry feelings and behaviour.'

Part B: Developing corrective self-talk skills

When you catch yourself either thinking or at risk of thinking conditioned unskilful thoughts in actual or potential anger-provocation situations, practise replacing them with corrective skilful thoughts.

Example
S – Situation: I am driving along and without any signalling a previously parked car abruptly pulls out in front of me causing me to slow down quickly to avoid an accident.
T(1) – Conditioned unskilful thought:
'You stupid bastard. What the f … do you think you're up to?'
C(1) – Consequences of conditioned unskilful thought:
Possibly anger verging on rage and an urge to ram the other car.
T(2) – Corrective skilful thought:
'Stay calm. There is no point in my upsetting myself over her/his inconsiderate driving.'
C(2) – Consequences of corrective skilful thought:
Possibly some minor anger that dissipates quickly without leading to hasty self-defeating action.

1. Work through the format of the above example in relation to an actual or potential anger provocation situation in your own life.
2. Use your corrective self-talk skills either in advance of and/or in actual anger provocation situations in real life.

Part C: Creating, rehearsing and enacting competent performance

Anger provoking situations often repeat themselves. Whenever you face an important situation where you think you are at risk of self-defeating angry feelings and behaviour, you can ask yourself the following questions:

'What are my goals in the situation?'

'What are appropriate verbal, vocal and body messages to achieve my goals?'

'How might the other person respond, and how can I handle one or more likely responses?'

Then, using coaching self-talk skills, rehearse in your imagination how to communicate skilfully in the situation. If and when you need to do so, enact your improved communication skills in real life.

ELEVEN Curbing Greed and Craving

As with curbing anger and aversion, curbing greed and craving is a problem not just for clients, but for therapists and the general public too. Greed means an intense or excessive desire for something – for example food, money or sex. Craving can be a characteristic of greed when it implies a longing for or yearning for something or someone to which a person is excessively attached. The emphasis in this chapter is on greed and craving centred around materialism or attaching excessive value to acquiring, accumulating and consuming wealth.

To date, with important exceptions like Horney (1937) and Fromm (1976), there has been little in the psychotherapy literature regarding the constricting effects of capitalism and consumerism on people's capacity to be fully human. However, the need to curb greed and craving has been a major emphasis in religious traditions such as Christianity and Buddhism. For example, Christ said 'It is easier for a camel to go through the eye of a needle, than for a rich man to enter the kingdom of God' (Matthew 19: 24). The Quaker tradition, which grew from Christian roots, emphasizes simplicity, moderation and not letting oneself be governed by one's possessions (Smith, 1998). Quakers value the idea of stewardship and the early Quakers with their plain dress 'viewed their possessions as held in trust, not for their own or for their children's benefit but for the Lord's work' (Hubbard, 1974, p. 136).

Buddha's Four Noble Truths teach that suffering is caused by craving and that the cessation of suffering is achieved by the elimination of craving. The Buddhist religious tradition views suffering as created by three main categories of spiritual pollutions or afflictive emotions and torments of the mind: namely, tendencies to greed, hatred and delusion. The Buddha's teachings advocate (Thitavanno, 2002, p. 203):

All things should not be attached to,
As it causes suffering, not happiness.
The more we attach to it, the more we suffer.
Because of detachment one can always be happy.

For the vast majority of ordinary people who are not monks and who have work, family and other commitments, Jesus Christ's emphasis on giving up one's possessions and the Buddha's emphasis on detachment raises issues of what are appropriate or balanced levels of attachment to material possessions. When considering such issues, virtually everyone living in North America, Europe and Australasia can realize that, by Third World standards, they are extremely rich.

A number of illusions can contribute to sustaining material greed and craving. Each of these illusions contains some truth, but it is the unbalanced way in which they are often held that turns them into illusions. First, there is the illusion of unlimited progress, the idea that technological and economic advances will automatically make for a happier, more just and better world. Economic advances have taken numerous people out of the misery of economic poverty. However, there still remains a huge gap between the richer and poorer nations. Furthermore, with improved communication, there exists a much greater chance than before of dangerous resentments building up in the Third World because of this disparity. In addition, economic and technological advances have created environmental degradation, global warming and the dangers of nuclear war. Second, there is the illusion that increasing happiness can be gained through ever-increasing wealth and consumption. Increases in gross national product do not necessarily result in increases in gross national happiness. Also, on the individual level, once a certain level of economic sufficiency is obtained, increments in happiness through having more money tend overall to be small and by no means guaranteed (Argyle, 1987).

Third, there is the illusion of greater wealth automatically bringing increased freedom and liberation. This ignores the important distinction between external liberation and internal liberation. Religious traditions like Buddhism heavily emphasize internal liberation. Despite high levels of affluence, minds that are riddled with cravings for acquiring, accumulating and consuming wealth are definitely not internally liberated from the suffering, struggles and restriction of choice that such cravings create. Fourth, there is the illusion of personal immunity from greed and craving. For virtually everyone living in the West, excessive economic desires are so built into the fabric of people's upbringing and daily existence that it is impossible to remain immune from their effects. Since many individuals possess little or no awareness of whether and how they are being dehumanized by greed and craving, they have little or no motivation to liberate themselves from these tendencies.

The costs of greed and craving

Acquiring, accumulating and consuming wealth are not inherently bad. There are many sound reasons for being skilled at these activities: for example, economic security for oneself and one's family and the chance to have increased quality and choice in life. However, in varying degrees, people living above subsistence levels are confronted with the issue of deciding when enough is enough and whether and when the costs of acquiring and consuming wealth outweigh the benefits. Fromm distinguishes between functional and pathogenic consumption (Fromm, 1976, 1993). Functional consumption involves individuals in consuming wealth for rational and psychologically healthy reasons in order to lead more human and fulfilled lives. Pathogenic consumption has entailed in it the notion of excess, just as going beyond a balanced diet to eating too much food is not good for individuals.

Material craving leads to mental suffering and alienation based on a false assumption that more is necessarily better. Instead of possessing calm and peaceful minds, *Homo consumens* creates an agitated mind inwardly enslaved to acquiring and consuming material possessions. For many people dehumanization can come from having too much as well as too little. The American, European and Australasian dreams have become strongly associated with consumption, without due regard to the insidious effects of greed and craving on people's capacity to attain levels of happiness and fulfilment deeper than the ephemeral levels provided by keeping buying new cars, new clothes and so on.

One of the main ways in which craving can lead to mental suffering is that individuals are never permanently satisfied. Instead, they feel the need to have new sensations to keep underlying feelings of emptiness and boredom at bay. People can become alienated from themselves by over-identification with their possessions – 'I am what I possess'. Furthermore, people can add to their alienation by consuming in such a way as to package themselves to be acceptable to significant others, for instance 'Others will accept me more if I have this Gucci handbag', rather than being firmly grounded in their own sense of worth.

Fromm identifies as part of a 'marketing character' the tendency for people in Western societies to cease to value themselves as humans and instead see themselves as commodities to be bought and sold on the employment and personality markets (Fromm, 1976). For many people, for instance factory assembly-line workers, some feelings of alienation in the processes of acquiring wealth are inevitable because they may have restricted choices in where and how they can work. However, alienation in the process of consumption is less inevitable because such people have more choice in how they spend their money outside their work settings than in how they earn it in them. Furthermore, individuals can choose to avoid the alienation and emotional impoverishment stemming from overly valuing their own and others' worth in materialistic terms.

One of the main symptoms and causes of greed and craving is that of a comparing, competing and judging mind. The extent to which people are happy with their financial lot often reflects their position in the groups by which they are judging themselves. Those continuously seeking not only to keep up with others but to surpass them and move into new social comparison groups are likely to maintain their mental suffering. Envy and jealousy can also be mental costs stemming from material greed and craving. Sometimes people seek to emulate those whom they envy, whereas others seek to bring them down to their own level. Another mental cost of greed is that people clutter their lives with unnecessary material possessions and then worry about them rather than leading lives of greater simplicity.

Greed and craving can also contribute to impaired relationships, with finer and more generous feelings being ignored or repressed. People can be so busy in the search for money and status that they provide insufficient attention and time to their nearest and dearest, thus impoverishing both themselves and others. A danger is that people approach their relationships as consumer items – 'What can I get out of them?' – rather than wanting to share the best of themselves with others and to help them become happier and more fulfilled. Another way of stating this is that people relate to one another in 'I-it' rather than in 'I-thou' terms (Buber, 1958). Selfishness, egocentricity and narcissism preclude a full experiencing of the essence of oneself and of others. Other outgrowths of greed and craving can include cheating, stealing and corruption, all of which are at the expense of others – sometimes staggeringly so.

Up until now the focus of this discussion has been on the costs of greed and craving for mental health and psychological wellbeing. However, greed can also have physical health costs. Many of the stress problems of modern life are worsened, if not caused, by people becoming trapped in vicious cycles of ever increasing wants and consumption. One aspect of this phenomenon is that of individuals engaging in over-occupation in which they work harder and harder to purchase goods that they do not really need. Pathogenic consumers can also create physical and mental stresses by becoming over-extended in terms of bank loans and credit card debt. Physical symptoms associated with such stress problems include fatigue, burn out, breakdowns, ulcers, hypertension and cardiovascular disease.

Fears associated with greed and craving

Fears associated with greed and craving can stimulate acquiring, accumulating and consuming wealth. Many of these fears have some basis in reality, but their exaggeration leads to irrational greed. For instance, people can be realistically afraid of not having enough money to meet everyday needs and emergencies but that is different from entertaining unrealistic thoughts and images about being destitute and hence developing a hoarding mentality. Furthermore, some fears prompting an excessive desire for money may be more because of its symbolic meaning rather than because of the money itself. For example, worries about status and positions in pecking orders may underlie attachments to obtaining increases in incomes and salaries.

What are some fears that contribute to pathological consumption? The consumer culture is so widespread that it is often hard for people to retain conscious autonomy over their spending. Furthermore, the line between sane and pathological consumption becomes harder to detect when a degree of pathological consumption becomes normative. Many people shop too much because this gives them a temporary feeling of happiness that assuages the insufficient self-esteem and sense of meaninglessness that they inwardly feel. The process of buying can provide feelings of power and release from boredom. The outcomes of buying can provide feelings of renewal and confidence, however short lived they may be. Consumption may also help people who possess the illusion of permanance assuage their anxieties about death and dying. Buying new things can be a defence against acknowledging the process of physical aging, deterioration and ultimate non-being. Furthermore, hedonism can provide a sense of aliveness while it lasts.

Consumption is very much a social as well as a private act. In consumer societies, people can define themselves to others not just by what they need to spend, but by what they can afford to spend, whether it is paid for by cash or on credit. Social fears attached to excessive consumption include being unlovable, being isolated and not being perceived to be as successful as other people. This process can start at a very early age with children's need for approval by their peers being manipulated by advertising into purchasing decisions. Parents can feel under pressure to buy unnecessary items for their children as a way of retaining their affection and, sometimes, to help them gain acceptance with other children and their parents. Throughout life, people who are insecure about their self-worth make social comparisons that can lead to purchasing behaviours to prove that they are as good as or better than others. Items of conspicuous consumption, such as expensive clothes, cars and houses, are bought for their intended effect on others and not just for their functional or aesthetic use. Furthermore, social groups can have rules that encourage their members to engage in pathogenic consumption at risk of exclusion and being considered 'cheap'.

Dealing with greed and craving

As with dealing with anger and aversion, dealing with greed and craving is a mixture of curbing poor human-being skills and cultivating good ones.

Some clients may require assistance in overcoming self-denial and acknowledging their material wants, but more are likely to have problems in which issues of greed and craving form a part. Short of full-blown addictions to activities such as shopping and gambling, which are not the focus of this discussion, there are many guises in which greed and craving may be present as issues in therapy. Some clients may have financial problems caused by their inability to restrict their spending and to assess properly the risks of getting into debt. Sometimes financial difficulties can lead to other problems such as juvenile delinquency. Differences over earning and spending money are one of the major sources of marital distress and breakdown, with partners offering differing views about what constitutes justifiable spending. Stress related problems frequently have a component of clients seeking to acquire and consume MORE, MORE, MORE ... NOW, NOW, NOW or seeking to please dependents with such expectations.

In capitalist economies greed can motivate entrepreneurial activity, innovation and a work ethic, but many people in Western societies are confronted with the realization that having material possessions does not necessarily bring happiness, meaning and fulfilment in life. Exploring issues related to acquiring, accumulating and consuming wealth is often highly relevant to clients with concerns about choice of study, work and lifestyle. The nature of work is changing with less job security than previously and, therefore, both employed and unemployed clients may gain from understanding irrational money-related pressures that they may place on themselves. Other clients may have problems in which they are reacting to the perceived harshness of a materialistic culture by dropping out of it or rebelling against it in destructive rather than constructive ways. Both clients and therapists alike may want to work on liberating themselves from the insidious effects of living in an acquisitive and consumer society so that they gain more awareness and autonomy in how they live. For some, their goals will involve moving beyond what Fromm calls the 'pathology of normalcy' (Fromm, 1995) to attain supra-normal levels of human sympathy and mental cultivation in which they focus much more than before on serving and helping others.

To deal comprehensively with the topic of material greed and craving involves examining social, economic and political structures. This is outside the scope of the present review. Issues of greed and craving are so pervasive in Western societies that they affect both therapists and clients. However, this very pervasiveness may be the reason why most psychotherapy writers and researchers have fought shy of seeing it as a problem. The following discussion focuses on how therapists and clients, and, by implication, personal practitioners, might improve certain mind skills and communication/action skills to counteract the dehumanizing tendencies of wanting and spending too much. Although it is not focused on here, some clients may require long-term psychotherapy to help them to attain basic levels of self-esteem in which they are less inclined to crave for external sources of affirmation, such as new clothes, cars or computers.

Improving clients' mind skills

Within the context of good collaborative working relationships, therapists can work with clients to address issues of greed and craving under whatever guise they may present themselves in therapy. The goal is not self-denial, but rather to assist clients in moving away from creating insane pressures to acquire, accumulate and consume wealth to saner, more balanced and autonomous ways of thinking and acting.

Improving clients' awareness

The first condition for overcoming tendencies to greed and craving is for clients to become aware of their existence. Therapists can assist clients to listen to their feelings and physical reactions more deeply so that they acknowledge when they are suffering because of placing excessive pressures on themselves. Furthermore, in instances where clients are exploring what values really matter in their lives, therapists can help them to listen more sensitively to what members of the Quaker tradition call the 'still small voice within'.

Therapists can help clients to explore and become more aware of the consequences of greed and craving for themselves and for others. As part of their inner exploration, some clients may appreciate therapists drawing their attention to Fromm's distinction between the having and being modes of existence (Fromm, 1976, 1993, 1995). In the *having* mode of existence people's relationship to the world is one of possessing and owning. They make everybody and everything, including themselves, their property. In the *being* mode of existence, there are two forms. One form of being means aliveness and authentic relatedness to the world. The other form of being refers to the true nature, the true reality, of a person or thing.

Therapists can also help clients look both inwards and outwards to become more aware of the sources of greed and craving and how inner and outer forces contribute to sustaining these feelings. Therapists can assist clients to raise their consciousness of the insidious pressures to acquire and consume in Western capitalist cultures so that they may then have more choice.

Improving clients' rules

Therapists can assist clients to detect demanding rules connected with greed and craving that contribute to their suffering and alienation.

Egocentric greed-engendering rules, probably originating in childish demandingness, permeate Western cultures. Fourteen examples of such rules are provided in Box 11.1. This list is illustrative and by no means comprehensive.

Box 11.1: Illustrative demanding rules conducive to greed and craving

'I must get what I want now, now, now.'
'I must have more, more, more.'
'I must always be happy.'
'I must always keep having new sensations.'
'I must always keep having new possessions.'
'I must have approval.'
'I must compete.'
'I must compare.'
'I must judge.'
'I must have prestige and status.'
'Others must see how successful I am/we are.'
'I/we must have a high standard of living.'
'I/we must keep up with my/our peers and neighbours.'
'The environment in which I live must be perfect.'

Clients' use of words like 'must', 'ought' and 'should' may provide clues to underlying demanding rules. Unpleasant feelings like high levels of anxiety, being depressed, low self-worth, irritability, apathy and boredom, when allied to a materialistic lifestyle, may be traced to demanding rules concerning greed and craving. Clients may also have thoughts indicative of excessive attachments to material things – for example, comparing, competing with and judging themselves and others in ways that emphasize money. Furthermore, clients may be engaging in self-defeating actions that belie excessive attachment to acquiring, accumulating and consuming material possessions: for example, overworking, taking unnecessary financial risks, and consuming above their means.

Once identified, therapists can assist clients in challenging and disputing rules conducive to material greed and craving by means of functional disputing and empirical disputing (Ellis and MacLaren, 1998). Functional disputing questions include 'How is always needing to have new possessions helping you?' and 'How is accumulating more and more possessions helping you?' and 'What are the consequences of continuing to think (or behave, or feel) this way?' Typical empirical disputing questions include 'Where is the evidence for your rule (specify)?' and 'Where is the proof that your rule (specify) is accurate?' Therapists and clients need to understand that many demanding rules connected with greed and craving are widely held in Western societies and that, when challenging clients' personal demanding rules, they may be challenging cultural rules and myths as well. Clients wishing to attain supra-normal levels of mental cultivation and human sympathy are especially likely to challenge rules reflecting the 'pathology of normalcy' rather than humanistic consciences.

Therapists can assist clients to restate demanding rules into preferential or rational rules. An issue in deciding what is a preferential rule is that of deciding what is an appropriate attitude to acquiring, accumulating and consuming material possessions. Answers to these questions are likely to reflect therapists' and clients' levels of mental cultivation and human sympathy. For example, two clients may have the same demanding rule 'I must have a high standard of living'. One client may be satisfied in restating this as a preferential rule within the confines of what is normal in Western culture: for instance, 'I would prefer to live very comfortably, but I also want to lead a balanced life in which I have quality time for relationships and recreation.' Another client might wish to state a preferential rule going beyond what is normal in Western culture: for example, 'I would prefer to live very comfortably, but I also want to assist others by sharing my discretionary wealth and to help future generations by not consuming natural resources excessively'.

Improving clients' perceptions

There are many ways in which clients' unskilful perceptions may contribute to greed and craving. For example, clients may overly focus on possessions lacking in their lives and insufficiently acknowledge and appreciate what they have. This tendency sets them up for a constant search for what is missing only to find that attaining one goal just brings the next one into focus and that they are never satisfied. Such clients possess unrealistic perceptions regarding the concept of ENOUGH. They have received insufficient assistance from their culture and significant others in thinking through such questions as 'When is enough, enough?' or 'What are the consequences of choosing to perceive that I never have enough?' and 'What constitutes autonomous consumption in a consumer society designed to create artificial wants and desires?'

Clients may perceive themselves in far too materialistic terms. Fromm observes 'Modern consumers may identify themselves by the formula:

I am = what I have and I consume' (Fromm, 1976, p. 27). Such clients lack a secure sense of their own worth as human beings. Furthermore, they may then apply the same formula to others: *Others are = what others have and what they consume.* The above may be overstated, but it reflects a common tendency to allow materialistic considerations unduly to influence judgements of self and others. One cost of this tendency is self-alienation in which people are looking for their source of value outside of themselves. Another cost is alienation from other people because true intimacy rests on relating to another's essential human qualities rather than their external material trappings. Furthermore, focusing on material possessions leads to a constant process of social comparison in which people's perceptions then lead to artificial feelings of superiority and inferiority.

When dealing with problems of craving, therapists can assist clients to explore the concept of enough. Asking basic cognitive therapy questions like 'Where is the evidence that you *do not* have enough (specify)?' and 'Where is the evidence that you *do* have enough (specify)?' may help certain clients to attain more balanced appraisals of their situations. Another basic cognitive therapy question is 'Are there other ways of perceiving your situation?' Therapist and client can then work together to develop alternative ways of perceiving the client's current situation in regard to acquiring, accumulating and/or consuming wealth.

Therapists can also help clients to become more aware of and challenge the reality of any tendencies to think of their own and others' value as human beings in material terms. Clients can be assisted to identify different ways of viewing themselves and others – for instance, accepting themselves and others regardless of material considerations. Furthermore, they can be helped to explore what qualities they really value in themselves and others. Where appropriate, as a corrective against tendencies to see themselves as commodities, therapists can assist some clients to explore and list their strengths and assets as human beings.

Clients can also be helped to identify cognitive errors or tricks of the mind and learn to counteract them. Two common thinking errors are black-and-white thinking and arbitrary inference (Beck and Weishaar, 2000). Examples of black-and-white thinking are clients who think in terms of being either very rich or very poor or of being either accepted by everybody or accepted by nobody. In arbitrary inference, clients draw conclusions without supporting evidence or in the face of contradictory evidence. For instance, a man who provides an average standard of living for his family might conclude 'I'm a failure as a husband and a father'. Such a person might be encouraged to list qualities of good husbands and fathers and then search for evidence affirming or negating his performance against such criteria. Assuming he was negatively distorting how he saw himself, he might then conclude 'I'm a good husband and father after all'.

After identifying and questioning erroneous thinking and automatic perceptions regarding acquiring, accumulating and consuming wealth, therapists can assist clients to state more accurate perceptions. For example, a client who previously over-emphasized seeing his worth in money terms might arrive at a more balanced perception: 'Having sufficient money is important, but I have many human qualities that are also important, for instance loving my wife and children. I will be happier if I acknowledge and develop myself more as a person as well as continue paying prudent attention to my finances.'

Improving clients' self-talk

Therapists can help clients with greed and craving-related problems to improve how they talk to and instruct themselves. As with anger and aversion, clients can improve in two main categories: calming self-talk and coaching self-talk. Clients who feel the impulse to go out and spend unwisely can use calming self-talk statements like 'keep calm', 'calm down' and 'relax'. They can also conduct a dialogue with themselves to cool their impulses to consume so as to make more rational purchasing decisions. Box 11.2 lists some calming self-talk and questions that clients might use for this purpose. Those clients concerned with developing higher levels of human sympathy can also ask 'Could the money be put to better use helping those genuinely in need?'

Box 11.2: Illustrative self-talk and questions for calming impulses to purchase

'Think it over.'
'Sleep on it.'
'Be strong, don't give in.'
'Do I really need it?'
'Do I really want it?'
'Will I really be happier if I purchase (specify)?'
'What else could I do with the money?'
'Where is it going to go?'
'What is wrong with what I've got?'
'Can I get more/better use out of what I've got?'

'Can I comfortably afford it?'
'What is the level of my debt?'
'What are the interest payments on my debt?'
'Do I really care what they think?'
'Am I being selfish/narcissistic/egocentric?'

Thought stopping and thought switching are two self-talk skills in which therapists can train clients to interrupt the excitement, energy and images stimulating unwise consumption. With both procedures, clients need to agree what thoughts and images are unhelpful. In thought stopping, clients learn to shout inwardly to themselves 'stop' as soon as they become aware of these thoughts and images (Wolpe, 1990). Clients who like thinking visually can also imagine a large flashing sign saying 'STOP'. Since the thoughts and images are likely to return, clients may need to repeat the procedure again and again.

Thought switching, which is basically a distraction skill, can be performed after thought stopping or on its own. In thought switching, clients switch from tempting thoughts and images about unwise consumption to those either unconnected with it, for instance an upcoming football match, or inhibiting it, for instance how short of money they will be at the end of the month.

Clients can use coaching self-talk to instruct themselves how to think more skilfully when creating rules, perceptions and explanations relevant to greed and craving. Such coaching is likely to take them through sequences of identifying unskilful thinking, challenging it, restating it in more skilful forms, and then practising using their improved skills in imaginary and everyday situations. Clients can also use coaching self-talk to improve their performance in targeted communication/action skills relevant to acquiring, accumulating and consuming wealth – for instance, being assertive with manipulative sales persons. Some of these communication/action skills are reviewed in the next section. Suffice it for now to say that such coaching self-talk should focus on vocal and bodily as well as verbal communication. Clients can also use coaching self-talk when rehearsing targeted communication/action skills in their imaginations.

Improving clients' explanations

One of the main reasons why clients sustain greed and craving is because they give themselves unskilful explanations about what it takes to be happy and fulfilled in life. Bombarded with advertising messages from an early age and living in a materialistic culture, it can be easy to fall into the trap of thinking *My happiness = What I have and I consume*. Clients can be assisted in exploring what they really need to be happy and content in life. Undoubtedly material considerations will play a part, but they need not just to search for deeper human values, but to appreciate the things that they take for granted, for instance in their relationships and in nature. Clients may also need to develop more realistic attitudes towards life: for example, relinquishing childlike illusions that it is possible to be happy all the time, understanding the importance of working hard at meaningful activities, and coming to terms with the fact that suffering is an integral part of life.

Therapists can assist clients to make more accurate explanations for their acquiring, accumulating and consuming wealth decisions. Many may think that such decisions are made by their independent selves when in fact there are numerous causes and conditions shaping their view of themselves and hence their decisions. For example, clients may be insufficiently aware when their consumption has a compulsive quality about it grounded in learned demanding rules, faulty automatic perceptions and inaccurate explanations. As mentioned earlier, therapists can help raise clients' awareness of the materialistic pressures that exist in contemporary Western cultures so that they may gain more autonomy in face of them. Therapists can also help clients to explain to themselves that ultimately they are the main agents of their inner liberation from greed and craving and, therefore, it is their personal responsibility to develop mind skills that, in turn, should lead to more skilful communications and actions in this area. Those clients wishing to demonstrate higher levels of human sympathy through generosity and service may have to work extra hard in assuming responsibility for their inner liberation from greed.

Improving clients' communication/action skills

Therapists can also assist clients to develop communication/action skills to curb greed and craving. This is a broad area and only a few illustrative strategies are provided here. Therapists can assist clients to practise mindfulness-of-breathing skills when faced with temptations to make unnecessary purchases. Therapists can also help clients to devise alternative recreational activities that help them to keep away from stores and shopping malls. Some clients may require assistance in developing budgeting skills and then rewarding themselves when they stay within budget. Clients may also need to develop assertion skills, such as saying 'no' to people inviting them out on shopping expeditions and to salespersons in shops. Some clients may need to change the company they keep to less materialistic friends who do not reinforce their consuming behaviour.

Clients with problems living beyond their means and consuming too much can also develop skills of moderation and of simple living. They can strive to implement the nineteenth-century American writer Henry Thoreau's advice to stop frittering away their lives in detail and 'Simplify, simplify' (Thoreau, 1995). As part of this process, they can reorient their lives so that engaging in non-material activities plays a larger part. Such non-material activities include family dinners where members share their lives and interests, picnics, walks, and cups of tea or coffee with friends. Clients may develop hobbies that do not require large amounts of money – for example, jogging, hiking or cycling. Furthermore, clients can resist temptations to buy goods so that they can show off to their peers. They can also value their existing possessions more and so use them longer and better.

Clients can also curb tendencies to greed and craving by reducing the amount of unskilful money-related communication in which they engage. Topics of money-related conversation include talking about recent purchases, future consumption, real-estate values, stock market prices, people's incomes, and about rich friends and acquaintances. For some clients a shift to more simple living and to engaging in less money-related communication will involve learning to value themselves and others in less materialistic terms.

Another area in which some clients may need to improve their skills is in living more ethically where money is concerned. Regarding prevention, clients may need to stop unethical communications and actions such as lying, cheating and in other ways exploiting others. Some clients, possibly the more wealthy ones, may need to become more aware that just because they can get away with some behaviours legally – for instance by clever accounting, this does not always make them ethical. Regarding cultivating positive ethical behaviours, clients can develop their skills of generosity, helping and service, the topic of Chapter 14.

Improving clients' mind skills and communication/action skills

Although they are treated separately above, therapists working within the skilled client model focus on assisting clients to improve both their mind skills and their communication/action skills. Unless clients change the way they think in relation to greed and craving, there is little likelihood of them changing their external behaviour. Therapists and clients also need to focus on maintaining changes in clients' behaviour, because clients may find it easy to fall back into old habits of wanting and spending. Clients can consolidate their skills by rehearsing and practising them both during therapy sessions and in homework assignments.

Clients can also identify and remind themselves of the gains from changing their irrational acquiring, accumulating and consuming wealth behaviours. Such gains are the reverse of the costs of greed and craving enumerated earlier in this chapter. An obvious gain of spending less is that clients then have more resources. Clients can acknowledge feeling more content and less stressed once they have taken themselves off the consumption treadmill. Furthermore, they may feel more authentic and self-accepting and less alienated once they stop valuing themselves so much in material terms. Their intimate relationships may be sounder and they may feel less alienated from friends and acquaintances once they stop comparing and competing with them so much. Their physical health may be better and they may be less prone to stress problems and heart attacks. Clients may also be helped to maintain curbing their greed and craving by the rewards they obtain from being generous and serving others.

Practices

Practice 11.1: Dealing with greed and craving in therapy and self-therapy

Part A: Therapy

One person acts as therapist and the other as client. The therapist assists the client to identify a specific situation in which the client has either exhibited or is at risk of exhibiting destructive greed and craving. Using the skilled client model described in Chapter 7, the therapist works with the client to agree on a shared definition of her/his greed and craving problem in skills terms. Therapist and client should start by identifying one mind skill to improve and one communication/action skill to improve and then, if necessary, build on this. Next, the therapist and the client discuss interventions for improving the client's skills. Afterwards, if appropriate, they can reverse roles.

Part B: Self-therapy

Acting as a self-therapist, identify a specific situation in which you have exhibited or are at risk of exhibiting destructive greed and craving. Using the skilled human being model described in Chapter 15, work with yourself to define your greed and craving problem in skills terms. Start by identifying one mind skill to improve and one action skill to improve and then, if necessary, build on this. Next identify and implement strategies for improving your skills.

Practice 11.2: Dealing with greed in personal practice

The following are just some of the ways that you can deal with greed in personal practice.

Part A: Assessing yourself

1. To what extent and how are you subject to greed and craving in each of the following areas:

   - acquiring wealth;
   - accumulating wealth;
   - consuming wealth?

2. If you are subject to greed and craving in one or more of the above areas, explore and identify some of the underlying fears that motivate or 'drive' your feelings and behaviour. Such fears include:

   - destitution;
   - not being seen as successful;
   - not being liked;
   - not being socially acceptable;
   - boredom and a sense of meaninglessness;
   - being considered cheap;
   - death;
   - any other fears not mentioned above.

3. Apart from unrealistic fears, what are some of the influences that restrict the rationality and autonomy of your consuming behaviour?
   Possible influences include advertising, family pressures, peer group pressures, social climbing, low self-esteem, difficulties in delaying gratification, illusion of an independent self, illusion of permanence, and specific poor mind skills and communication/action skills, among others.

4. Answer the following questions about your consuming behaviour

   - What are good criteria for deciding when enough is enough?
   - Where is the evidence that you do not have enough?
   - Where is the evidence that you do have enough?
   - Regarding having enough, are there other ways of perceiving your situation?
   - Will you ever be satisfied with what you have?

5. What do you really value about:

   - yourself;
   - those whom you love;

- your friends;
- life.

To what extent do material considerations play a part in your answers?

Part B: Developing corrective self-talk skills

When you catch yourself either thinking or at risk of thinking conditioned unskilful thoughts in actual or potential situations connected with greed, practise replacing them with corrective skilful thoughts. For example:

S – Situation: I am attracted to an expensive item in a shop that I cannot really afford.
T(1) – Conditioned unskilful thought:
'Come on. You deserve to pamper yourself a little. Everyone else does.'
C(1) – Consequences of conditioned unskilful thought:
Possibly either going in and purchasing the item on impulse or obsessively ruminating about it and then going and purchasing it.
T(2) – Corrective skilful thought:
'Stay calm. The impulse to buy will pass and later on I can rationally consider whether I want and can afford it.'
C(2) – Consequences of corrective skilful thought:
Delaying the purchase and thinking about it rationally later.

1. Work through the format of the above example in relation to an actual or potential greed evoking situation in your own life.
2. Use your corrective self-talk skills either in advance of and/or in actual greed evoking situations in real life.

Part C: Communicating and acting differently

What are some of the ways in which you can communicate and act differently if unwise consumption is a problem for you? These ways include:

- using mindfulness of breathing skills;
- keeping away from stores and shopping malls;
- developing budgeting skills and rewarding yourself for staying in budget;
- developing assertion skills for saying 'no';
- changing the company you keep to less materialistic friends;
- developing skills of simple living;
- using existing possessions longer and better;

- being less ready to show off material possessions;
- spending less time talking about money and possessions.

In addition, think of other ways not mentioned above.

Where appropriate, practice your skills of communicating and acting differently in order to avoid unwise consumption.

TWELVE   Cultivating Goodwill, Sympathetic Joy and Gratitude

Cognitive humanistic therapy adopts the position that all individuals have an innate capacity for goodness as well as for aggressive and destructive behaviour. Humans can develop and cultivate their minds so that they can actively demonstrate more of their potential for human sympathy. The next three chapters focus on cultivating skilful mental states and behaviours. If clients, therapists and others are to become more fully human, they must go beyond curbing the unskilful to developing and practising the skilful. Chapters 12 and 13 focus on cultivating what the Buddhist religious tradition calls the four Divine Abodes of lovingkindness, sympathetic joy, compassion and equanimity. Here, for ease of communication to a non-Buddhist audience, the word goodwill is used instead of lovingkindness. Furthermore, to emphasize its importance, gratitude is treated separately rather than being incorporated into the other qualities. Chapter 14, the third of the cultivating skilful mental states and behaviour chapters, focuses on cultivating generosity, helping and service.

Some humanistic writers, such as Fromm and Maslow, raise the question of whether human nature is basically selfish. Fromm views an attitude of love towards oneself as joined with an attitude of love towards others. Ability to love others and oneself are not alternatives in that inability to love others represents insufficient self-love rather than an excess of it (Fromm, 1956). Similarly, Maslow writes in terms of healthy and unhealthy selfishness and of healthy and unhealthy unselfishness. Whereas unhealthy selfishness and immature unselfishness stem from emotional insecurity and poverty, healthy selfishness and mature unselfishness tend to be a phenomenon of personal abundance stemming from relative basic gratification (Hoffman, 1996). Maslow's concept of unhealthy unselfishness echoes the point made at the start of Chapter 10 about some people wanting to take a psychological bypass and focus on cultivating supra-normal qualities without adequately addressing the skills of attaining normal functioning first. Healthy unselfishness and healthy selfishness go together. Unfortunately, both Fromm and Maslow are rather stronger on describing the human condition than on suggesting practical steps whereby therapists can assist clients to become more loving human beings.

Much of Western psychotherapy appears to focus on assisting clients to lead happier and more fulfilled lives for their own sakes. A reason for this individualistic focus may be that mostly originators of Western approaches to psychotherapy insufficiently realize the extent to which cultural pathology can interact with, stimulate and reinforce individual pathology. Western societies are highly materialistic, competitive and market driven. Without deliberately intending it, capitalistic economic systems can relentlessly influence people to be egocentric, unhealthily selfish and narcissistic. Both therapists and clients can bring such values to the therapy situation and remain relatively unaware that they do so. It can be hard to address some problems adequately when they become so intimately connected to basic unexamined assumptions held by many therapists and clients.

The next three chapters assume that, in order to become more fully human, individuals need to be assiduous in promoting and nurturing the welfare of others as well as their own. The more mentally cultivated clients and others become, the more they are able to fuse attaining their own personal goals with feeling goodwill towards and serving others. Even when striving to attain normalcy, it can be helpful for clients to focus on cultivating the skills addressed in the next three chapters. For instance, angry clients can be helped by learning to view others in more loving and compassionate ways and to behave more generously towards them. For those clients and other people wishing to attain supra-normal levels of functioning, it is absolutely essential that they develop, cultivate and practise mind skills and communication skills that enhance others' interests and not just their own.

Cultivating positive qualities like goodwill, sympathetic joy, compassion and equanimity can be seen as steps along the way to inner liberation and to greater connectedness with others. Clients can learn to become freer from the negativity and aversion that contribute to their feeling alienated and separated from their fellow humans. Religious leaders like the current Dalai Lama and the late Mother Teresa have commented on the emotional poverty of much of Western life. In one of her speeches, Mother Teresa commented: 'In the West, there is loneliness which I call the leprosy of the West. In many ways it is worse than our poor in Calcutta. In Calcutta the poor, they share' (Chawla, 1992, p. 214). It is easy to get very caught up in personal agendas, such as one's career, family and mortgage, and to start judging others positively or negatively in terms of their usefulness in advancing these agendas. Cultivating more the loving human qualities can assist clients and others to move away from hard heartedness in the direction of human heartedness. Clients and therapists alike can learn to become strong enough to liberate themselves further from the prisons of their separate existences by cultivating skills of thinking and communicating more benevolently towards others.

Cultivating goodwill

Goodwill goes further than acceptance of others to wishing actively that they be well and happy. In Buddhism, goodwill or lovingkindness is the foundation upon which the qualities of compassion, sympathetic joy and equanimity rest. The Dalai Lama defines lovingkindness as the wish that all sentient beings may enjoy happiness (Dalai Lama, 2001). Often this is expressed as 'May I be well, may I be happy; May others be well, may others be happy.' Instead of looking from outside to inside and waiting for other people to have goodwill towards them, therapists can encourage clients to look from inside to outside and, of their own accord, generate goodwill towards others. Clients are more likely to succeed in doing this if they feel accepting and affirming towards themselves in the first place.

There are many positive benefits if clients and others train their minds to develop the skills of goodwill towards others. They are less likely to fall prey to fear, anger and aversion based on seeing the world as an unnecessarily threatening place. The world is full of negativity and the more loving people can become the less likely they are to spread ill will, which in turn generates further animosity. By projecting an image of goodwill, they are less likely to stimulate hostile behaviour from others. By transforming and liberating their hearts and minds from undue bad feelings and being prepared to search for the good in their fellow humans, they are more likely to enjoy better relationships with others and more serenity in themselves. Furthermore, those seeking to attain higher levels of mental cultivation and human sympathy are more likely to engage in acts of generosity and service above and beyond those for people in their immediate circles of engagement.

Improving clients' mind and communication skills

Improving clients' mind skills so that they may exhibit more goodwill is both a matter of clearing away the hindrances and promoting desirable ways of thinking. Already in Chapter 10, the mind skill of altering demanding rules conducive to anger and aversion to more preferential rules was reviewed. Rules that encourage judgement, competition and comparison are hindrances to feeling goodwill towards others. In his bestseller *Tuesdays with Morrie*, Albom tells the story of his professor Morrie

Schwartz who, when watching a basketball game in the Brandeis University gym in which the students were shouting 'We're number one, we're number one', at one point rose and yelled 'What's wrong with being number two?' (Albom, 1997). Rules that encourage greed and craving can also interfere with feeling goodwill and lovingkindness towards others.

Perhaps creating more accurate perceptions is the most important mind skill on which to focus when assisting clients to feel more goodwill towards other humans. Therapists can assist clients to challenge their illusions. For instance, they can challenge the illusion of an independent self by helping clients to acknowledge their dependence on others and the goodwill that is due to them on this count. Clients can challenge the illusion of permanence by realizing that their own lives and the lives of others are transitory and that it is tragic under these circumstances to go round generating unnecessary ill will rather than exhibiting goodwill. Therapists can assist clients to see how their mental inefficiency is contributing to their inability to be more loving and that they can assume responsibility for developing better mind skills and, hence, communicating more goodwill. Therapists can also help clients to challenge their illusion of differentness and replace it with the reality of perceiving universal sameness. If clients are worthy of respect and goodwill from their fellow humans, they need to show respect and goodwill towards them too.

In addition, therapists can assist clients to challenge the bad-animal view of human nature that justifies relating to many others on the basis of ill will rather than goodwill. Instead, clients can be helped to gain a more positive perspective on the human potential that justifies goodwill towards others as part of the process of striving to create a better world. For example, clients' tendencies to think negatively towards others can be challenged by asking them to recall loving people, requesting that they remember the good acts done for them by other people, and helping them to see the good points of others rather than relentlessly focusing on their weaknesses.

Often clients who think ill of most other people are projecting their view of themselves onto others. Such clients may need assistance to get in touch with their own innate goodness rather than to continue demeaning themselves. For example, clients can be actively encouraged to focus on good qualities in themselves, good things they have done in the past, and good intentions they may have for the future. Writers like Fromm and Maslow acknowledge that many people repress and fear what is good about themselves in addition to their bad qualities. The author's therapeutic experience is that most clients are far more skilled at saying what is wrong with them than at identifying what is right. Clients may need skilled therapeutic assistance when accessing their softer and kinder feelings about themselves and others.

Therapists can assist clients in creating accurate explanations for acquiring, cultivating and maintaining goodwill and the other positive qualities addressed in this and the following chapters. Clients can be assisted to see that if they are to become more mentally cultivated and show more human sympathy they must ultimately assume personal responsibility for developing these qualities. Therapists can help liberate clients from self-defeating explanations like 'Others must make the first move before I can show goodwill', 'The fact that I do not show more goodwill is other people's fault' and 'Others are responsible for making sure that I become a more skilled and loving human being'. Such explanations can be challenged and replaced. For instance, the first of the above statements might be changed to, 'It might be easier if others made the first move in showing goodwill, but it is my responsibility both to myself and to my fellow humans to show goodwill wherever feasible.' Clients may need to work hard to understand emotionally as well as intellectually that the extent to which they become more loving persons depends on their effort and their willingness to renounce self-defeating explanations, however comfortable and superficially reassuring they may be. Those clients seeking to attain higher levels of goodwill need to develop a rock-hard commitment to cultivating the appropriate mind skills and communication skills.

Therapists can also help clients use the mind skills of creating self-talk and creating visual images to develop their capacity to feel and show goodwill towards others. Clients can use self-talk to alert themselves when they are judging, comparing and competing and switch to kinder self-talk about another: for instance, 'May you be happy.' Often in Buddhist lovingkindness meditation practices, individuals are encouraged to use self-talk to cultivate loving feelings towards themselves prior to focusing on others: for example, 'May I be happy, kind, loving and peaceful' (Walsh, 1999, p. 107). Another version is 'May I be filled with lovingkindness, may I be well, may I be peaceful and at ease, may I be happy' (Kornfield, 1993, p. 20). Perhaps during the first twenty-minute or so practice session, meditators will only direct their goodwill towards themselves. Then they may branch out: for instance, they may visualize a benefactor, someone in their life who has truly cared for them: 'May he/she be happy, kind, loving and peaceful'. After this they can gradually expand to include relatives, friends, neighbours, groups of people and the human species. Meditators can also practise feeling goodwill towards difficult people in their lives, even those that they hate. Clients too can learn from using contemplative practices such as the above to cultivate their capacity to feel and show goodwill.

Clients can use coaching self-talk and visualized rehearsal to improve their communication skills of demonstrating goodwill. For example, some may choose to imagine moving and speaking in ways that are gentle, non-aggressive, peaceful and serene. Clients can adjust to their personal styles the way they communicate goodwill by means of their verbal, vocal and bodily messages. Simple things can mean a lot when communicating goodwill: for instance, smiling at people and visibly taking an interest in their happiness. Clients can practise skills of communicating goodwill in numerous situations in their everyday lives. Such communication may be with casual contacts, for instance with the staff in shops and petrol or gas stations, or with those with whom they are more intimately connected. Clients can also learn to monitor their communication to identify and edit out comments that may be competitive, demeaning and hurtful to others. Avoiding communicating ill will and causing others to feel inferior is important in creating an atmosphere of respect, psychological safety and goodwill.

Cultivating sympathetic joy

Cultivating the capacity to feel and communicate sympathetic joy is another way in which clients and other people can gain inner liberation from negativity and improved relationships with others. Sympathetic joy, which is grounded in goodwill and lovingkindness, means rejoicing in others' good fortune. It entails the ability to be genuinely glad at others' happiness and success. Sharing sympathetic joy is not just a matter of going through the motions of being a 'nice' person, but involves giving a sincere gift of delight and pleasure from both one's heart and one's head. People who show sympathetic joy rise beyond the confines of everyday negativity in ways that enhance both their own and others' happiness.

The opposite of sympathetic joy is the German idea of *schadenfreude*, being happy at another's misfortune. Many people experience either varying degrees of ambivalence or negative feelings at others' happiness and good fortune. Often people see another's happiness and good fortune as threatening in some ways to their own: for example they can assume that it means there is less for them. Judging, comparing and competing, they set themselves up for negative feelings of jealousy and envy. In Australia, such tendencies go by the name of 'the tall poppy syndrome' in which successful people (tall poppies) need to be cut down to size. There are numerous strategies people can employ to avoid acknowledging one another's good fortune and success. One strategy is to ignore it and pretend it never happened, for instance, by quickly changing the subject and then never talking about it. Another strategy is to dilute it and make out that the success is nothing out of the ordinary; in fact one might have achieved it oneself if one had bothered to make the effort. A further strategy is to attack the motivation of successful people as selfish, when they perform well, and boasting, when they talk about it. Still another strategy is to refocus the conversation on oneself and start extolling the virtues of one's own achievement.

Maslow (1971) uses the term counter-valuing to refer to people's unconscious tendencies to fear those who are talented because they make them feel aware of their lesser worth, even if they do not intend to. However, it is not just outstanding achievement that can generate unease but just the experience of another being happy. The old saying 'misery loves company' can hold true and clients may come from environments where their happy moments are not shared. Furthermore, clients themselves may have poor skills at feeling and showing sympathetic joy partly because they have rarely received it themselves.

Improving clients' mind skills and communication skills

Some clients may need longer term psychotherapy to raise their level of self-esteem so that they can genuinely share sympathetic joy. However, many clients and those seeking to become more fully human may gain from specifically focusing on developing, cultivating and maintaining the human-being skill of sympathetic joy. To date, working in this area seems to have been more the preserve of religious traditions than of psychotherapy. Furthermore, this is an area in which many therapists and therapy trainers may benefit from focusing in their own lives. The history of psychotherapy is littered with bitterness – for example, the relationship between Freud and Jung – and psychology and psychiatry departments have more than their fair share of rivalries, negative gossip and back stabbing. There is an aphorism 'the loftier the ideals, the dirtier the politics', which suggests how hard it can be for members of the helping professions to show sympathetic joy to one another.

Therapists can help raise clients' awareness of how they feel, think and communicate when faced with another's happiness or success. Clients can get in touch with a range of feelings from genuine delight to threat, jealousy and envy. Therapists can provide healing emotional climates where clients feel safe to acknowledge and strengthen more positive and sympathetic feelings towards others that they may have been repressing or ignoring. Therapists can also help clients become more aware of their shadow side and assist them to use their greater awareness of negative and unwanted feelings as a stimulus for exploring the thoughts and mental processes contributing to them.

Creating rules is an important mind skill area to explore when exploring hindrances to feeling, thinking and communicating sympathetic joy. Rules connected with judging, comparing and competing with other people can both lower personal self-esteem as well as contribute to negative feelings towards others. In addition to exploring such rules, therapists can assist clients to explore their rules about people disclosing happiness and success to them in their relationships. Regarding sharing happiness, some clients may possess demanding rules such as 'Others must not be happy' and 'When others are happy they must not talk about it'. Regarding sharing good fortune and success, clients may possess demanding rules like 'People must not talk about their good fortune' and 'People must not bring their successes to my attention'. To some extent, even when done unassumingly, there is a taboo against talking about one's successes in Western culture because it can be construed as boasting and ego-tripping at the listener's expense.

Therapists can assist clients to detect and dispute such underlying demanding rules that may be inhibiting feeling and communicating sympathetic joy. Furthermore, they can help clients become more aware of the negative consequences of maintaining such rules and the positive consequences of liberating themselves to show more sympathetic joy. Therapists can help clients to state demanding rules as preferential rules. For instance, in close relationships it is very important that couples are able to talk about what they perceive as their strengths and weaknesses honestly. If a couple were to possess a relationship rule 'People must not bring attention to their success', this might be reworded to become the preferential rule that 'Our relationship will be happier if each of us feels comfortable in sharing our successes and failures'. Then partners might feel freer to show one another sympathetic joy when appropriate. The same holds true for work situations in which developing rules about honest communication may liberate colleagues to show more sympathetic joy when they genuinely feel it.

Many ways exist in which therapists can assist clients to challenge inaccurate perceptions that act as impediments to sympathetic joy. Clients can be assisted to show sympathetic joy to themselves. Underneath their social personas, clients may be consciously and subconsciously thinking 'I'm not good enough. I'm not good enough. I'm not good enough.' To maintain a consistent self-picture however negative it may be, many clients ignore or dilute the impact of their successes and emphasize their shortcomings. Such clients need to get more in touch with their strengths and to become much more aware of when they are thinking, feeling, communicating and acting effectively. Clients who have lapsed into bad habits of self-denigration may need to acknowledge their strengths and assets again, again and again.

Clients can also be assisted to challenge illusions that interfere with sympathetic joy. For instance, the illusion of an independent self may interfere with acknowledging the extent to which showing feeling, thinking and showing sympathetic joy enhances relationships with others and lessens feelings of alienation from them. Clients can be assisted to replace the illusion of differentness with the reality of universal sameness. The illusion of differentness can preclude clients from fully participating as part of the human race and so being able to feel and show sympathetic joy to a wide variety of people rather than just to members of their own family, clan and race. Furthermore, if clients perceive others as similar to themselves, two beneficial outcomes for showing sympathetic joy may result. First, clients are more likely to empathize accurately with others when they are happy and successful. Second, they are more likely to be sensitive to the consequences of their behaviour on others, including when either showing or withholding displays of sympathetic joy.

Without necessarily realizing it, some clients perceive that life is a zero-sum game in which one person's winning must necessarily involve the other person losing. This win-lose attitude can create lose-lose outcomes in which both parties suffer the consequences of their shortsighted selfishness. Good personal relationships, such as marriages, depend on teamwork in which partners help one another to develop as much of their human potential as is realistic. In intimate relationships, showing sympathetic joy is part of a win-win mutually enhancing process and the same holds true for most other relationships. Where possible, clients should avoid making their showing of sympathetic joy too conditional on how other people are behaving. As Maslow writes: 'Psychological success is a non-zero-sum game because everyone can win. Rather than seeking to defeat someone else, it is better to seek excellence and perfection in one's own accomplishments.' (Hoffman, 1996, p. 68).

Clients may also use self-talk skills to feel, think and show more sympathetic joy. For example, when they catch themselves at risk of falling into conditioned patterns of negativity at another's happiness and good fortune, they can calm themselves down and think matters through. When calmer they may be in stronger positions to identify and correct the thoughts contributing to negative feelings such as jealousy and replace them with more sympathetic thoughts. As part of this process clients may use coaching self-talk as they work on challenging and changing demanding rules and inaccurate perceptions that interfere with feeling and showing sympathetic joy. Clients can also use coaching self-talk as they employ active listening skills in which they accurately understand another's good fortune and show them by how they respond that they have clearly heard their happiness. Furthermore, where appropriate, clients can use coaching self-talk to send appropriate verbal, vocal and body messages for disclosing sympathetic joy. Such verbal disclosure messages include 'well done', 'congratulations', 'I'm delighted', and 'I'm really happy for you'. Needless to say disclosing happiness verbal messages need to be accompanied by genuine vocal and body messages.

A final point is that clients may need to use sympathetic joy judiciously. For example, if after careful reflection, they consider showing too much sympathetic joy will make another person conceited, they need to take this into account. Furthermore, clients should be careful not to allow themselves to be psychologically abused by insecure people who constantly want to talk about their achievements. In such instances, clients can use skills of setting limits assertively.

Cultivating gratitude

Gratitude is grounded in goodwill and lovingkindness and is closely related to the ability to feel, think and show sympathetic joy. The feeling and thinking component of gratitude is that of being genuinely thankful for something positive either done for one or something otherwise positive in one's life – for instance, good health. Thus the human-being skill of gratitude comes from both heart and head. The communication/action component of gratitude is that of showing appreciation to those from whom one has received kindness and help. There is a happy synergy in that gratitude affirms both the grateful and the thanked. The more mentally cultivated people become, the more they are able to open their hearts to the blessings they receive from others and to show gratitude as a way of sharing their appreciation of their good fortune.

The author concurs with Maslow who regarded gratitude as an extremely important, but badly ignored aspect of emotional health. Towards the end of his life Maslow, who died in 1970, came to view the widespread presence of ingratitude in American society as a definite sign of emotional pathology (Hoffman, 1996). The same holds true for contemporary British and Australasian cultures where much of the time, as in America, individualism and a sense of entitlement hold sway. Many factors may contribute to this lessening of gratitude. Previously, people relied on their communities, villages, and extended families to take care of them. Because people needed each other more for their very existence they placed a higher value on one another's contribution to their lives. Furthermore, although welfare state provision represents a caring society, an unintended side effect may be to encourage a further weakening of family ties and hence gratitude for family support, because people can rely on the state in emergencies rather than on one another. In rapidly changing consumer-driven and technology-driven societies, gratitude for the wisdom and contribution of older people is less likely to be felt and expressed.

Improving mind skills and communication skills

Therapists can help clients become more aware of feelings that enhance and inhibit expressing gratitude. Clients' ability to feel gratitude may vary according to whom they have in mind. For example, it may be easy to express gratitude to close friends, but sometimes harder to express it to parents. In the latter case clients' feelings of gratitude may be tinged with ambivalence especially if the parents have been or continue to be controlling and possessive. In some instances, therapists may need to help clients to work through feelings of anger so that they attain a degree of forgiveness of others so that they can truly feel gratitude to them. In intimate relationships, partners may develop interaction patterns in which each feels unappreciated by the other. As part of relieving the distress in such relationships, clients can be assisted to feel and express gratitude to one another. This can initiate a virtuous cycle in which it becomes easier to be more mutually appreciative. In good marriages both partners are able to get in touch with and express feelings of gratitude, appreciation and celebration of the very existence of one another.

Clients' demanding rules can provide a fertile breeding ground for hindrances to feeling and showing gratitude. For instance, clients' exaggerated sense of entitlement may be expressed in such rules as 'I must have whatever I want as my right', 'Others must be perfectly attentive to my welfare', and 'Others must show gratitude and appreciation for everything I do'. Other demanding rules that can inhibit gratitude are 'I must never forgive', 'I must not show gratitude' and 'Others should not expect gratitude.' Rules that encourage competing, comparing and judging can also be impediments to feelings of gratitude. Once identified, key demanding rules require being disputed or challenged and restated as preferential rules.

Therapists can also assist clients to feel and show more gratitude by challenging their illusion of permanence. Clients can be asked to imagine that people close to them are about to die and what feelings of gratitude they would like to express to them right now when it is still possible. Clients can also be requested to imagine that their own deaths are imminent and how they might use their remaining life and say goodbye to the persons they love best. Clients' hearts can also be softened so that they are more likely to show gratitude by challenging the illusion of difference and replacing it with the reality of universal sameness. Furthermore, clients who are able to discard the illusion of human badness are likely to be in stronger positions to express gratitude to their fellow humans than those who are still stuck with a jungle outlook.

Clients' feelings of gratitude may be inhibited if they tend to focus too much on perceiving their own and others' negative qualities. More balanced appraisals make it easier to express gratitude, because positive qualities are more likely to be noticed and appreciated. Some clients may perceive the process of being grateful in negative ways – for instance, either as weakness, putting oneself under an obligation, or sucking up.

Such clients can be assisted to examine the reality of their perceptions and change them, where appropriate. Those receiving gratitude may also need to distinguish when the gratitude is a genuine expression of thanks or when they are either being manipulated or just participating in social rituals.

To become more grateful, some clients may benefit from working on the mind skill of creating explanations. For instance, clients may explain the problems in their lives as being due to the shortcomings of their parents and other people. Clients who provide such explanations may be triply inaccurate: first, by being insufficiently aware of the good things others have done for them; second, by ignoring their own roles creating their problems; and third, by insufficiently acknowledging their responsibility to work for change. Arriving at more balanced explanations may make it easier to show gratitude. Clients may also fail to show gratitude to others when they explain too much of their success to themselves and insufficiently notice how they have been helped by others. Therapists can assist such clients to examine the evidence for how they became and are successful and then help them to be more generous in feeling and showing appreciation for others' efforts.

Therapists can assist clients to use self-talk to feel and show more gratitude. When clients find themselves at risk of falling into conditioned patterns of either not feeling or not demonstrating the gratitude they do feel, clients can calm themselves down, listen to their feelings more closely and, where appropriate, show their appreciation. Furthermore, when calmer, clients who feel inhibited in showing gratitude can ask themselves 'What is going on here?' and if necessary coach themselves in addressing any demanding rules, unrealistic perceptions and inaccurate explanations that may be getting in the way.

Clients can also coach themselves in the verbal, vocal and body messages of communicating gratitude and then practise these skills both in their imaginations and in actual situations. Communicating gratitude needs to go beyond the rituals of being polite to giving another genuine appreciation. Such appreciation may be shown in numerous ways with the most obvious ones being to say sincerely 'thank you' and 'I appreciate what you've done'. Other ways of showing gratitude include appreciative looks, smiles, hugs and kisses, sending notes and poems, and being there for others when needed. Sometimes gifts can be an appropriate way of showing gratitude so long as the givers are genuinely expressing appreciation rather than trying to relieve themselves of a feeling of obligation or having some other ulterior motive. Over the course of long-term relationships, partners can show gratitude by treating one another with respect and engaging in numerous caring acts that give credence to verbal expressions of appreciation. When expressing gratitude, clients may need to pay attention to communicating the appropriate amount. It is possible to be too effusive as well as too muted, although if done sincerely probably effusiveness is a fault on the right side. Expressions of gratitude should be backed up by appropriate actions, for example acts of caring, or else they may just be viewed as empty words.

Practices

Practice 12.1: Cultivating goodwill skills

As appropriate, conduct those parts of this practice that seem most helpful either with one person acting as therapist and another as client or as part of personal practice.

The term goodwill/lovingkindness is used throughout to give readers the choice of using whichever word has the most meaning for them when doing the practice. Alternatively readers can think in terms of using both goodwill and lovingkindness together.

1. Either the therapist assists the client to recall or you recall loving people whom she/he/you either know or have known personally or know about and admire. For each one, what makes them so special at feeling, thinking and communicating goodwill/lovingkindness?
2. Either the therapist assists the client to assess or you assess how well she/he/you feel/s, think/s and communicate/s goodwill/lovingkindness to her/his/your

    *   self;
    *   partner (if applicable);
    *   relatives;
    *   friends;
    *   neighbours;
    *   casual contacts (for example, in shops);
    *   work or study colleagues;
    *   other relevant groups of people (please specify).

3. What mind skills and communication/action skills does the client (or do you) need to improve to feel, think and communicate with more goodwill/lovingkindness? Start by identifying one mind skill and one communication/action skill to improve and then, if necessary, build on this.
4. Conduct a personal experiment for a specified period of time (one day, two days, a week) in which the client consciously tries to (or you try to) feel, think and communicate with goodwill/lovingkindness towards one or more persons or categories of people chosen in advance. At the end of the experiment evaluate what happened and the positive and negative consequences of feeling, thinking and communicating differently.

Practice 12.2: Cultivating sympathetic joy skills

As appropriate, conduct those parts of this practice thought most helpful either with one person acting as therapist and another as client or as part of personal practice.

1. Either the therapist assists the client to imagine or you imagine a good thing happening to someone held dear making that person very happy. Then imagine feeling, thinking and communicating sympathetic joy to that person. Afterwards, repeat this activity for a liked but less close person, for a neither particularly liked nor disliked person and for a difficult person.
2. Either the therapist assists the client to assess or you assess how well she/he/you feel/s, think/s and communicate/s sympathetic joy to her/his/your

    - partner (if applicable);
    - relatives;
    - friends;
    - neighbours;
    - casual contacts (for example, in shops);
    - work or study colleagues;
    - other relevant groups of people (please specify).

3. What mind skills and communication/action skills does the client (or do you) need to improve to feel, think and communicate with more sympathetic joy? Start by identifying one mind skill and one communication/action skill to improve and then, if necessary, build on this.
4. Conduct a personal experiment for a specified period of time (one day, two days, a week) in which the client consciously tries to (or you try to) feel, think and communicate with sympathetic joy towards one or more persons or categories of people chosen in advance. At the end of the experiment evaluate what happened and the positive and negative consequences of feeling, thinking and communicating differently.

Practice 12.3: Cultivating gratitude skills

As appropriate, conduct those parts of this practice thought most helpful either with one person acting as therapist and another as client or as part of personal practice.

1. Either the therapist assists the client to make or you make a list of significant people at each of the following stages of life (where relevant).

    - infancy and childhood;
    - adolescence;

- young adulthood;
- middle age;
- post-middle age.

For each person either the client or you write(s) down some specific ways in which these people made positive contributions to her/him/you. Then the client or you evaluate(s) whether she/he/you has communicated sufficient gratitude for the different contributions cited.

To whom either does the client or do you want to make amends for her/his/your past or present lack of gratitude? If relevant, make and implement a plan to put matters right by thanking at least one of the persons identified.

2. Either the therapist assists the client to imagine or you imagine her/him/your self to be either dying or about to be executed. What would either the client or you cherish, hold precious and be thankful for in life? What would the client or you want to say to each of the people that she/he/you love/s best?

3. What mind skills and communication/action skills does the client (or do you) need to improve to feel, think and communicate with more gratitude? Start by identifying one mind skill and one communication/action skill to improve and then, if necessary, build on this.

4. Conduct a personal experiment for a specified period of time (one day, two days, a week) in which the client consciously tries to (or you try to) feel, think and communicate with gratitude towards one or more persons or categories of people chosen in advance. At the end of the experiment evaluate what happened and the positive and negative consequences of feeling, thinking and communicating differently.

THIRTEEN Cultivating Compassion and Equanimity

This chapter continues the emphasis on cultivating positive human-being skills not just for their own sakes, but as antidotes to negative emotions, thoughts and communications. Arguably the Western psychotherapy literature insufficiently emphasizes cultivating the positive as a weapon against the negative. For example, Deffenbacher, Oetting and DiGiuseppe (2002), in their review of empirically supported anger management interventions, fail to mention this aspect of dealing with the problem. This is despite the fact that cultivating feelings of compassion has the potential to be an important antidote for feelings of anger and aversion. Angry or greedy clients require assistance in developing positive qualities as part of the process of curbing negative ones when they try to transform how they approach their lives and relationships.

Cultivating compassion

Compassion for the suffering of others is central to the practice of Christianity and Buddhism. The life and death of Jesus Christ exemplified that of a person dedicated to relieving the suffering of others. For instance, Christ's commandment to 'Love thy neighbour as thyself' (Mark 12:31) and his parables like those of the Good Samaritan and the Prodigal Son emphasize the virtue of compassion. As Martin Luther King observes the Good Samaritan was not only a good man, but a great man, 'because he had the capacity to project the "I" into the "thou," and to be concerned about his brother' (King, 1986, p. 284).

The Buddha's life and teachings also heavily emphasize compassion. Compassion is regarded as one of the three cardinal virtues of the Buddha, the other two being purity and wisdom (Thitavanno, 1995). Despite attaining Enlightenment, the Buddha spent the remaining 45 years of his life enduring the daily hardships of human existence to teach the *dhamma*. The Dalai Lama stresses the importance of cultivating an other-concerned attitude and defines compassion as 'not being able to stand the enslavement of others to suffering without doing something about it' (Dalai Lama,

2002, p. 100). He considers that it is through the inspiration of compassion that people engage in the virtuous practices that lead to Enlightenment. The world's other major religious traditions, for instance Islam, Taoism, Confucianism and Judaism, also highly value compassion (Walsh, 1999).

So far cultivating compassion has not been a major focus in the Western psychotherapy and counselling literature. The Viennese psychiatrist Alfred Adler (1870–1937), with his stress on social interest or social feeling (Ansbacher and Ansbacher, 1956; Adler, 1997, 1998), has probably come closest to advocating the importance of compassion. The German word for social interest is *gemeinschaftsgefühl*, which literally means feeling for the community. Social interest involves the ability to move beyond egocentricity to identify and empathize with others and the community. This empathic identification can be expanded to include all humankind and animals, plants and the cosmos. Taking the broader perspective, the human quest for social interest is above all a struggle to attain the ideal communal form in which humanity has reached its final stage of perfection. From the viewpoint of Adlerian therapy, if clients develop inferiority complexes, they are always looking out for their own interests rather than those of others and thus not having any sense of community. The main task of therapy is to help clients with inferiority complexes strengthen their social interest and thus become less self-centred. As with the Buddhist focus on compassion, Adler regarded social interest as an innate potential requiring conscious development.

Erich Fromm's (1976) emphasis on developing a humanistic conscience also implies the importance of developing a compassionate attitude. One of the key characteristics of Fromm's 'New Man' is that of making the full growth of oneself and one's fellow human beings the supreme goal of living.

Of the modern psychotherapeutic writers Aaron Beck has emphasized people's need to break out of the prisons of their egocentricity and hostility and treat one another more compassionately both on the personal level (Beck, 1988) and on the group and national levels (Beck, 1999). As an antidote to group narcissism, Beck writes of humanistic altruism in which others are seen as fellow human beings and not as stereotyped members of a group. The mind-set of the narcissistic-expansive orientation, in which one group or nation is superior and others are potential enemies, restricts compassion to members of the superior group. Alternatively, assumptions characterizing the altruistic-humanistic orientation include the following: all people are equal and worthwhile, outsiders are potential friends, no group has a prior claim, all lives are sacred, and if I help outgroupers it makes me a better person (Beck, 1999). Those who mediate conflicts need to help participants shift from the limited compassion of the narcissistic-expansive orientation to the much broader compassion of the altruistic-humanistic orientation.

Dimensions of compassion

Compassion literally means suffering together with another or others. It connotes sympathy and pity based on fellow feeling. Perhaps the opposite of compassion is self-pity where, instead of transcending their egocentricity to focus on others' suffering, people wallow in feeling sorry for themselves. A useful distinction exists between growth-motivated compassion and deficiency-motivated compassion. The former is based on self-love and abundance, while the latter is fragile and may represent a projection of people's longing to be treated compassionately themselves and thus, perhaps, an underlying self-pity.

There are numerous benefits of mature compassion. The capacity for an other-concerned attitude protects people from the dangers of self-centredness by helping them to get their own problems into perspective. Compassion can dissolve alienation and separation from other individuals, groups and the human species. In addition, compassion can act as a powerful antidote to aggression and aversion in that compassionate people can acknowledge the suffering of others and do not just focus on their own. Highly mentally developed and compassionate people see beneath unskilful surface behaviour to understand its roots in ignorance and in insufficiently developed mind skills and communication/action skills. They are sufficiently liberated from conditioned ways of reacting to avoid agitating themselves with inappropriate anger and behaving in self-defeating ways. Instead they attempt to think with reason and behave with love. Furthermore, treating other people with kindness and respect, they are more likely to be treated this way themselves. On a broader level, the more groups and nations can react with compassion to one another, the more likely they are to find non-violent solutions to their problems.

Compassion and suffering are inextricably interwoven. The intellectual dimension of cultivating compassion is that of developing a greater understanding of the nature of suffering, one's own as well as that of others. The Western emphasis on the pursuit of happiness may make it hard to switch to a more Eastern perspective in which acknowledging the pervasiveness of suffering throughout life and trying to ameliorate it plays a much larger role. The concept of suffering was reviewed in Chapter 3. Elements of suffering identified there included the universal experiences of birth, aging, dying, death, sickness and the loss of physical powers. Further aspects of suffering include psychological suffering through emotional crippling, failure to acquire and maintain good mind skills and communication/action skills, inability to find meaning in life, and realizing too little of one's potential for innate goodness. Many people in the West may see suffering as the failure to reach an average level of psychological functioning; a more Eastern perspective is that even normal people suffer because they have still to attain supra-normal levels of mental cultivation and human sympathy.

To acknowledge another's suffering intellectually is insufficient. Compassionate people also need the capacity to be emotionally open to this suffering and to empathize with the sufferer in an 'as if' way. True compassion requires heart as well as head. Being open to another's suffering can bring about a softening of heart and mind. Consequently, clients and others need to train their minds to broaden and deepen their capacity to empathize with those who suffer. Threat, anxiety, anger and aversion are emotions that can interfere with being open to another's suffering. For example, the amount of suffering in the world is so enormous that some may fear being overwhelmed by their emotions if they acknowledge more of its existence. Furthermore, being open to suffering has the potential to threaten people's happiness and sense of adequacy, especially if these qualities are not firmly grounded. Reactions to suffering can include disgust, aversion and not wanting to know about it. When people's suffering is accompanied by aggressive behaviour, anger may be another emotion blocking the experience of compassion. Cultivating being open to suffering entails a gradual step by step process of transforming one's heart and mind and working through psychological defences against acknowledging the reality of suffering. Furthermore, being open to suffering entails getting more in touch with one's own capacity for human sympathy and social feeling and addressing defences against being good.

Compassion needs to go still further than intellectually acknowledging the reality of suffering and being emotionally open to specific instances of it. Compassionate people also require the capacity to act in appropriate ways to relieve the suffering of others. Compassion must become not just the wish that others be free from suffering but the willingness and, if possible, the ability to do something about it. The next chapter on generosity, helping and service addresses issues and skills connected with communicating and acting with compassion. Those committed to relieving suffering may also need to address the social, political and economic structures that create the conditions under which many people suffer, a topic beyond the scope of the present book.

Improving mind skills and communication/action skills

Therapists can help clients to become more aware of their feelings of compassion and to value, nurture and express them. Clients can understand that the potential for feelings of compassion is part of their evolutionary heritage, but that they need to take responsibility for nurturing this potential. Therapists can assist clients to see more clearly some of the advantages of getting in touch with their compassionate feelings. Furthermore, therapists can help clients to become more aware of and understand more deeply the feelings of anxiety and aversion that they may feel when faced with situations requiring compassion. Such negative feelings can be used as the starting point for self-exploration rather than accepted as the end point of what clients truly feel.

All people have some good in them but many are afraid to acknowledge their softer more tender feelings. Maslow considered that pertinent questions to ask about everyone were 'How much, to what extent does he or she possess saintliness?' and, 'How scared is he or she of this saintliness? How much is he or she repressing it' (Hoffman, 1996, p. 91). Therapists can encourage clients as they confront their fears about being more compassionate. Helping clients to get more in touch with feelings of compassion often means working through deeply held mental and behavioural habits that keep them impoverished by their egocentricity. The shift towards feeling, thinking and acting compassionately is usually a gradual process of inner transformation and not a Big Bang experience.

Addressing the mind skill of creating rules is highly relevant to overcoming hindrances to compassion. Demanding rules that contribute to anger, aversion, greed and craving diminish clients' compassion. Irrational rules involving comparing, competing and judging interfere with understanding others' suffering with empathy. Box 13.1 lists some demanding rules that can interfere with compassion. Each of these demanding rules breeds alienation and separation from others rather than fellow feeling for them. Some of the demanding rules, such as needing to be seen as tough and strong, reflect cultural pressures not to show the softer side of one's human nature. Therapists can assist clients to detect and articulate these and other demanding rules that may be barriers to compassion.

Box 13.1: Illustrative demanding rules hindering compassion

My/my family's pursuit of happiness must always come first.
My happiness and mental wellbeing must not be challenged by others' suffering.
I must not allow myself to get upset at others' misfortune.
I must not be naïve in feeling compassion.

I must not be foolish in feeling compassion.
I must not be impractical in feeling compassion.
I must be in control of my emotions.
I must not be weak and tender hearted.
I must be seen as tough and strong.
My group/nation must be right at all costs.
Other people (e.g. the poor) must always look after themselves.
People who do bad things must be severely punished.
Might on my side must always be right.

Therapist and client can challenge and dispute demanding rules by means of functional disputing – for instance 'How is having the rule "Other people must always look after themselves" helping you?' – and empirical disputing – for instance, 'Where is the evidence that other people (such as the poor) must always look after themselves?' As in the following example, therapists can also assist clients in restating compassion-hindering demanding rules into compassion-enhancing preferential rules.

Demanding rule: 'Other people (such as the poor) must always look after themselves'.
Preferential rule: 'I would prefer people to be self-reliant, but often there are environmental and personal circumstances that mean that individuals and groups require a helping hand in life'.

Clients and self-therapists need to work hard to remember, rehearse and practise their new preferential rules, so that they can more readily use them in real-life situations.

Therapists can assist clients to be more compassionate by helping them to challenge false perceptions or illusions maintaining hard heartedness rather than human heartedness. The illusion of an independent self can be challenged by helping clients to reflect on their own experience of being happy when treated with compassion and affection by others (Dalai Lama and Cutler, 1998). Clients then gain insight into how others may feel when treated with compassion by them. Furthermore, they may become more aware that humans are interdependent in needing to give and receive compassion. The illusion of an independent self can also be challenged by making clients more aware that, just as much of their own behaviour results from the causes and conditions of their upbringing and environment, so the same is true for other people.

The illusion of a permanent self can be challenged by helping clients to become more aware of their need for compassion in light of the fragility of their own lives and how others therefore also need compassion during their short stays on earth. Anything that therapists can do to break down the illusion of differentness and replace it with the reality of universal sameness is likely to enhance compassion by helping clients to become more empathic by projecting their 'I' into other people's 'thou'. Illusions of superiority based on compensations for inferiority feelings, group identification, race, creed and financial status may each need to be addressed as part of the process of enhancing compassion. Challenging the illusion of human badness may also be important in getting people out of a jungle outlook into seeing the potential for good in others and how this can be enhanced by treating them compassionately.

In instances of antagonism and aversion, opponents can enhance compassion and empathy by 'accepting the principle that although one's perspective *feels* real and legitimate, it could be biased and totally wrong' (Beck, 1999, p. 231). Beck considers the following are questions people can ask about the possible fallibility of their perspectives:

- Is it possible that I have misconstrued the apparently offensive behaviour of another person or group?
- Are my interpretations based on real evidence or on my preconceptions?
- Are there alternative explanations?
- Am I distorting my image of the other person because of my own vulnerabilities or fears?

Beck uses the term 'decentring' for the process of distancing oneself from a self-centred and potentially invalid perspective about a situation to reframe the meaning of that situation with the objectivity of an impartial observer. Such decentring increases the possibility of an empathic understanding of another's perspective, which in turn may be the doorway to feeling more compassion for them. Therapists can help clients to develop and use decentring skills to enhance their capacity for compassion.

Therapists can help clients to perceive the nature of suffering more accurately. Some clients may be blocked from perceiving when others need compassion because they possess poor skills of understanding their own suffering. For instance, clients who drive themselves too hard may also place unfair demands on others because they possess limited insight into both parties' suffering. In such instances, therapists can assist clients to understand their own suffering better as part of the process of empathizing with, then feeling compassion for, and then altering their behaviour to relieve others' suffering. Within the context of collaborative working relationships, therapists can assist clients to develop more accurate perceptions of the nature of suffering, their own current capacity for compassion and their potential for change.

Therapists can enhance compassion by assisting clients to explore and, if necessary, challenge and restate the meanings that they attach to feeling compassion. If clients attach negative labels like weak, soft and unmanly to feeling compassion, therapists can ask them for evidence why this is the case. Therapists can also help clients to see that truly skilled people combine tough mindedness with tender heartedness and that often the softest people are those who are strongest.

The mind skill of creating explanations has much relevance for whether people cultivate or curb compassion. For example, feelings of compassion for poor people can be lessened or entirely blocked by explaining their poverty as due to laziness, stupidity and a mentality that expects welfare handouts. Compassion for poor people can be further diminished by explaining one's own more fortunate financial situation as solely or mainly the result of the efforts of an independent self. In cases where others are less fortunate than clients, therapists can assist clients to explore the reality of their explanations for others seemingly being less successful. Some clients may gain from being helped to see that people's position in life is heavily influenced by environmental circumstances and the extent to which they have been helped to acquire and maintain good human-being skills. Such mainly learned human-being skills include the extent to which people have been helped to develop poor skills or good skills of assuming personal responsibility for making the most of their lives. By challenging and replacing false explanations, therapists and clients can work to enhance clients' capacity for compassion. As part of this process clients may require their therapists' help in learning to accept more responsibility for developing high levels of compassion and social feeling.

Therapists can assist clients to enhance compassion by improving their creating self-talk and creating visual images skills. By using these skills clients can develop greater compassionate identification with both individuals and groups of people. Adler suggests that social feeling involves an evaluative attitude towards life clearly expressed by the words of an unnamed English author 'To see with the eyes of another, to hear with the ears of another, to feel with the heart of another' (Ansbacher and Ansbacher, 1956, p. 135).

The Buddhist religious tradition has many self-talk and visual image practices designed to enhance compassion. An important meditation practice for the purpose of counteracting selfishness and encouraging people to open themselves to others' suffering is that of *Tong-Len*, 'giving and receiving' (Dalai Lama and Cutler, 1998, pp. 212–16). First, meditators visualize on one side of themselves a group of people who desperately need help, suffer greatly and live under conditions of poverty, hardship and pain. Then on the other side meditators visualize themselves as the embodiment of a self-centred person. And then in between the suffering group of people and the selfish representation of themselves, meditators view themselves as neutral observers. Next they are instructed to notice which side they naturally incline towards.

After that, meditators focus their attention on the needy and desperate people. They direct all their positive energy towards them. They mentally give them their successes, their resources, their collection of virtues. When they have done that, they visualize taking upon themselves all the needy people's suffering, problems and negativities. The Dalai Lama provides an example of doing this practice: visualizing an innocent starving child from Somalia and mentally taking upon oneself all the child's suffering, poverty, starvation and deprivation, and mentally giving to the child one's facilities, wealth and success. Sometimes, in this practice, giving positives precedes receiving negatives and sometimes the reverse is true.

Another Buddhist meditation practice to enhance compassion is that in which the meditator imagines someone who is acutely suffering or in a very unfortunate situation. Then the meditator tells herself or himself: 'that person has the same capacity for experiencing pain, joy, happiness, and suffering that I do' (Dalai Lama and Cutler, 1998, p. 129). The next step is to try to allow a natural feeling of compassion to arise toward that person. Next the meditator is directed to think how strongly she or he wishes that person to be free of that suffering and then to resolve to help that person be relieved from their suffering. In conclusion, for the last few minutes of the meditation, the meditator tries to generate in his or her mind a compassionate and loving state.

In a further Buddhist practice to enhance compassion, phrases such as 'May you be free of your pain and sorrow' or 'May you find peace' are directed at a specific person with great physical and mental suffering as the meditator remains cognizant of that person's difficulties. Then meditators can progress to directing their compassion to other people such as themselves, a benefactor, friend, difficult person and all living beings (Salzberg, 1995, pp. 116–17).

When clients feel aversion in the face of suffering, they can use calming self-talk to manage their anxiety and then use other mind skills as appropriate, for example challenging a compassion-hindering demanding rule (see Box 13.1). The use of coaching self-talk is implicit when using any mind skill – for instance, clients need inwardly to ask and respond to questions when testing the reality of perceptions contributing to anger and aversion and thus inhibiting compassion. Therapists can also assist clients to use coaching self-talk to facilitate compassionate actions. As a start, clients can use appropriate coaching self-instructions to refrain from doing harm to others. In addition, clients can use coaching self-talk to improve their empathic listening skills so that they are able to understand others' viewpoints more compassionately. Furthermore, clients can challenge themselves to behave humanely in specific situations by asking themselves questions like 'What is the compassionate way to speak?' and 'What is the compassionate way to act?' As appropriate, they can then coach themselves in the verbal, vocal and body messages of speaking and acting compassionately in upcoming situations. As part of this process, clients can rehearse targeted behaviours in their imaginations.

Cultivating equanimity

In everyday usage, equanimity means mental composure and the ability to retain equilibrium, poise and inner peace, especially in times of misfortune. Much of psychotherapy aims to help clients achieve equanimity: for example, it forms an important part of learning to manage emotions like anxiety, anger and depression. Equanimity is also highly valued by the world's major religious traditions. For instance, the example of Jesus Christ in the last days of his life was one of supreme equanimity in the face of betrayal and adversity.

In Buddhism, equanimity means possessing a balanced mind. An underlying assumption about equanimity, found especially in the Mahayana Buddhist tradition, is that all people are equal because each person contains the pure Buddha nature or potential for enlightenment within them. Furthermore, everyone is equal in that each individual desires to be happy and to overcome suffering. People are viewed as essentially neutral and whether they become either friends or the enemy depends on many factors. As such, equanimity requires that compassion be unconditional, without any discrimination or partiality (Dalai Lama, 2001).

Equanimity along with goodwill or lovingkindness, sympathetic joy and compassion are Buddhism's four Divine Abodes. Equanimity helps balance the other three qualities with the recognition that things are the way they are. For example, people with equanimity accept both that great suffering exists both throughout the world and in specific situations and that there are limits on their ability to feel and act compassionately in the face of it. Equanimity involves the capacity to let go and accept the world as it is and stops people from trying to control the uncontrollable. In such circumstances, equanimity describes the feeling of an understanding calmness of mind when qualities like lovingkindness, sympathetic joy and compassion are either insufficient or inappropriate (Thitavanno, 1995). However, this kind of equanimity is very different from allowing oneself to be lulled into a false sense of detachment that results in callousness rather than appropriate concern for others.

Irrespective of whether people are religious in traditional ways or not, there are many advantages to possessing equanimity or a balanced mind. One advantage is that of possessing a sense of inner strength, having faith in one's ability to deal with life's challenges. Another advantage is that of facing problems in a reflective and cool-headed way without the agitation of distracting emotions and over-engagement. Equanimity does not mean absence of emotion but the ability to stay composed and clear minded in the face of stresses, misfortune, difficult people and whatever other suffering life presents. People who have cultivated equanimity are more likely to act creatively in such situations with reason and compassion and not react in conditioned and unhelpful ways. They are also more likely to take into consideration the root causes of situations and not just their surface manifestations. As equanimity does not imply total detachment from the world but rather appropriate and balanced attachment to it, this quality can help provide people with the strength and courage to undertake and persist in relieving the suffering of others. Furthermore, to the extent that people cultivate the positive quality of equanimity they are more able to curb negative tendencies to anger, aversion, greed and craving.

Another advantage of cultivating equanimity is that it leads to a sense of mental calmness and inner peace. The goal of this quieting of the mind is summed up in the well-known serenity prayer that is often attributed to Reinhold Niebuhr.

> God, give us the serenity to accept what cannot be changed,
> the courage to change what should be changed,
> and the wisdom to distinguish one from the other.

A further advantage of equanimity is that people exhibiting this characteristic on a daily basis communicate a sense of calmness and goodwill that can heal, affirm and encourage those with whom they come into contact. In addition, their mental and physical composure will often, but not invariably, help others to become calmer and more rational when dealing with difficulties and differences. Possibly the practice of equanimity, entailing a reflective inner strength and a quiet and unassuming presence, is an ideal more valued and practised in Asian than in Western cultures.

Improving mind skills and communication/action skills

One way to improve clients' capacity for equanimity is to address their tendencies to create demanding rather than preferential rules. In Buddhism, equanimity is viewed as a buffer against becoming too attached to the other three Divine Abodes. Demanding rules underlie over-involvement in the qualities of goodwill/lovingkindness, sympathetic joy and compassion.

Clients can place unrealistic pressures on themselves if they think 'I must feel goodwill', 'I must feel sympathetic joy', and 'I must feel compassion'. Therapists can increase clients' equanimity by assisting them to alter into preferential rules any demanding rules they identify about feeling and expressing these positive qualities. Focusing on the skill of creating preferential rules can also be useful for helping clients to calm down and think before acting. Equanimity entails a capacity to clear a space for reflective thought rather than being continuously emotionally engaged in what is happening and feeling the pressure to take action, as is often the case in the West. Clients can explore and alter demanding rules that interfere with balanced reflection: for instance, 'I must take action soon when faced with problems.'

Addressing demanding rules centred on the theme of control of the vicissitudes of life is important in learning to feel, think and act with equanimity. Ellis goes beyond advocating unconditional self-acceptance (USA) and unconditional other-acceptance (UOA) to advocate unconditional life-acceptance (ULA) (Ellis, 2001). Unconditional life-acceptance means learning to accept and to live with conditions that one really does not like and cannot change. In rational emotive behaviour therapy there are at least two elements to fostering unconditional life-acceptance. The first element is to detect, dispute and alter into a preferential rule any demanding rule that contributes to insufficient acceptance of the realities of life. Examples of such rules include 'Life must be fair', 'All people must be honest', 'I must never be made unemployed', 'There must never be terrorist incidents' and 'There must never be natural disasters, like forest fires or earthquakes'.

The second element is to identify and dispute the derivatives of demanding rules based on conditional life acceptance. Two important derivatives that contribute to low frustration tolerance (LFT), as contrasted with high frustration tolerance (HFT), are 'awfulizing' and 'I can't stand-it-itis'. Take the example of a client who has the demanding rule 'I must never be unemployed' and who then, because of economic circumstances outside of his or her control, gets laid off. First the client agitates himself or herself disproportionately because of the rigidity of the demanding rule about never being made unemployed. Then the client further disturbs himself or herself with thoughts like 'This is absolutely awful' and 'I can't stand it'. Thus, demanding rules and their derivatives can set clients up for 'double trouble' in losing equanimity. Clients and others wishing to obtain greater high frustration tolerance (HFT) and hence more equanimity need to improve their skills of turning demanding rules into preferential ones and in dealing with counterproductive derivatives of demanding rules. Furthermore, they need to work on developing and implementing a philosophy of unconditional life-acceptance, which approximates a passable definition of equanimity.

Regarding the mind skill of creating perceptions, therapists can assist clients to perceive the advantages of cultivating equanimity and the disadvantages of insufficient mental composure. Clients can also improve their equanimity by challenging their illusions. The illusion of an independent self can lead to pride and to agitating oneself by putting one's ego on the line unnecessarily. Helping clients to acknowledge that their constructions of themselves and of others are heavily influenced by past and current causes and conditions can help them to become less egotistical, more compassionate and mentally calmer.

Therapists can also help clients become more mentally balanced by assisting them to challenge the illusion of permanence. A central feature of equanimity is learning to accept the reality of the rising and passing of phenomena and to understand that life is a process of continuous change. Consequently clients can learn to perceive the necessity of letting go and of accepting situations that they cannot change. Since an important part of equanimity is that of accurately perceiving rather than unduly fearing the reality of death and coming to terms with the transient nature of human existence, some clients may need to do therapeutic work in this area. When living through difficult situations, clients can also acknowledge the impermanence of phenomena by using time projection (Lazarus, 1984). In time projection, clients imagine themselves at some point in the future, say six months from now, looking back on their current difficulties and thus gaining a much better perspective on them.

Regarding the illusion of mental efficiency, clients can examine the reality of their perceptions about themselves, others and situations to see whether they are unduly upsetting their mental composure. Then, where appropriate, they can arrive at more balanced perceptions. Clients can also be assisted to challenge the illusion of differentness so that they perceive all humanity to be the same as themselves and equal, thus avoiding unsettling their equanimity by prejudice and partiality. Where necessary, clients can work on challenging the illusion of human badness to arrive at a more balanced view of the human condition and of humankind's potential for positive change. Clients with jungle outlooks are continuously on their guard for threats and as such are incapable of creating the high degree of inner peace that is a defining characteristic of equanimity.

Therapists can also assist clients to improve their skills of creating explanations conducive to cultivating equanimity. For example, clients can learn that it is their responsibility to work towards being more mentally balanced and physically composed. Clients learn to explain that they generate their own over-involvement when showing too much compassion or sympathetic joy and that, consequently, it is their responsibility to develop more equanimity in such situations. Therapists can also assist clients to learn that they are responsible for the emotional climates that they create for themselves and for others. In situations where clients want to create calm and composed atmospheres, they need to accept the responsibility for feeling, thinking and communicating accordingly.

Therapists can assist clients to improve their skills of developing self-talk and visual images conducive to equanimity. Simple calming self-talk statements include 'calm down' and 'slow down'. Clients can also make reflective self-talk statements like 'Let's think things through and take a balanced approach'. Kornfield describes a Buddhist meditation on equanimity in which the meditator begins by repeating the phrase 'May I be balanced and at peace'. Then the meditator, acknowledging that all created things arise and pass away, lets herself or himself rest in the midst of them and repeats 'May I learn to see the arising and passing of all nature with equanimity and balance. May I be open and balanced and peaceful.' Then the meditator, acknowledging that all people are heirs to their own karma and to the conditions and deeds they created, repeats 'May I bring compassion and equanimity to the events of the world. May I find balance and equanimity and peace' (Kornfield, 1993, p. 331). In another Buddhist meditation practice, Salzberg encourages meditators to generate equanimity towards a range of people by means of phrases including 'May we accept all things as they are', 'May we be undisturbed by the comings and goings of events' and 'I will care for you but cannot keep you from suffering' (Salzberg, 1995, p. 152).

In the Buddhist religious tradition, mindfulness of breathing is the most highly recommended and widely practised route to equanimity. Therapists with appropriate backgrounds can instruct clients in how best to do this. Therapists can also assist clients in identifying the verbal, vocal and body message components of communicating good skills of equanimity. To clarify how to communicate with equanimity, therapists can request that clients contrast imagining themselves when agitated and lacking composure and then when calm and composed. Furthermore, clients can search for people that they know personally, others whom they know about and figures from the past to act as models and guides in how to communicate with equanimity. Such good exemplars are likely to use skills that include thinking before speaking and then speaking in balanced and respectful ways, listening calmly and attentively, and avoiding distracting body messages. Equanimity does not mean that clients need to be non-assertive. Instead they can be assertive and show inner strength by using the minimum amount of outer strength necessary to communicate their messages adequately. Furthermore, by using coaching self-talk and visualized rehearsal, clients can privately practise their skills of communicating with equanimity before using them in specific public situations.

Practices

Practice 13.1: Cultivating compassion skills

As appropriate, conduct those parts of this practice thought most helpful either with one person acting as therapist and another as client or as part of personal practice.

1. Either the therapist assists the client to recall or you recall

   - One or more situations where she/he/you *have not* been treated with compassion. When treated like this how did she/he/you feel, think and act?
   - One or more situations where she/he/you *have* been treated with compassion. When treated like this how did she/he/you feel, think and act?

2. Either the therapist asks the client to choose or you choose a person to whom you are close. Imagine what it is like to be that person, what gives him or her happiness and joy in his or her life now, what brings him or her suffering and pain. Imagine what hurts or burdens that person has to deal with, hidden as well as observable ones. Then, perform this practice with someone else, possibly a person with whom you are currently experiencing difficulty.

3. Either the therapist asks the client to choose or you choose a person to whom you are close – this may be either the same person chosen in the second part of this practice or someone different. Imagine how it is for that person and try to empathize with him or her as he or she goes through the various seasons of life. Imagine the person as a new born baby, an infant, a toddler, a child, a young adult, in middle age, in early old age, in decline in old age, dying and when dead. Acknowledge a common humanity with this person and feel compassion for his or her suffering and for his or her wish to be happy. Then, perform this practice with someone else, possibly a person with whom you are currently experiencing difficulty.

4. For each of the following categories of people either the therapist assists the client to think about, imagine, understand and feel compassion for their suffering or you think about, imagine, understand and feel compassion for their suffering:

   - yourself;
   - partner (if applicable);
   - a relative;
   - a friend;
   - a neighbour;

- a work or study colleague;
- a difficult person or enemy;
- other relevant groups of people (please specify).

If appropriate, for at least one of these people imagine doing your best to relieve their suffering and then possibly engage in specific compassionate communications and actions towards them as well.

5. Either the therapist assists the client to perform or you perform the *Tong-Len*, 'giving and receiving' meditative practice. In this practice she/he/you give(s) all her/his/your facilities, wealth and success to a desperately needy and suffering person or group of persons and take(s) upon herself/himself/yourself all their suffering, pain and deprivation.
6. What mind skills and communication/action skills does the client (or do you) need to improve in order to feel, think and communicate with more compassion? Start by identifying one mind skill and one communication/action skill to improve and then, if necessary, build on this.
7. Conduct a personal experiment for a specified period of time (one day, two days, a week) in which the client consciously tries (or you try) to feel, think and communicate with compassion towards one or more persons or categories of people chosen in advance. At the end of the experiment evaluate what happened and the positive and negative consequences of feeling, thinking and communicating differently.

Practice 13.2: Cultivating equanimity skills

As appropriate, conduct those parts of this practice thought most helpful either with one person acting as therapist and another as client or as part of personal practice.

1. Either the therapist assists the client to practise or you practise your mindfulness-of-breathing skills to achieve more equanimity.
2. Either the therapist assists the client to get into or you get into a calm and reflective state of mind. Then practise repeating each of the following sentences:

> 'May I be balanced and at peace.'
> 'May I learn to see the arising and passing of nature with equanimity and balance.'
> 'May I bring compassion and equanimity to the events of the world.'
> 'May I find balance and equanimity and peace.'

This practice may be extended to offering equanimity to others, for example a relative or friend, by repeating 'May she/he be balanced and at peace' and so on.

3. Either the therapist assists the client to reflect on or you reflect on the benefits of balance and equanimity. As part of this process it may also help to reflect on the disadvantages of losing equanimity – for instance, by over-involvement in goodwill/lovingkindness, sympathetic joy, gratitude and compassion.

4. Either the therapist assists the client to imagine or you imagine a serious misfortune happening to her/him/you that has the potential to cause loss of equanimity. Then either the client imagines or you imagine

   • how she/he/you would think, feel and communicate when badly losing equanimity in addressing the misfortune; and
   • how she/he/you would think, feel and communicate when maintaining equanimity in addressing the misfortune.

5. What mind skills and communication/action skills does the client (or do you) need to improve in order to feel, think and communicate with more equanimity? Start by identifying one mind skill and one communication/action skill to improve and then, if necessary, build on this.

6. Conduct a personal experiment for a specified period of time (one day, two days, a week) in which the client consciously tries (or you try) to feel, think and communicate with equanimity towards one or more persons or categories of people chosen in advance. At the end of the experiment evaluate what happened and the positive and negative consequences of feeling, thinking and communicating differently.

FOURTEEN   Cultivating Generosity, Helping and Service

Human beings have the capacity to cultivate their social instincts by training their minds so that they can communicate and act in ways that help and affirm others. The fruit of high levels of mental cultivation is the capacity to demonstrate great human sympathy. At its higher levels human sympathy requires not just deep and widespread feelings of compassion, but the human-being skills of consistently showing generosity and helpfulness and living a life of service committed to affirming others. As civil rights leader Martin Luther King observed 'Life's most persistent and urgent question is, What are you doing for others?' (King, 1996, p. 17). Alfred Adler also emphasized that the value of a person's social interest was in what they actually did or accomplished for society (Adler, 1997). Compassion and love must be proved in generous deeds and acts of service. An other-centred attitude requires other-centred actions.

Cultivating generosity and helping

Generosity and helping others involve giving, which in turn raises questions of what is a gift and what is the motivation for giving or helping. The Buddha repeatedly emphasized generosity and helping others and always started with new practitioners by teaching them to practise being generous. He regarded the power of a gift to be determined by three things: the purity of the giver, the purity of the receiver, and the purity of the gift itself, meaning whether or not it had been ethically acquired. In Buddhism, giving is regarded as one of the six perfections – the others being morality, patience, concentration, effort and wisdom – that demonstrate practical intention to become Enlightened. The Dalai Lama observes that giving includes (1) donating material things such as money, clothing and food; (2) giving love; (3) giving the teachings of spiritual doctrines and practices, and (4) giving relief from fearful situations to all beings (Dalai Lama, 2002). Each of the four Buddhist Divine Abodes of lovingkindness, compassion, sympathetic joy and equanimity express generosity and helping others.

The Christian religious tradition also heavily emphasizes generosity and helping others. Christ's life is an example of generosity in his miracles, in his teachings, and in his willingness to sacrifice his life so that others might be redeemed. Christian missionaries see it as their duty to spread the gift of Jesus' teachings to others. Butt (2002) makes an interesting distinction between being a Christian, that is being a member of the Christian community, and being Christian or Christ-like, engaging in the generous and helpful behaviours that characterized how Christ treated others. Truly committed Christians aim to emulate Christ and to cultivate generosity by giving of themselves as well as of their possessions. Mother Teresa provides the example of a rich man who, after giving a big donation to her home for the dying at Kalighat, still wished to give something of himself. To achieve this personal contribution, he then came regularly to the hospice, talked to the dying people and helped them to bathe and shave (Chalika and Le Joly, 1996). Mother Teresa sometimes emphasized that the poor are often more generous than many of the rich. Unlike the man in the above example, some rich people suffer from emotional poverty and are crippled in their capacity to be generous and to give of themselves.

Individuals can give to and help one another in many different ways including being loving partners and parents, listening in ways that affirm others, participating in the community, working ethically, offering kind words and looks to strangers, sharing knowledge and skills, and helping the sick and the suffering. They can also benevolently and generously give time, effort, food, shelter, medicine and money to the poor, be they either in their own or in developing countries. Refraining from harming others by anger, aversion, greed and craving is another way in which people can give to one another. Driving one's car provides daily opportunities for restraining anger and responding generously: for instance, by allowing pedestrians to cross the road, by letting another person take a parking space, by allowing other cars to enter a stream of traffic and by not hogging the road. Generosity and helping others does not stop with the present generation in that people can give to future generations by assisting young people to develop their full humanity and by protecting the natural environment for them and succeeding generations to enjoy.

Motivations for giving and helping

In Buddhism, generosity is a way of making merit on the path across many lifetimes to enlightenment. The Buddhist concept of making merit regards gifts of food and money to monks, temples and to the less fortunate as a privilege as well as a duty. Many Buddhists engage in genuinely compassionate giving, but sometimes gifts to Buddhist temples are a form of insurance against unfortunate rebirths in future lives. In Christianity giving is a way of showing love of God and of Jesus Christ through helping even the least of one's fellow humans. Whether a person is a humanist or religiously oriented, ideally giving comes from a sense of abundance in which the act of giving emotionally enriches both receiver and giver.

Purity of intention in giving is very important. For example, insecure parents may give money and other presents to children as ways of controlling them, compensating for insufficient generosity by spending too little time with them, and hiding feelings of inability to offer real love. In some societies, giving is seen as a way of establishing positions in pecking orders and of obtaining corrupt favours. Furthermore, generous and helpful acts can be a form of self-aggrandizement in which the fruits of generosity must be widely seen and appreciated.

Box 4.1, which depicts five levels of human sympathy, can also be seen as a measure of the purity of a giver's or helper's intentions. At the lowest or egocentric level, when people give or help they seek some advantage in return. As such, giving and helping may be viewed as the prelude to taking. At the second or restricted level of human sympathy, giving and helping still mainly depend on how useful the receiver is perceived to be, although the level of manipulation is less than at the egocentric level. The third or reciprocal level represents the motivation for giving and helping that predominates in Western societies. People invest in relationships in which they exchange emotional, physical and material gifts and help to selected individuals in such a way as to give roughly the same amount as they receive. Such social exchanges are often ritualized, for instance, at Christmas, birthdays and anniversaries. There may be some giving and helping to people outside of immediate family and social circles, but this is likely to be small because most people's circle of active compassion does not extend very far. At the fourth or enhanced level, people have cultivated their human sympathy to the point where they can act compassionately on a regular basis both within and beyond their immediate circle. The fifth or committed level of human sympathy is attained by relatively few people who have strongly cultivated the finer aspects of their human potential, possess highly developed humanistic consciences and seem to exhibit a deep vocation for enhancing themselves, others and humankind.

Improving mind skills

Therapists can work with clients to help them become more aware of their feelings of generosity and urges to help others. Creating greater awareness of compassionate feelings usually has the effect of stimulating greater awareness of generous and helpful feelings. As a rule of thumb, the more therapists can assist clients to gain in self-esteem, the more these clients are likely to react generously and help others. Therapists can help clients to acknowledge the importance of getting in touch with their generous and benevolent feelings and to understand that such feelings are part of their evolutionary heritage. By using active listening skills, therapists can assist clients to listen to and explore their inner voices. Clients can catch glimpses of their generous impulses and be helped to acknowledge them more fully rather than repressing them and nipping them in the bud. Some clients may be assisted to acknowledge their potential for generous feelings and actions by becoming more aware of the good and helpful things they have done for others and their effects on the recipients. As part of this process clients can explore how they felt about doing these good deeds.

To create greater awareness of their potential for generosity and for helping others, therapists can encourage clients to experiment with acting more generously and being more helpful in specific situations. Therapists can then help clients to evaluate the effects of their changed behaviour on themselves and others. Clients can also be assisted to explore their fears about and resistances to giving and helping. They can be helped to examine why sometimes it is so difficult to let go, to relinquish time, effort and possessions, to move beyond feeling compassion and to respond generously and helpfully to other people's plight.

Therapists can assist clients to identify demanding rules that interfere with being generous and helping others. Demanding rules that enhance anger, aversion, greed and craving may need to be curbed as part of this process. Furthermore, demanding rules hindering compassion may require addressing. Box 14.1 lists some demanding rules that can interfere with clients being generous and helpful. Some of these rules – for instance, 'I must always look out for number one' – are obviously egocentric. Other rules – for instance, 'I must be generous to and help only my family and friends' – are less egocentric, but nevertheless limiting. Some of the demanding rules reflect underlying fears: for instance of destitution (as in 'I must keep everything for a rainy day/retirement/old age'), of being too gullible (as in 'I must not let others take advantage of me'), of being socially unacceptable, as in 'I must not make others uncomfortable by talking about my generosity and good works', and of acknowledging one's innate goodness, as in 'I must not accept my generous and helpful impulses'. One of the rules, 'I must do everything', illustrates using perfectionism as a way of either doing nothing or never being satisfied with what one does. The demand for approval in relation to generosity, 'Recipients of my generosity and help must be eternally grateful', is likely to weaken motivation, because approval cannot be guaranteed. It also obscures the main purpose of generosity, which is to benefit recipients. The rule 'Being generous and helping others must always be easy' may both interfere with giving in smart rather than foolish ways and in maintaining generosity when faced with difficulties.

Box 14.1: Illustrative demanding rules hindering being generous and helping others

I must always look out for number one.
I must always get something in return if I give or help.
I must be generous to and help only my family and friends.
I must be generous to and help only people like me (my social class, group and so forth).
I must not be more generous and helpful than other people.
I must keep everything for a rainy day/retirement/old age.
I must be seen to be generous and helping others even when this is not the case.
I must not be a bleeding heart.
I must not let others take advantage of me.
Others must see me as tough minded.
I must not be seen to be generous and good.
I must not make others uncomfortable by talking about my generosity and good works.
I must not accept my generous and helpful impulses.
I must do everything.
Recipients of my generosity and help must be eternally grateful.
Being generous and helping others must always be easy.

Therapists, as we have seen, can help clients to challenge their rules by means of functional disputing – for instance, 'How is having the rule "being generous and helping others must always be easy" helping you?' – and of empirical disputing, for instance, 'Where is the evidence that being generous and helping others must always be easy?' Therapists can assist clients to restate demanding rules into preferential rules. Continuing the above example, therapist and client may engage in a discussion about the practicalities of being generous and helping others. The therapist could assist the client to see that being serious about maximizing the benefits of generosity and helping others can involve developing a set of skills – selection of suitable recipients, giving appropriately, evaluating – rather than just throwing money at people and problems. Furthermore, clients can be assisted to see that they run greater risks of not getting the outcomes they want if they fail to develop applied generosity and helping skills.

Demanding rule: 'Being generous and helping others must always be easy.'

Preferential rule: 'Being and staying generous and helping others to best effect requires judgement and skill.'

Therapists can assist clients to challenge perceptions and illusions that inhibit generosity and helping others. Maintaining the illusion of an independent self can block clients from seeing how dependent they have been on others' kindness for all that they enjoyed in the past and enjoy now. Acknowledging their dependence on fellow humans can help clients to feel and act more generously and kindly towards them. The illusion of permanence with regard to themselves and others can lead clients to defer generous and benevolent acts. Clients may require assistance in acknowledging that wealth and possessions are impermanent or as the sayings go 'You can't take it with you' and 'If you're not careful you're going to end up the richest person in the cemetery'. Clients can be encouraged to see that life is limited and that good deeds need to be done in the present rather than at some vague date in the future. Without being foolhardy, clients can enjoy the pleasures of giving and of helping in their lifetime.

Therapists can also help some clients lessen or overcome their illusions of differentness so that they have a wider circle of empathic identification with others and can hence act more generously and benevolently towards them. By mentally trading places and seeing themselves as equal to others, clients can sense the impact that their generous and helpful actions might have on them. Therapists can also help clients to challenge the illusion of human badness. One way to do this is for therapists to assist clients to a greater awareness of their own generous and helpful impulses, feelings and actions. Clients who can accept the reality of universal sameness should then see that all others are capable of similar generous and helpful feelings and actions as them.

Cultivating generosity and helping others involves clients in being honest in acknowledging both the brighter and darker aspects of themselves. Clients may need help in perceiving that they are capable of making positive contributions to others' lives, not just financially but in numerous other ways. Some clients require assistance in overcoming self-doubt and self-denigration and in valuing their past and current contributions to others. This can be a feature of people, including psychotherapists, who have reached a state of burnout from helping others. Certain clients may have a highly inflated sense of their own generosity and helpfulness to others, sometimes combined with a 'holier than thou' attitude. Within the safety of good therapeutic relationships, such clients may become more secure and feel less need to make themselves out to be more saintly than they are.

Therapists may need to assist clients in exploring the complexity of their motivation for giving and for helping others in order to understand when it is not as pure as they might like. Then therapists can help clients address the impurities, for instance tendencies towards seeking approval, possessiveness or self-aggrandizement. Most clients consider that they are reasonably generous, helpful and well-meaning human beings. However, they may have difficulty in realizing that arguably the average level of generosity and helping others in Western countries falls well below that required for responsible care of one's fellow humans, especially people outside of one's immediate circle of acquaintance. Those clients seeking to attain the higher levels of demonstrating human sympathy need to perceive their current limitations honestly as part of the process of becoming more fully human.

Clients may also require help in perceiving that cultivating generosity and helping others entail both developing a set of skills and then maintaining these skills to the point where they become habits. Some of the skills of being generous and helping others are the mind skills discussed in the current section. Other skills entail how best to plan and perform generous and helpful actions. Clients are likely to initiate and to maintain generous and helpful actions if they can perceive the advantages of behaving this way. These advantages include pleasure in making others happy – or at the very least lightening their burden in life – and increased self-esteem from helping others without seeking anything for oneself.

Clients are also more likely both to initiate and to maintain generous and helpful actions if they perceive them positively and avoid getting tricked into perceiving them negatively. As mentioned in Chapter 5, negative words and labels attached to helping others include 'do-gooders', 'bleeding hearts', 'interfering bastards', 'softies' and 'suckers'. Where necessary, therapists can assist clients to attach positive meanings to generosity and helping others including 'making a contribution', 'showing compassion', 'relieving suffering', 'easing another's burden', 'creating happiness' and 'being a good human being'.

In the previous chapter, mention was made about how the explanations clients create can impede or enhance their capacity for compassion. Since compassion is often the stimulus for generosity and helping, clients need to beware of creating explanations that are unfair and derogatory to individuals and groups to whom they might be giving money or other assistance. It is easy to fall into the trap of blaming others for their misfortunes. Such rationalizations provide convenient ways of avoiding the challenge to be generous in doing something to help. Clients and others who are genuinely concerned with assisting others can do so in ways that enhance their self-reliance, where possible helping them learn to fish rather than providing them with fish – though this too may be necessary until they get on their feet.

Clients can create explanations that make it more likely that they will engage in generous and helpful actions. Some of these motivating generosity and help explanations focus on themselves: for instance, 'I can make a contribution', 'I can make a difference', and 'I have a responsibility to help my fellow humans'. Other explanations can focus on the actual or potential recipients of generosity and help. For example, one of the explanations of Mother Teresa's 'listening groups' of co-workers for befriending and visiting the elderly in their homes was 'Very old people love to have somebody to listen to them and let them talk, even when they have to tell the story of thirty years ago. To listen, when nobody else wants to listen, is a very beautiful thing' (Chalika and Le Joly, 1996, p. 64). The same explanation holds good for those befriending the elderly in Western societies.

Explanations that motivate the author to help underprivileged school-children in Thailand include 'Young people can make a bigger contribution to their societies if they gain knowledge and skills' and 'Children will have more energy to work and play if they have enough rice to eat for lunch'. Therapists can also assist clients to challenge and replace explanations that interfere with being generous and helping others. Such explanations include 'There is so much suffering that it is not worth bothering' and 'I've been badly treated in the past, so why should I help others?' Clients may also need to realize that failure to help in some situations makes them accomplices in the suffering of others.

Clients may need to learn that there is a causal connection between developing good applied generosity and helping skills and the extent to which they benefit others through their help. A reason why some kind people either do not help as much as they would like or become exploited is that they are insufficiently rigorous in how they invest their time, effort and money. Being generous and helping others smartly is likely to relieve much more suffering than taking too little care.

Clients can enhance their generosity and help by improving their calming and coaching self-talk skills. Clients who become conscious of resistances to generosity and helping others can calm themselves as a prelude to exploring the mental processes and feelings that contribute to them. Clients can also use calming self-talk to clear a psychological space for either deciding how to help in a specific instance or for making a comprehensive action plan for their help. A further instance in which clients might use calming self-talk is when dealing with disappointments and setbacks in relation to their help. For example they may feel insufficiently appreciated by recipients of their giving. When calmer, clients are more likely to think through these issues rationally and then act appropriately.

In Buddhist practice, people can cultivate their willingness to be generous and help others by repeatedly thinking and telling themselves 'May I become able to help all beings' (Dalai Lama, 2002, p. 220). Non-Buddhists can give themselves similar self-talk to motivate their generosity and help. For example, at the start of each day they can ask themselves 'How can I help make someone happy or relieve their suffering today?' Whenever clients use any of the mind skills discussed in this section to improve generosity, they need to coach themselves in the steps involved in implementing them. Clients can also coach themselves as they implement the communication and action skills of generosity and helping others. For instance, clients who want to be generous and help in systematic ways can coach themselves through the steps of developing action plans for these purposes. Clients can also use coaching self-talk when preparing for various upcoming situations, such as discussing with staff of voluntary agencies potential gifts of time, effort and/or money and rehearsing how best to communicate with alienated young people when doing community service.

Clients can use creating visual images skills to enhance their ability to be generous and help others. For example, they can imagine role models of genuinely caring people whose concern for others inspires them. They can also imagine themselves competently performing generous and helpful acts and visualize the beneficial consequences of these good deeds for the recipients.

Improving communication and action skills

The discussion in this section focuses on individual giving and helping rather than on taking social action to address the structures that create and contribute to others' suffering. Let us assume that a client wants to initiate a habit of greater generosity and/or of helping others more. Therapists can assist such clients to use getting started skills. Systematic approaches to changing behaviour usually begin by establishing a baseline of how clients currently behave in the area in question, for example the nature and frequency of and, if relevant, the sums of money involved in their generous and helpful actions to those less fortunate. Clients can be requested to list those generous and helpful actions that they can remember performing in a stipulated time period, say the last three months. Either alternatively or in addition, clients can keep monitoring sheets recording their current generous and helpful actions. From examining their behaviour, many clients may realize that they are already engaging in generous and helpful actions, so improvement or change is more a matter of building upon existing actions than initiating new ones. Other clients may be challenged to acknowledge how little they do that is generous and helps others.

Clients can be encouraged to view improving their generosity and helping skills and building habits of being generous and helpful as a process in which they experiment with changed actions and then learn from their experiences. It is probably best for clients to start small and then progressively increase their generosity and help at rates that are both realistic and comfortable for them. Therapist and client can design experiments that encourage clients to change their behaviour. Box 14.2 depicts five steps in a simple experiment in which therapist and client participate to improve a client's capacity to be generous or to help in other ways.

Box 14.2: Experimenting with being more generous and helpful

1. *Assess.* Therapist and client collaborate to assess what generous or otherwise helpful actions the client currently engages in and how she or he feels about them.

2. *Formulate changed actions.* Therapist and client clarify goals and identify specifically how the client wants to be more generous or helpful: for instance, by visiting a local HIV/AIDS hospice or by donating £100 or $100 for a chosen purpose.

3. *Make an 'If ... then ...' statement.* The 'if' part of the statement stipulates how the client is going to engage in at least one specific new generous or helpful action. The 'then' part of the statement indicates the consequences for others and for themself that the client predicts will follow from their changed action(s).

4. *Implement the targeted actions.* The client enacts the targeted changed generous/helpful action(s) in real life. If necessary and feasible, the client rehearses the changed action(s) beforehand.

5. *Evaluate.* It is important that the client develops self-monitoring skills, so initially the client should be requested to evaluate the processes and outcomes of their changed actions on their own. Afterwards the therapist can assist the client to process what they have learned from their experiences and then discuss what to do next.

Therapists can assist clients wanting to cultivate habits of generosity and of helping others to develop skills of systematically making action plans. The purpose of such plans is to ensure that clients allocate time, effort and financial resources to the people or causes that they want in the proportions that they want. Where money is involved, the sums need not be large because a series of small gifts can be made with great love, care and effectiveness. As Mother Teresa observed 'not all of us can do great things – but all of us can do small things with great love'. Similarly, there is a passage in the Bible where Jesus Christ extolled a poor widow's contribution to the treasury of two copper coins above those of the rich contributors. Jesus observed 'For they all contributed out of their abundance; but she out of her poverty has put in everything she had, her whole living' (Mark 12:44).

Box 14.3 outlines six steps in making and implementing a generosity/ helping others action plan. Clients can take a progressive approach to making action plans for giving time, effort and money. If the time frame of an action plan is, say, one year, it can be revised annually and possibly enlarged in subsequent years. Revisions can involve adding or dropping some recipients and, in other ways, changing the way the help is provided or money spent in an upcoming year. Enlargements of action plans can involve both increasing the amount of time, effort and/or money given and also increasing the number of recipients.

Box 14.3: Making and implementing a generosity/helping others action plan

1. *Establish general goals.* Use goal-setting skills to decide on the overall amount of time, effort and/or money to be allocated, the time frame for allocation, the underlying values that guide the generosity, and the broad areas in which the help might be given.

2. *Generate options.* Use information-gathering skills to find out about charities, schools, community centres, hospitals, old people's homes, hospices, or other worthy agencies and individuals in the broad areas identified for offering help.

3. *Evaluate options.* Use assessment skills to evaluate potential recipients of help or donations in terms reflecting one's purposes in giving, trustworthiness, efficiency, and any other relevant criteria. Site visits may be a useful part of this process.

4. *Refine goals and allocate resources.* Use goal-setting skills to refine the purposes and values of one's generosity and help and to select recipients and allocate time, effort and/or financial resources to them.

---

5. *Implement giving and helping.* Prior to giving and helping, use contracting skills to ensure that there are clear agreements about how gifts of time, effort and/or money are to be used. Since trust is vital to continued relationships, take precautions to avoid unnecessary misunderstandings. Where appropriate, practice the appropriate skills for giving and helping skilfully before and during doing so.

6. *Monitor and evaluate.* Use monitoring and evaluating skills to ensure that the help or funds are being used for the intended purposes in the most efficient way possible. Furthermore, monitor and evaluate your own behaviour in order to improve your generosity and helping others skills.

Cultivating generosity and helping others entails building up sustainable habits of doing this skilfully. The author finds it useful to make annual generosity action plans, because not having to start from scratch each time eases the habit of consistent giving. Furthermore, annual action plans can bring continuity into making donations as well as offering opportunities for giving differently and more. Though this may be less possible in the West, living in Thailand, a country where there is much poverty, the author takes somewhat of a 'hands on' approach to making donations and deals directly with the recipient schools and agencies. This kind of personal involvement minimizes administrative expenses and ensures that money is used for the intended purposes. Furthermore, taking a 'hands on' approach to investing in people enables the author to give something of himself. For instance, in dealing with one educational institution the author takes part in selecting the scholars, meets them individually twice a year, identifies the areas on which they can use extra tuition, and encourages them. In all instances where the author gives money to schools and other agencies, he knows the staff personally, consults with them about their needs, and encourages them in their fine work.

'Hands on' generosity and helping can require helpers to communicate skilfully with verbal, voice and body messages. Therapists can work with clients to improve communication skills that they agree are insufficiently good. For example, clients require competent active listening and questioning skills when consulting with staff of helping agencies to identify if, where and how best to give time, effort and/or money. When doing voluntary work, in addition to active listening skills, clients need skills of tactfully showing involvement and assisting those whom they help to address any problems that they uncover together. Clients may also require assertion skills: for example, when contracting with voluntary or charitable agencies, for making sure their help and/or donations are used as intended, and for either saying no to or setting limits on requests for time, effort, emotional involvement and money. In instances where clients are helping people from other cultures they require sensitivity as to how best to communicate within the framework of that culture.

Cultivating service

Dictionary definitions of service focus on helping or doing work for others or for the community. However, service may be defined further to mean fusing one's own interests with an other-centred approach to living. Thus service entails individuals assuming responsibility for becoming more fully human by striving to develop and to demonstrate high levels of mental cultivation and human sympathy for others and for the human species. Some of the key human-being skills of taking an other-centred or service-centred approach to living have been covered in this and the previous chapters, namely calming and disillusioning the mind; curbing anger, aversion, greed and craving; and cultivating goodwill, sympathetic joy, gratitude, compassion, equanimity, generosity and helping others. Cultivating service involves CHT clients, therapists and personal practitioners in general in undertaking a firm and ongoing commitment to developing positive qualities and curbing negative ones.

Whence come the sources of motivation for cultivating service? Cultivating service is heavily emphasized in the world's main religious traditions. Often the concept of vocation or calling is used to describe the strong feeling that committed members of those religions possess to serve God and their fellow humans. Jesus Christ's life and death was an example of service to others. Christians are inspired to serve by their love of God and of Jesus, by Christian teachings, and by the examples of service of past and present Christians. Furthermore, they are supported in cultivating service by the fellowship of the Church.

Within Buddhism, the Mahayana tradition especially emphasizes following the *bodhisattva* or 'awakening warrior' path of compassionate service. The Dalai Lama writes: 'When we have developed our sense of compassion to the point where we feel responsible for all beings, we are motivated to perfect our ability to serve them. Buddhists call the aspiration to attain such a state bodhicitta, and one who has achieved it, a bodhisattva' (Dalai Lama, 2001, p. 119). The *bodhisattva* ideal is that of striving for greater insight, compassion and enlightenment at the same time as being actively engaged in relieving the suffering of others. It is an ideal that inspires and motivates Buddhist monks and lay people alike.

The *bodhisattva* vow is an undertaking to dedicate one's life to seeking enlightenment as a *bodhisattva* for the benefit of all beings. To emphasize the dedication to service involved in the bodhisattva path, the Dalai Lama sometimes quotes the final verse from the eighth-century Indian master Shantideva's *Guide to the Bodhisattva's Way of Life*:

> As long as space remains,
> As long as sentient beings remain,
> Until then, may I too remain,
> And dispel the miseries of the world.

A major theme of this book is that humanists, both religious and non-religious, are also motivated and inspired to cultivate service. Humans are social animals whose evolutionary history has been that of group living. Chapter 2 mentioned the seeds of a humanistic conscience existing in the social instincts. In Chapter 9, without denying the human potential for aggressive destructiveness, a case was made for innate human goodness. Serving and helping others is a central part of the human potential. However, for personal, social psychological and cultural reasons, many already reviewed, most individuals develop their potential to serve at levels representing the 'psychopathology of the average' (Maslow, 1970) or the 'pathology of normalcy' (Fromm, 1995). There are many outstanding exceptions, but all too often people stunt and repress their capacity for sharing beyond their immediate self-interest. In doing so, they miss opportunities for serving their fellow humans and of finding important sources of meaning and satisfaction in this process.

Human beings, however, are not just the victims of their evolution. With their capacity for reflective thought, both as individuals and as a species, they can assume responsibility for their own evolution. Present unsatisfactory levels of motivation for sharing and service can be challenged and improved. With technological advances bringing not only great benefits but huge risks to the survival of the planet, the human race faces an imperative challenge to pay more attention to how best to motivate and cultivate effective service. The vast majority of the world's population are either not members of religious organizations or just paying lip service to their religious beliefs. Both inside and outside academic institutions, much more progress needs to be made in developing a psychologically grounded, yet multidisciplinary, humanistic worldview that serves as an alternative to current religious worldviews for non-believers and as a complement to them for their adherents. Such a humanistic worldview would celebrate core human values that transcend non-religious and religious divisions and provide a rationale for allowing huge numbers of people to cultivate more of their innate motivation for service.

Within psychology and psychiatry, with the pioneering writings of humanists such as Alfred Adler, Carl Rogers, Erich Fromm and Abraham Maslow, a start has already been made in developing a humanistic world-view. Cognitive behavioural writers like Albert Ellis and Aaron Beck have also made valuable contributions to this effort. However, there seems to be a paucity of recent writing that builds upon their work to present a contemporary worldview that extols the human capacity for reason and love and acknowledges the importance of motivating people to cultivate service for others' benefit. As material sufficiency is increasingly attained in the West, becoming more fully human will be one of the main challenges, if not the main personal and societal challenge, of the twenty-first century. Psychology and psychotherapy have a crucial role in providing the theory, research, knowledge and applied skills to meet this challenge.

Cognitive humanistic therapy entails psychotherapy students and psychotherapists – and some clients too – committing themselves to something akin to the *bodhisattva* path of Buddhism. Therapists wishing to work with clients in mental cultivation CHT should be further along the path in terms of possessing the human-being skills of human sympathy and mental cultivation than their clients. Becoming a better therapist and becoming a better person overlap (Maslow, 1976). Both in their work and private lives, helping service professionals can be personal practitioners who daily commit themselves to the humanistic ideal and path of cultivating service. Many therapists and other people of goodwill undertake this commitment already. The next and final chapter includes some practical suggestions for implementing a service-oriented mentality.

Practice

Practice 14.1: Cultivating generosity and helping skills

This practice, which can be performed by doing those parts thought most beneficial, may be carried out, as appropriate, either in conjunction with therapy or in personal practice.

1. Either the therapist assists the client to recall or you recall:

    *   generous and helpful actions that she/he/you has or have received in the past and are receiving now – acknowledge the feelings generated by these generous and helpful actions and their practical impact in her/his/your life;
    *   generous and helpful actions that she/he/you have performed in the past and/or are performing now – acknowledge the feelings in

others and yourself generated by these generous and helpful actions and their practical impact in other people's lives;

- past and current generous and helpful actions of other people that she/he/you has or have heard about or seen – acknowledge the feelings in others and yourself generated by these generous and helpful actions and their practical impact in other people's lives.

2. For each of the following categories of people either the therapist assists the client to identify or you identify one or more specific generous or helpful actions that might in some way, however small, ease or relieve their suffering and make them happy:

- yourself;
- your partner (if applicable);
- a relative;
- a friend;
- a neighbour;
- a work or study colleague;
- a difficult person or enemy;
- other relevant groups of people (please specify).

3. What mind skills and communication/action skills does the client (or do you) need to improve to feel, think and communicate more generously or to be more helpful to another or others in a specific situation? Start by identifying one mind skill and one communication/action skill improve and then, if necessary, build on this.

4. Following the step-by-step guidelines provided in Box 14.2, the therapist assists the client to conduct and evaluate an experiment in which she/he performs one or more specific generous or helpful actions (possibly an action or actions identified above in part 2 of this practice). Alternatively, Box 14.2 may be adapted so that it becomes a personal practice experiment about performing and evaluating one or more specific generous or helpful actions.

5. Following the guidelines provided in Box 14.3, the therapist assists the client to develop and implement a 'generosity/helping others action plan'. Alternatively, the steps in Box 14.3 may be performed as a part of personal practice.

FIFTEEN   Personal Practice

Much of any approach to therapy takes place outside of therapists' offices. This is especially likely to be the case with an approach like cognitive humanistic therapy with its emphasis on skilling clients to prevent and manage problems in their daily lives and with its added focus on attaining higher levels of mental cultivation and human sympathy. As mentioned in Chapter 6, personal practice refers to a range of activities or practices performed by clients and others independently of therapists. Personal practice may be performed either in conjunction with therapy, or as a continuation of work performed during therapy, or, in varying degrees, involving little or no prior or present contact with therapists. Some skills and strategies for personal practice are now presented for each of CHT's adaptation and mental cultivation components. Nonetheless, it should be remembered that these two components overlap and interact and, accordingly, the same personal practice skills and strategies can be relevant to both components.

Adaptation CHT

Negotiating homework during therapy, personal coaching after therapy, and conducting self-therapy are three important ways in which personal practice skills and strategies may be used to attain adaptation CHT goals. Each way is now briefly reviewed.

Negotiating homework

Since the goal of adaptation CHT is to build clients' self-helping skills, formal and informal homework assignments focusing on the transfer of skills learned in therapy to outside of therapy are always an integral part of the process. On many occasions therapists find it useful to discuss with clients homework activities or practices that they might undertake before their next session. Homework assignments include rehearsing and then trying out improved skills in everyday life and filling out self-monitoring and skills-building worksheets. Other assignments can entail reading self-help books, listening to cassettes, watching videotapes and observing people with good communication and action skills.

One of the central problems in assigning homework activities or practices is that of motivating clients to do them. Greenberger and Padesky (1995) suggest nine useful guidelines for increasing the chances of client compliance. The first three guidelines are to make assignments small, assign tasks within the client's skill level and make assignments relevant and interesting. The next three guidelines are: to collaborate with the client in developing learning assignments, provide a clear rationale for the assignment and a written summary, and begin the assignment during the session. The final three guidelines are: to identify and problem solve impediments to the assignment, to emphasize learning, not a desired outcome, and show interest and follow up in the next appointment.

Sometimes, changing a way of communicating or acting requires clients to give up long-established habits. Here, it can be especially important for therapists and clients not to agree on too difficult an activity too soon. When possible, they should try to build in some early successes to encourage clients to persist in working on their skills.

Some clients return to non-supportive, if not downright hostile environments. If so, therapists may need to prepare clients more thoroughly prior to suggesting they implement their improved communications and actions outside of therapy. Such preparation may include devising strategies for coping with negative feedback.

At the conclusion of negotiating homework, therapists can signal a joint progress review by letting clients know that, when they next meet, they will ask them how they fared in their assignments. Clients who know that their therapists are interested in and supportive of their attempts to complete homework assignments are more likely to be motivated to do so, provided that therapists avoid becoming controlling and judgmental.

Personal coaching

In adaptation CHT, therapists use a combination of facilitating and training to impart self-helping skills to clients. Let us take the analogy of a coach, who is training or instructing people in the skills of a sport such as swimming, tennis or golf. Good sports coaches help clients internalize the knowledge and skills they require so that they can be their own personal coaches once formal coaching ends. Similarly, good therapists assist clients to become their own personal coaches in using, maintaining and, where possible, improving the targeted mind skills and communication/action skills once therapy ends.

Therapists can assist clients to become effective personal coaches by helping them to understand clearly the choices they need to make in implementing each skill. Both therapists and clients require a commitment to formal and informal homework assignments as a bridge between the therapist as coach during therapy and the client developing the skills to be their own coach once therapy ends. Therapists can enhance clients' abilities to be personal coaches by training thoroughly so that the material really sinks in, and training diversely so that clients have the ability to respond flexibly to different situations once on their own. Therapists can also help clients to become effective coaches by training them in strategies for anticipating and handling difficulties and setbacks. Relevant books, client manuals, handouts and client records of work performed during therapy are other tools that can support former clients in being effective personal coaches once therapy ends.

As personal coaches in using and maintaining skills targeted during therapy, former clients require good mind skills. For instance, they may need to challenge demanding rules, such as 'Maintaining my improved skills must always be easy', and restate them as preferential rules such as 'There is no such thing as cure' and 'I need to keep practising my improved skills so that using them becomes progressively easy'. Former clients should strive to monitor and perceive their good and poor skills accurately. They need to check any tendencies to discourage themselves by paying disproportionate attention to setbacks rather than to successes.

Former clients can use coping self-talk to deal with 'hot' thinking connected with temptations to revert to former self-defeating ways of communicating and acting. For instance, in high-risk situations they can coach themselves to say 'Stop ... think ... calm down' and then instruct themselves in what to do. Further instructions include telling themselves that cravings will pass, engaging in distracting activities, and reminding themselves of the benefits of maintaining their improved skills and of the costs of giving in. Former clients can also use affirming self-talk to maintain their improved skills: for instance, 'Well done', 'I hung in there and coped', and 'I'm happier now that I'm using my improved skills'.

As personal coaches, former clients require accuracy in explaining the causes of positive and negative events as they implement and maintain their improved skills. For instance, where justified, it can be important that they inwardly explain the cause of their successes relates to factors within their control such as effort, willingness to take reasonable risks, and use of targeted skills.

Self-therapy

Self-therapy entails systematically working with oneself as though being one's own therapist. Box 15.1 shows how the skilled client model of the psychotherapy process can be shortened and modified to become a self-therapy process model. The skilled human being model requires knowledge and skills in how to work within the cognitive humanistic frame-work, so it is likely in the first instance to be of most use to former clients and to students, therapists, supervisors and others in the helping professions conversant with the framework. It is also conceivable that some lay people might, of their own accord, acquire sufficient knowledge and skills about cognitive humanistic theory and practice to use the skilled human being model on their own. Self-therapy poses many problems and challenges. Insufficient motivation may be a problem at each stage of the skilled human being model. Furthermore, people's resistance to being honest about them-selves can interfere with engaging in and persisting in self-therapy.

Box 15.1: The skilled human being model

Stage 1: Relating
Main task: Form an internal collaborative working relationship

Phase 1: Pre-self-therapy contact

Establish the conditions for self-therapy. Where appropriate, acknowledge self-therapy's relevance and importance and also find a suitable location for it.

Phase 2: Starting self-therapy

Go to your quiet space, relax, focus inwards and become calmer and more centred. Help yourself to access, acknowledge and experience more about yourself and your problem(s) and/or areas for becoming more fully human. Select a problem or area as the initial focus for self-therapy.

Stage 2: Understanding
Main task: Assess and formulate a definition of your problem and/or area for becoming more fully human

Phase 1: Assessing

Assess your selected problem and/or area for becoming more fully human by gathering information to understand yourself better. Search for specific evidence to test ideas about possible poor skills and then review all available information to suggest which skills might require improving.

> ### Phase 2: Formulating a definition in skills terms
>
> Arrive at a preliminary definition in skills terms of your problem and/or area for becoming more fully human by specifying the mind skills and communication/action skills that you want to improve.
>
> ### Stage 3: Changing
> ### Main task: Achieve change and the maintenance of change
>
> ### Phase 1: Using skills-building strategies
>
> Select and implement strategies for managing the current problem and/or area for becoming more fully human and improving relevant mind skills and communication/action skills for now and later.
>
> ### Phase 2: Terminating and personal coaching
>
> Consolidate your skills for use afterwards and plan how to maintain them when, and if, self-therapy ends. Coach yourself in using and maintaining your skills, monitor your progress, retrieve lapses and, where possible, integrate your improved skills into your daily living.

In the homes of many people who follow the Buddhist religious tradition there is a shrine in front of which family members meditate. Similar to this idea, people also need to identify a suitable location or quiet space for self-therapy where they can escape from the external and internal clatter of everyday life and access their thoughts, feelings and basic human nature more deeply. This is not always easy where family life is involved. Where possible the furnishing of the self-therapy space should be comfortable, but not too comfortable, and the décor should be restful. Clipboards, notepads, activity sheets and even small whiteboards can be useful working aids during self-therapy sessions and for keeping records. Some people, perhaps especially those in the helping professions, may find their offices more conducive to self-therapy than their homes.

Self-therapy involves engaging in a collaborative working relationship with oneself. Self-therapists are their own facilitators and trainers. Starting self-therapy, and indeed starting any self-therapy session, entails a period of entry or of transition into a calmer and more inwardly focused state of being. In therapist-client work, the therapist is there to facilitate the change of gear from the frenetic hurly-burly of everyday life to this more contemplative state in which underlying as well as surface feelings have space to emerge. Self-therapists have to achieve this state on their own.

It may help in the entry period to close one's eyes. In addition, some may find the basic techniques of breathing meditation helpful: for example, focusing on the process of breathing in and breathing out and, when distracting thoughts occur, gently bringing one's mind back to attending to one's breathing. Tensing and relaxing groups of muscles – for example facial muscles, arm muscles, trunk of body muscles and leg muscles, may help some people too. Possibly up to the first five minutes of a self-therapy session might be taken up with entry activities to create the emotional climate for working. At the end of this period, people can choose whether it is better to open their eyes or keep them shut for longer to facilitate the focusing inwards and centring process.

Given the difficulties of self-therapy, perhaps it is best to focus on either one problem or one area for becoming more fully human at a time. The use of the term 'area' for becoming more fully human in addition to the term 'problem' is deliberate to indicate that the skilled human being model can be used for mental cultivation self-therapy as well as for adaptation self-therapy. Examples of adaptation problems on which to work include those connected with relationships, study, work, leisure, and health. Examples of mental cultivation areas for becoming more fully human include becoming less caught up in consumerism, increasing one's ability for feeling and thinking compassionately, and actively helping others less fortunate than oneself.

Let's take the example of Tessa, a graduate student coming to the end of a helping profession course and needing to look for a full-time job. Tessa is familiar with the cognitive humanistic theoretical framework and has already completed the stages and phases of self-therapy up to the point of formulating a definition in skills terms of her problem. Tessa then uses the two-column format and proceeds to write out on a clipboard hypotheses about the skills that she needs to improve to interview more competently when getting a job (see Box 15.2). Alternatively, Tessa could have written her hypotheses without using columns – this is a matter of individual preference.

The process of any self-therapy session can be seen as having three phases: entry, working, and ending. In the entry phase, self-therapists become calm, centred and inwardly focused. The nature of the working phase depends on a variety of factors such as whether it is an initial or follow-up session. The ending phase can entail such activities as reviewing the session, adding to records, clarifying homework tasks, if necessary thinking about when to hold the next self-therapy session, and mentally returning to the world.

Box 15.2: A self-therapy definition in skills terms for managing job interviews better

**Mind skills
I need to improve**

Creating self-talk

- use more calming self-statements
- use coaching self-statements before/during/afterwards

Creating rules

- Challenge and restate rules such as 'I must be perfect' 'Everyone must approve of me'

Creating perceptions

- Reality-test and alter perceptions like 'Interviews are a contest' 'I can never do well in job interviews'

**Communication/action skills
I need to improve**

Answering questions better

- verbal messages briefer and more focused answers
- vocal messages speak more slowly, clearly and louder
- body messages use better eye contact, stop waving my arms about, smile more

---

Mental cultivation CHT

How can clients, former clients, therapists and others cultivate and implement a service-oriented mentality or disposition in which they fuse their own interests with those of others and humanity? This section looks at some ways in which those engaging in personal practice can develop their human-being skills for attaining higher levels of human sympathy and mental cultivation, be it either concurrently with therapy, after therapy, or independent of therapy. The following suggestions are illustrative rather than exhaustive. Without losing their essence, individuals may find ways of adapting any or all of the following suggestions to suit their preferences.

Possessing a humanistic vision

A starting point for being a successful personal practitioner in attaining higher levels of human sympathy and mental cultivation is that of articulating some idea or vision of the sort of person one is trying to be. The cognitive humanistic approach merges religious and psychotherapeutic insights to provide a vision of the skills required for being more fully human. The concluding section of the previous chapter mentioned Buddhism's *bodhisattva* path and ended with the observation that practitioners of cognitive humanistic therapy's mental cultivation component needed to commit themselves to something akin to this path.

In Buddhism, there is a also a *bodhisattva* vow that allows *bodhisattvas* to dedicate themselves to following the path to enlightenment at the same time as actively relieving the suffering of others. Box 15.3 presents 'a humanist's vow' based on the underlying values and skills of cognitive humanistic therapy. Adherents of the cognitive humanistic approach can repeat, repeat and repeat again this vow to identify and remember some of the key skills for being fully human. Essentially the vow provides a vision statement or set of guidelines for cultivating some of the finer aspects of a humanistic self-concept. Such a self-concept then provides the foundation or motivating source for communicating and acting humanely.

The components of the vow go some way to articulating the elements or human-being skills required for cultivating what Fromm termed a humanistic conscience. Fromm wrote: 'Humanistic conscience is not the internalized voice of an authority whom we are eager to please and afraid of displeasing; it is our own voice, present in every human being and independent of external sanctions and rewards' (Fromm, 1949, p. 158). The seeds of being fully human and for developing and implementing a humanistic conscience are implanted as part of humankind's evolutionary heritage. However, it is up to human beings, individually and collectively, to cultivate their growth and maintenance.

Box 15.3: A Humanist's Vow

I commit myself to cultivating the following human-being skills:

- I commit myself to calming my mind.
- I commit myself to disillusioning my mind.
- I commit myself to curbing anger and aversion.
- I commit myself to curbing greed and craving.
- I commit myself to goodwill/lovingkindness.
- I commit myself to sympathetic joy.
- I commit myself to gratitude.
- I commit myself to compassion.
- I commit myself to equanimity.
- I commit myself to generosity and helping.
- I commit myself to service for other human beings.

It is one thing to state a humanist's vow and another much more difficult thing to implement it in one's daily life. The Dalai Lama observes of Buddhist practice that it is a constant battle within to replace previous negative conditioning or habituation with new positive conditioning. However, through constant familiarity, training and practice people can transform themselves (Dalai Lama and Cutler, 1998). Similarly, Christian practice entails Christians in a constant struggle to overcome prior conditioning and live according to the teachings and example of Jesus Christ.

Cultivating and implementing an other-centred attitude or service-oriented mentality entails a journey of inner and outer transformation in which personal practitioners struggle, sometimes backslide, yet hopefully make progress along the path. On the way practitioners are constantly going to be confronted with negative aspects of their conditioning that they have internalized and regarded as parts of their natural or independent selves. They are also likely to get glimpses of and be confronted with positive aspects of their underlying nature. Gaining greater awareness of both positive and negative feelings and behaviour can threaten current self-concepts and therefore evoke anxiety and possibly defensiveness. Personal practitioners may need to face and work through fears associated with both their brighter and shadow sides in order to gain greater insight into and understanding of their thoughts, feelings and communication/ actions.

The process of changing to improved mind and communication skills may also generate much anxiety. When striving to reach the heights of the human potential, conditioned ways of thinking, feeling and communicating/ acting can still be hard to shake off. As with Christian and Buddhist practice, inner and outer transformation entails familiarity, training and practice so that implementing higher levels of positive human-being skills becomes increasingly habitual. For both non-religious and religious humanists, the cognitive humanistic framework outlined in the book is intended to provide a useful tool to guide the process of becoming a better human being.

Withdrawing and contemplating

Built into the practice of religion is the rhythm of withdrawal and involvement. In Christianity and Buddhism, this entails setting regular times aside for prayer and meditation, respectively. Humanist personal practitioners can either set aside regular times for withdrawal and contemplation or engage in these activities as necessary. For over 40 years, Erich Fromm conducted a daily self-analysis in which he discovered something new or deepened already known-material (Fromm, 1993). Cognitive humanism involves a reflective approach in which practitioners strive for inner liberation so that they can proactively shape their lives to become more fully human. The alternative is that of constantly being at the whim of conditioned reactions to external events.

On a regular basis, personal practitioners can clear temporal and psychological spaces to become more inwardly focused. Sometimes, as with self-therapy, using mindfulness-of-breathing skills can provide a good bridge for moving from outside to inside. In these mini-retreats, personal practitioners can do numerous things to support attaining and maintaining higher levels of human sympathy and mental cultivation. For some, it may help just to calm down and allow their minds to become less agitated and more centred in order to enable them to handle either the remainder of the day or a particular problem better. Practitioners can also attempt to listen more deeply to their social instincts that form the basis of their humanistic conscience. They can then process past problems and attempt to think through present and future problems more thoughtfully and compassionately.

In addition, at the beginning of the day, practitioners can ask themselves relevant service mentality-oriented questions: for example, 'How can I use this day positively for others as well as myself?' and 'Who needs my help today?' At the end of the day they can review whether they utilized the day as planned (Dalai Lama and Cutler, 1998). They can also perform brief monitoring reviews focused on those human-being skills on which they may be working at the time. Furthermore, they may use withdrawal time to engage in some of the contemplative and other practices presented in this and other books for curbing negative and cultivating positive qualities and skills.

Another possibility is to conduct self-therapy during withdrawal and contemplation periods. A personal example is that of the author using a brief self-therapy session to overcome his resistance to moving beyond good intentions to commit publicly to donating his fees for an upcoming workshop tour of the UK to a Chiang Mai charity called Agape Home. At that time Agape Home, run by Canadian Christian missionaries with mainly Thai staff, provided residential care in a suburban hostel for about 35 babies and children with HIV-AIDS. In the past the author had contributed modestly to their then current project of building a new hostel in rural surroundings that would house more than 100 children and provide some facilities for mothers too. The result of the author's self-therapy on improving his mind skills and communication skills was that shortly afterwards he invited the Agape Home director to lunch and committed the workshop tour funds to the charity.

Correcting unskilful thinking

Attaining and maintaining higher levels of human-being skills is an ongoing process of making skilful as contrasted with unskillful choices. As Maslow observed 'To make the growth choice instead of the fear choice a dozen times a day is to move a dozen times a day towards self-actualization' (Maslow, 1971, p. 47). Personal practitioners need to be careful not to perpetuate the illusions of an independent self and of mental efficiency. Instead they need to realize that their 'selves' are heavily influenced by their past and current conditioning and weakened by their mental inefficiencies. Individuals can cultivate and implement humanistic consciences by using their capacity for reflective thinking; for example, by becoming more aware of and correcting ingrained habits of unskilful negative thinking.

Working to counteract unskilful thinking can be done as part of therapy and during private periods for withdrawal and contemplation. However, correcting negative thinking is also a form of mental house cleaning that frequently needs to be performed 'here-and-now' as unskilful thoughts arise. Attaining and maintaining high levels of mental cultivation and human sympathy entails continuously working to address issues of inner or mental liberation. Those who are mentally free have attained high levels of mental *response-ability* and *choice-ability*.

People have underlying tendencies to be humane, but all too frequently their conditioned reactions interfere with thinking, feeling and showing the positive qualities listed in 'a humanist's vow'. Practitioners need to develop skills of inner dialoguing in which they talk back to their unskilful thinking. They can become aware of those skill areas in which they have developed ingrained habits of negative thinking, become alert when they fall into such thinking, and then immediately engage in corrective thinking. Box 15.4 illustrates how to do this in regard to negative thoughts and images that interfere with goodwill/lovingkindness, sympathetic joy and generosity/helping. A further example of correcting unskilful thinking was provided in Practice 10.3 in regard to curbing anger. Practitioners can develop and use skilful thinking responses that have most meaning and work best for them. It is important to correct repeatedly unskilful negative thoughts and images when they occur, so that increasingly humane and skilful thoughts become engrained in one's repertoire of mental responses in their stead.

Box 15.4: Illustrative examples of correcting negative thinking

Goodwill/lovingkindness

T (1) Conditioned unskilful thoughts
Any critical thoughts and images about another person or their behaviour held without good reason.

T(2) Corrective skilful thoughts
'May she/he be happy and free from suffering.'
'There I go again judging people superficially.'
Visualize showing goodwill to that person.

Sympathetic joy

T(1) Conditioned unskilful thoughts
Any thoughts and images that contribute to feeling diminished by another's success and happiness.

T(2) Corrective skilful thoughts
'I'm delighted at her/his success and happiness.'
'Because someone else succeeds I am not less of a person.'
Visualize showing sympathetic joy to that person.

Generosity/helping

T(1) Conditioned unskilful thoughts
Any thoughts that block getting in touch with wishes to share money, time, effort or other resources in ways that might be mutually affirming.

T(2) Corrective skilful thoughts
'I can make a positive difference to her/his life.'
'I feel more of a person when I help others.'
Visualize being generous/helping in that situation.

Cultivating skillful communications/actions

In addition to inner transformation, implementing a service-oriented mentality entails outer transformation to show consistently the qualities contained in the humanistic vision and dedicated to in 'a humanist's vow'. To put it colloquially, personal practitioners have to keep working so that they 'walk the walk' in addition to 'talking the talk' and 'thinking the thought'. Though the skill areas in the humanistic vision may sometimes require large actions, they invariably also require small, daily actions so that practitioners change in the direction of other-centredness, but not at the expense of legitimate self-interest. In each of the skill areas for cultivating service, thinking better can lead to communicating and acting better, which in turn is likely to feed back into thinking better.

Personal practitioners need to struggle constantly to attain liberation not just from conditioned unskilful ways of thinking, but conditioned unskilful ways of communicating and acting as well. This is partly a process of checking themselves when they become aware that they are either engaging in, or might engage in, actions contrary to qualities like goodwill/lovingkindness, sympathetic joy, gratitude, compassion, equanimity and generosity and helping. However, practitioners can also actively and consistently cultivate these positive qualities in everyday life. For example, without waiting to be asked, practitioners can strive to show more goodwill/lovingkindness at home, at work, and in other areas of their daily lives. They can take 'here-and-now' opportunities to show sympathetic joy and gratitude as occasions arise. They can also work on a daily basis to understand and behave towards those with whom they interact with equanimity and compassion. Furthermore, they can take and create opportunities to show kindness and generosity.

Implementing a humanistic vision, as the word vision implies, can involve developing a visual as well as a verbal concept of the sort of person one wants to be. As such, possessing a humanistic conscience entails images as well as words to guide one's communications and actions. Developing and adhering to a humanistic vision and conscience requires strengthening by daily practice in which practitioners repeatedly take small steps to serve others as well as themselves. Repeated practice helps to build skilful habits and lays the groundwork for attaining higher levels in the different humanistic skill areas. Practitioners continuously need to act as personal coaches in formulating the thoughts and verbal, vocal and body messages that contribute to communicating and acting humanely in specific situations. In addition, where necessary, those practitioners with the required knowledge and skills can engage in self-therapy focused on the skill areas of demonstrating higher levels of human sympathy and mental cultivation.

Monitoring humanistic skills

Throughout this book, the point has been made that the goals and processes of CHT's adaptation and mental cultivation components overlap and interact. Nevertheless, the author has selected a range of human-being skills as essential for attaining supra-normal levels of human sympathy and mental cultivation. Those personal practitioners who are sufficiently versed in what each skill entails can monitor how skilful they are in each of the skills areas mentioned in 'a humanist's vow'. For example, they can rate their level of satisfaction with their skills in each area, for instance calming my mind, on a 1 to 9 scale, with 1 meaning 'very dissatisfied' and 9 meaning 'very satisfied' (see practice 15.1). Since ratings in each skill area are highly subjective, at best they can only provide a rough guide. In order to help their answers be independent from one another, some personal practitioners may choose to write down and then rate each skill area on a separate page. Before answering the final item on the log 'service for other human beings', it may help practitioners to gain an overall impression if they review all of their previous answers relating to specific skill areas.

Once a particular skill area is identified as in need of improvement, for instance sympathetic joy, the next step might be to break it down into overall ratings of mind skills and communication/action skills for sympathetic joy. Beyond that personal practitioners can then identify the specific mind skills and communication/action skills they need to improve.

Sources of strength and support

Following through on the humanist's vow and consistently implementing a humanistic vision requires courage, resilience and inner strength. There are many reasons why some personal practitioners may be tempted to give up the struggle. For example, if they have the poor mind skill of demanding approval they may not be able to cope with insufficient praise, indifference or even hostility to their efforts to be more humane. Another example is that of individuals whose compassion is limited by feeling overwhelmed by the amount of suffering in the world and threatened or repelled when confronted with face-to-face examples of it. Furthermore, helping and generosity can involve obvious costs in time, effort and money. As mentioned earlier, though the two components overlap, some people require adaptation CHT to attain normal functioning before participating in mental cultivation CHT to address issues of supra-normal functioning.

All persons who are sincerely committed to the humanistic path are ultimately personal practitioners, whether they are therapists, former clients or others. This raises the issue of what are the sources of strength that can help give personal practitioners the courage to persist. As many, if not most, people in Western societies show insufficient commitment to humanistic ideals, why follow them? Each individual needs to answer this question for herself or himself, but the following are some possible sources of strength and support.

The qualities in the humanistic vision represent the social part of humankind's underlying animal nature. Becoming more in touch with these qualities and thinking and acting skilfully in accordance with them is fulfilling a deep-seated evolutionary need. Humanistic qualities and skills are not add-ons in recent years; rather they are outer manifestations of what Darwin called the social instincts residing in the species-wide unconscious.

As well as fulfilling a valuable part of their evolutionary heritage, personal practitioners can gain further rewards from adhering to a service-oriented mentality. For instance, they can liberate themselves from much of the suffering and mental enslavement that is caused by narcissism, egocentricity and selfishness. By treating other people better, they may be treated better in return, although this is not always the case. In addition, they can either directly experience or imagine how their humane communications and actions are helping and have helped other people. If they receive expressions of gratitude, this may be rewarding. However, at the higher levels of human sympathy and mental cultivation people develop a 'give to give' mentality in which their positive actions are not heavily dependent on external approval or reciprocity. What is important to such people is that they live in accordance with the humanistic consciences that they have struggled to cultivate over the years. The sources of their self-respect and strength are inner- rather than outer-directed. Failure to live up to their humanistic consciences may lead practitioners to experience humanistic guilt, which is a healthy feeling so long as it is a genuine call to conscience, which is then heeded.

Nevertheless, it can be rewarding for personal practitioners to have the respect of persons whom they respect. The great religious traditions of Christianity and Buddhism support the importance of persons giving and gaining strength from one another. Effective practitioners are careful to seek out and cultivate friends and peers with similar humanistic values and aspirations. Such people can be important sources of support and offer inspiration by their example. Furthermore, although primarily self-reliant, personal practitioners can seek the support and insights of therapists, wise mentors and others to help them to become and stay more fully human.

Personal practitioners can also be inspired by the examples of those persons who have attained high levels of humanity, be they directly known to them or past or present public figures. Many people who either follow or want to follow the humanistic vision are religious and they are sustained in their efforts by their religious teachings, practices, exemplars and, hopefully, by supportive religious communities. For all practitioners, books, movies and television programmes that show the brighter side of humanity can also strengthen motivation to persist in following the humanistic path. Many inspirational books are referenced in the bibliography – for example biographies of Erich Fromm (Funk, 2000), Abraham Maslow (Hoffman, 1999) and Mahatma Gandhi (Fischer, 1997), Martin Luther King's collection of sermons published as *Strength to Love* (King, 1963), Mother Teresa's sayings for each day of the year published as *The Joy in Loving* (Chalika and Le Joly, 1996), and books by the Dalai Lama such as *The Art of Happiness* (Dalai Lama and Cutler, 1998) and *An Open Heart* (Dalai Lama, 2001).

As part of the struggle to become and to stay more fully human, practitioners also require compassion towards their own human frailty. When striving to attain higher levels of human sympathy and mental cultivation, personal practitioners should realize that this is a process that may take time and practice, practice and practice. They require equanimity and realism about their strength, progress and limitations. As a former UN Secretary-General observed 'Life only demands from you the strength you possess. Only one thing is possible – not to have run away' (Hammarskjöld, 1964).

Concluding comment

Cognitive humanism focuses on helping clients and others cultivate their capacity for reason and love. So far, psychology and psychotherapy have mainly emphasized helping clients to attain subnormal and normal levels of functioning and have insufficiently emphasized helping them to attain higher levels of or supra-normal human functioning. Furthermore, for the most part, psychotherapy theorists have inadequately recognized humankind's social instincts and their capacity to develop humanistic consciences representing enhanced levels of human sympathy and mental cultivation. The author intends cognitive humanistic therapy (CHT) to be a contribution towards redressing this balance. At the start of the twenty-first century it is imperative that more people are helped to develop a service-oriented mentality whereby, at the same time as affirming themselves, they are effective in affirming other people and the human species.

Practice

Practice 15.1: Personal practices for becoming and staying more fully human

1. If in broad agreement, repeat 'a humanist's vow' provided in Box 15.3 again, again and again until it really sinks in.
2. Using a 1 to 9 scale, with 1 meaning 'Very dissatisfied' and 9 meaning 'Very satisfied', rate how satisfied you are with your skills in each of the following eleven skill areas:

- calming my mind;
- disillusioning my mind;
- curbing anger and aversion;
- curbing greed and craving;
- cultivating goodwill/lovingkindness;
- cultivating sympathetic joy;
- cultivating gratitude;
- cultivating compassion;
- cultivating equanimity;
- cultivating generosity and helping;
- cultivating service for other human beings.

In what skill areas do you possess strengths? In what skill areas do you most need to improve?

3. For a stipulated period, say three, five or seven days, schedule a fifteen to twenty-minute withdrawal and contemplation period for your-self. During your mini-retreat you may engage in one or more of the following activities:

    - mindfulness of breathing;
    - listening more deeply to your feelings, especially your finer ones;
    - processing and thinking through present or future problems thoughtfully and compassionately;
    - asking yourself and answering service-oriented mentality questions;
    - performing brief monitoring reviews of specific humanist's skills;
    - engaging in contemplative and other practices presented in this and other books;
    - engaging in self-therapy;
    - other activities not mentioned above important to you.

4. For a stipulated period, say one day, monitor how skilfully you think in the skill areas contained in 'a humanist's vow'. Where necessary and feasible, engage in here-and-now corrective thinking for conditioned unskilful thoughts. Repeat this practice until it becomes part of your daily approach to living.
5. For a stipulated period, say one day, monitor how skilfully you com-municate and act in the skill areas contained in 'a humanist's vow'. Where necessary and feasible, engage in on-the-spot improvements for conditioned unskilful communications/actions. Repeat this practice until it becomes part of your daily approach to living.
6. Identify the sources of strength and support in your life for becoming and staying more fully human. Where appropriate, identify and seek out additional sources of strength and support.

Appendix: Some Research Implications

An important question is that of where research fits into cognitive humanistic therapy. The following are some points that address this issue.

1. Research consists of two overlapping components: creating ideas and evaluating them. All statements about approaches to the theory and practice of counselling and psychotherapy are attempts to articulate ideas relevant to understanding and helping patients and clients. As such, they are creations or accumulations of ideas that require assessment through evaluative research. The statement of cognitive humanistic therapy contained in this book represents an attempt to create ideas that overlap with, yet differ from, those of existing psychotherapies. Cognitive humanistic therapy's theory and practice require continuing, expanding, reorienting and building upon the psychotherapy research knowledge generated to date. If anything, the emphasis in contemporary psychotherapy research leans more heavily towards evaluating existing ideas than towards generating new and different ideas for later evaluation. This is a pity because over-emphasizing assessment at the expense of generating content stifles the creation and articulation of new or different ideas, which are the seeds of much successful evaluative research.

2. A research question of critical importance for humankind is that of what is a realistic and humane worldview for contemporary human beings. All people are personality theorists holding worldviews, sometimes tenaciously in face of conflicting evidence. Religious worldviews receive much attention. However, the kind of worldview that lends itself most to a scientific approach is that of humanism, since it makes no requirement to believe in unproven divine explanations. There exists a worldview vacuum for those who find that traditional religious worldviews are unconvincing. To date, in universities and elsewhere, insufficient effort has been made to generate and evaluate a sound humanistic worldview to fill that vacuum. Further pertinent research can provide many of the building blocks for stating a humanistic worldview that unites and affirms people rather than risks dividing and destroying them.

3. Continued research into humankind's evolutionary and genetic heritage is of great interest and importance for understanding human motivation, including what might be variously termed the social instincts, innate goodness, social feeling, and co-operative behaviour. In addition, continued research is necessary into the extent to which and how humankind can take more responsibility for its own evolution by developing and using its mental potential.

4. The question of whether there are universal human-being skills for effective living requires much more research attention than currently received. Elsewhere the author has suggested that this critical 'big picture' question urgently requires a major international research effort similar to the Human Genome Project to address the many and complex issues involved in answering it properly (Nelson-Jones, 2002c). Cognitive humanistic therapy, and indeed all psychotherapies, would be much more soundly based if such research were to be conducted successfully.

5. Curiously enough, the concept of 'mind' does not feature prominently in cognitive behavioural therapies like rational emotive behaviour therapy and cognitive therapy. Though extremely useful, as the twenty-first century progresses such therapies may increasingly be viewed as pioneering practical attempts to understand the mind and how to use it to live effectively and humanely. Much more useful research remains to be done to underpin cognitive approaches to therapy and living. Cognitive humanistic therapy hypothesizes that it is useful for people to develop a concept of mind and of mind skills. Relevant areas for research include the nature of mind, how best to divide its processes or functions into learnable skills, and how to train clients and people in general to assume more effective control over their mental processes. In addressing such questions, cognitive psychology and cognitive psychotherapy could probably interact more fruitfully than at present, with more attempts made to overcome the academic-practitioner divide.

6. Echoing Maslow's idea of the value of studying superior specimens, more research is needed into what constitutes high level or supranormal functioning. Maslow's work on self-actualizing people was descriptive rather than detailing the applied skills that highly self-actualized people used (Maslow, 1970). Research into high-level functioning needs to incorporate an applied focus that seeks to explain not only 'the what' but 'the how' of supra-normal functioning. To perform such research it is probably necessary to have the concept of human-being skills and then to break it down into its component parts.

7. The world's religious traditions seem to have much to offer psychotherapy in terms of articulating goals for being fully human.

Psychotherapy has much to offer the world's religious traditions in applied strategies, other than traditional strategies like prayer and meditation, for attaining humanistic goals within religious frameworks. Psychotherapy research might become both broader and deeper by incorporating more of a focus on examining processes and outcomes connected with religious aspirations like mental cultivation and human sympathy. Research into the psychology of religion might be stronger if it incorporated more of an applied emphasis by using tools adopted from psychotherapy. For instance, use of psychotherapy methods might well provide practical insights for Buddhists in how to think, feel and act more compassionately and for Christians in how to become and behave more like Jesus Christ.

8. Cognitive humanistic therapy relies heavily on using cognitive behavioural methods to attain both adaptation CHT goals and mental cultivation CHT goals. Much of the growing literature on empirically supported treatments supports the use of cognitive behavioural interventions for specific problems, for example sexual dysfunction, marital conflict and anger management. Thus this empirically supported treatment literature is highly relevant for adaptation CHT. However, to date there has been little or no research on mental cultivation CHT or on how to help people become better human beings. For example, the author cannot readily recall any studies on how to be more compassionate, generous or on how to feel and show more sympathetic joy.

9. Psychotherapy process and outcome research might sometimes be more useful if it emphasized cultivating positive qualities alongside or even instead of curbing negative qualities. For instance, research into anger management might be broadened to include helping clients to feel, think and act more positively towards others.

10. Perhaps existing psychotherapy research insufficiently takes into account the extent to which some of the problems of contemporary humans are systemic rather than individual. Psychotherapy research needs to identify and create strategies for dealing with problems inherent in contemporary society as well as to identify new ones that may arise in future. For example, in Western materialistic societies people can have problems with greed and craving without even realizing it. Sometimes the bigger their greed problem, the more successful they and others will regard them. Similarly, technological advances may be creating systemic problems without people being fully aware of what they are. Pertinent research areas include identifying psychological problems with systemic components, devising strategies to inoculate clients and others against them, and looking at ways of creating more humane and less stress-inducing societies.

Bibliography

Adler, A. (1997) *Understanding Life*. Oxford: Oneworld. First published in 1927.

Adler, A. (1998) *Social Interest: Adler's Key to the Meaning of Life*. Oxford: Oneworld. First published in 1933.

Alberti, R. E. and Emmons, M. L. (2001) *Your Perfect Right: Assertiveness and Equality in Your Life and Relationships* (8th edition). Atascadero CA: Impact.

Albom, M. (1997) *Tuesdays with Morrie: An Old Man, A Young Man, and Life's Greatest Lesson*. London: Warner Books.

Alford, B. A. and Beck, A. T. (1997) *The Integrative Power of Cognitive Therapy*. New York: Guilford Press.

Allport, G. W. (1964) The fruits of eclecticism: bitter or sweet? *Acta Psychologica*, **23**, 27–44.

American Psychiatric Association (2000) *Diagnostic and Statistical Manual of Mental Disorders* (4th edition). Washington DC: APA.

Ansbacher, H. L. and Ansbacher, R. R. (eds) (1956) *The Individual Psychology of Alfred Adler*. New York: Harper & Row.

Argyle, M. (1987) *The Psychology of Happiness*. London: Routledge.

Argyle, M. (1991) *Cooperation: The Basis of Sociability*. London: Routledge.

Argyle, M. (2002) State of the art: Religion. *The Psychologist*, **15**, 22–6.

Bandura, A. (1986) *Social Foundations of Thought and Action: A Social Cognitive Theory*. Englewood Cliffs NJ: Prentice-Hall.

Batchelor, S. (1997) *Buddhism Without Beliefs: A Contemporary Guide to Awakening*. London: Bloomsbury.

Beck, A. T. (1976) *Cognitive Therapy and the Emotional Disorders*. New York: New American Library.

Beck, A. T. (1988) *Love is Never Enough: How Couples Can Overcome Misunderstandings, Resolve Conflicts, and Solve Relationship Problems through Cognitive Therapy*. New York: Harper & Row.

Beck, A. T. (1999) *Prisoners of Hate: The Cognitive Basis of Anger, Hostility and Violence*. New York: HarperCollins.

Beck, A. T., Freeman, A. and Associates (1990) *Cognitive Therapy of Personality Disorders*. New York: Guilford Press.

Beck, A. T. and Weishaar, M. E. (2000) Cognitive therapy. In R. J. Corsini and D. Wedding (eds) *Current Psychotherapies* (6th edition). Itasca IL: Peacock, pp. 241–72.

Beit-Hallahmi, B. and Argyle, M. (1997) *The Psychology of Religious Behaviour, Belief and Experience*. London: Routledge.

Bowlby, J. (1979) *The Making and Breaking of Affectional Bonds*. London: Tavistock.

Buber, M. (1958) *I and Thou*. New York NY: Charles Scribner & Son.

Bugenthal, J. F. T. (1964) The third force in psychology. *Journal of Humanistic Psychology*, **4**(1), 19–25.

Buss, D. M. (1999) *Evolutionary Psychology: The New Science of the Mind*. Boston: Allyn & Bacon.

Butt, J. (2002) *The Role of the Christian Missionary*. Chiang Mai, Thailand. Unpublished Manuscript.

Carkhuff, R. R. (1987) *The Art of Helping* (6th edition). Amherst MA: Human Resource Development Press.

Chalika, J. and Le Joly, E. (eds) (1996) *The Joy in Loving: A Guide to Daily Living with Mother Teresa*. London: Penguin/Arkana.

Chawla, N. (1992) *Mother Teresa*. London: Arrow Books.

Chodren, T. (1990) *Taming the Monkey Mind*. Lutterworth: Tynron Press.

Cohen, D. (1997) *Carl Rogers: A Critical Biography*. London: Constable.

Confucius (1994) *Analects of Confucius*. Beijing: Sinolingua.

Corey, M. S. and Corey G. (1998) *Becoming a Helper* (3rd edition). Pacific Grove CA: Brooks/Cole.

Cormier, S. and Nurius, P. S. (2002) *Interviewing and Change Strategies for Helpers: Fundamental Skills and Cognitive Behavioral Interventions* (5th edition). Belmont CA: Wadsworth.

Dalai Lama, His Holiness the (1999) *Ethics for the New Millennium*. New York: Riverhead Books.

Dalai Lama, His Holiness the (2000) *The Transformed Mind: Reflections on Truth, Love and Happiness*. London: Hodder & Stoughton.

Dalai Lama, His Holiness the (2001) *An Open Heart: Practicing Compassion in Everyday Life*. New York: Little, Brown.

Dalai Lama, His Holiness the (2002) *How to Practice: The Way to a Meaningful Life*. London: Rider.

Dalai Lama, His Holiness the, and Cutler, H. C. (1998) *The Art of Happiness: A Handbook for Living*. Sydney: Hodder.

Darwin, C. (1859) *The Origin of Species*. London: Penguin.

Darwin, C. (1958) *The Autobiography of Charles Darwin*. New York: W. W. Norton. First published in 1887.

Darwin, C. (1998a) *The Descent of Man* (2nd edition). Amherst NY: Prometheus Books. First published in 1871.

Darwin, C. (1998b) *The Expression of the Emotions in Man and Animals* (3rd edition). London: HarperCollins. First published in 1872.

Deffenbacher, J. L., Oetting, E. R. and DiGiuseppe, R. A. (2002) Principles of empirically supported interventions applied to anger management. *The Counseling Psychologist*, **30**, 262-80.

Deffenbacher, J. L., Oetting, E. R., Huff, M. E., Cornell, G. R. and Dallager, C. J. (1996) Evaluation of two cognitive-behavioral approaches to general anger reduction. *Cognitive Therapy and Research*, **20**, 551–73.

Dryden, W. (2001) How rational am I? Self-help using rational emotive behaviour therapy. In E. Spinelli and S. Marshall (eds) *Embodied Theories*. London: Continuum, pp. 28–42.

Egan, G. (2002) *The Skilled Helper: A Problem Management and Opportunity Development Approach to Helping* (7th edition). Pacific Grove CA: Brooks/Cole.

Ekman, P. (1998) Universality of emotional expression? A personal history of the dispute. Afterward to Darwin, C. *The Expression of the Emotions in Man and Animals* (3rd edition). London: HarperCollins, pp. 363–93.

Ellis, A. (1977) *Anger: How to Live With and Without It*. Melbourne: Sun Macmillan Australia.

Ellis, A. (1980) Overview of the clinical theory of rational-emotive therapy. In A. Ellis and R. Grieger (eds). *Rational-Emotive Therapy: A Skills Based Approach*. New York: Van Nostrand Reinhold, pp. 1–31.

Ellis, A. (1991) Achieving self-actualization: The rational-emotive approach. In A. Jones and R. Crandall (eds) Handbook of Self-Actualization (special issue.) *Journal of Social Behavior and Personality*, **6**(5), 1–18.

Ellis, A. (1993) Reflections on rational-emotive therapy. *Journal of Consulting and Clinical Psychology*, **61**, 199–201.

Ellis, A. (2000) Rational emotive behaviour therapy. In R. J. Corsini and D. Wedding (eds) *Current Psychotherapies* (6th edition). Itasca IL: Peacock, pp. 168–204.

Ellis, A. (2001) *Feeling Better, Getting Better, Staying Better*. Atascadero CA: Impact.

Ellis, A and Dryden, W. (1997) *The Practice of Rational Emotive Behaviour Therapy*. London: Free Association Books.

Ellis, A. and MacLaren, C. (1998) *Rational Emotive Behavior Therapy: A Therapist's Guide*. San Luis Obispo CA: Impact.

Fischer, L. (1997) *The Life of Mahatma Gandhi*. London: HarperCollins.

Franck, F. (1991) *To Be Human Against All Odds*. Berkeley CA: Asian Humanities Press.

Frankl, V. E. (1955) *The Doctor and The Soul: From Psychotherapy to Logotherapy*. Harmondsworth: Penguin Books.

Frankl, V. E. (1963) *Man's Search for Meaning: An Introduction to Logotherapy*. New York: Washington Square Press.

Frankl, V. E. (1975) *The Unconscious God: Psychotherapy and Theology*. New York: Simon & Schuster.

Fromm, E. (1949) *Man for Himself: An Enquiry into the Psychology of Ethics*. London: Routledge & Kegan Paul.

Fromm, E. (1956) *The Art of Loving*. New York: Bantam Books.

Fromm, E. (1961) *Marx's Concept of Man*. New York: Frederick Ungar Publishing.

Fromm, E. (1976) *To Have or To Be?* London: Jonathan Cape.

Fromm, E. (1993) *The Art of Being*. London: Constable.

Fromm, E. (1995) *The Essential Fromm: Life Between Having and Being*. London: Constable.

Funk, R. (2000) *Erich Fromm: His Life and Ideas, An Illustrated Biography*. London: Continuum International.

Goldstein, J. (1994) *Insight Meditation: The Practice of Freedom*. Boston: Shambala.

Goleman, D. (1995) *Emotional Intelligence: Why It Can Matter More Than IQ*. London: Bloomsbury.

Greenberger, D. and Padesky, C. A. (1995) *Mind Over Mood: Change How You Feel by Changing The Way You Think*. New York: Guilford Press.

Greer, G. (1999) *The Whole Woman*. London: Anchor.

Hammarskjold, D. (1964) *Markings*. London: Faber & Faber.

Hart, W. (1987) *The Art of Living: Vipassana Meditation as Taught by S. N. Goenka*. New York: Harper & Row.

Hodge, S. (1999) *Tibetan Buddhism*. London: Piatkus.

Hoffman, E. (ed.) (1996) *Future Visions: The Unpublished Papers of Abraham Maslow*. Thousand Oaks CA: Sage.

Hoffman, E. (1999) *The Right to be Human: A Biography of Abraham Maslow*. New York: McGraw-Hill.

Horney, K. (1937) *The Neurotic Personality of Our Time*. New York: W. W. Norton.

Howard, A. (2000) *Philosophy for Counselling and Psychotherapy: Pythagoras to Postmodernism*. London: Macmillan.

Hubbard, G. (1974) *Quaker by Convincement*. Harmondsworth: Penguin Books.

Jones, A. (1994) Introduction. *The Koran*. London: J.M. Dent, pp. xi–xxvii.

Jung, C. G. (1966) *The Practice of Psychotherapy* (2nd edition). London: Routledge.

Jung, C. G. (1968) *Analytical Psychology: Its Theory and Practice*. New York: Vintage.

King, C. S. (1996) *The Words of Martin Luther King, Jr.* New York: Newmarket Press.

King, M. L. (1963) *Strength to Love.* Philadelphia: Fortress Press.

King, M. L. (1967) *Where Do We Go From Here: Chaos or Community?* New York: Harper.

King, M. L. (1986) I see the promised land. In Washington, J. M. (ed.) *Testament of Hope: The Essential Writing and Speeches of Martin Luther King, Jr.* San Franscisco CA: HarperSanFranscisco, pp. 279–86.

Kornfield, J. (1993) *A Path With Heart: A Guide Through the Perils and Promises of Spiritual Life.* New York: Bantam Books.

Lazarus, A. A. (1984) *In the Mind's Eye: The Power of Imagery for Personal Enrichment.* New York: The Guilford Press.

Lazarus, A. A. (1993) Tailoring the therapeutic relationship or being an authentic chameleon. *Psychotherapy*, **30**, 404–7.

Lazarus, A. A. (1997) *Brief but Comprehensive Psychotherapy: The Multimodal Way.* New York: Springer.

Lerner, H. G. (1985) *The Dance of Anger: A Woman's Guide to Changing the Patterns of Intimate Relationships.* New York: Harper & Row.

Lewinsohn, P. M., Munoz, R. F., Youngren, M. A. and Zeiss, A. M. (1986) *Control Your Depression.* New York: Prentice-Hall.

Loewenthal, K. M. (2000) *The Psychology of Religion: A Short Introduction.* Oxford: Oneworld.

MacLean, P. D. (1991) The triune brain. Appendix to F. Franck *To Be Human Against All Odds.* Berkeley CA: Asian Humanities Press, pp. 181–8. Reprinted from G. Adelman (ed.) (1987) *Encyclopedia of Neuroscience.* Boston MA: Birkhauser. Vol. 2, Appendix 1, 1235–7.

Maslow, A. H. (1962) *Towards a Psychology of Being.* New York: Van Nostrand.

Maslow, A. H. (1969) Towards a humanistic biology. *American Psychologist*, **24**, 724–35.

Maslow, A. H. (1970) *Motivation and Personality* (2nd edition). New York: Harper & Row.

Maslow, A. H. (1971) *The Farther Reaches of Human Nature.* Harmondsworth: Pelican.

Maslow, A. H. (1976) *Religions, Values, and Peak Experiences.* New York: Penguin.

Masters, W. H., Johnson, V. E., and Kolodny, R. C. (1986) *Masters and Johnson on Sex and Human Loving.* London: Pan Macmillan.

May, R. and Yalom, I. D. (2000) Existential psychotherapy. In R. J. Corsini and D. Wedding (eds) *Current Psychotherapies* (6th edition). Itasca IL: Peacock, 273–302.

Mead, M. (ed.) (1937) *Cooperation and Competition Among Primitive Peoples.* New York: McGraw-Hill.

Miller, J. and Van Loon, B. (1992) *Darwin for Beginners.* Cambridge: Icon Books.

Nelson-Jones, R. (1984) *Personal Responsibility Counselling and Therapy: An Integrative Approach.* London: Harper & Row.

Nelson-Jones, R. (1999) *Creating Happy Relationships: A Guide to Partner Skills.* London: Continuum.

Nelson-Jones, R. (2002a) *Essential Counselling and Therapy Skills: The Skilled Client Model.* London: Sage.

Nelson-Jones, R. (2002b) The skilled client. *Counselling and Psychotherapy Journal*, **13**(1), 10–13.

Nelson-Jones, R. (2002c) Are there universal human being skills? *Counselling Psychology Quarterly*, **15**, 115–19.

Nyanaponika, Thera (1962) *The Heart of Buddhist Meditation: A Handbook of Mental Training Based on the Buddha's Way of Mindfulness.* London: Rider & Company.

Oxford English Dictionary (2001) *OED Online.* http://dictionary.oed.com, Oxford: Oxford University Press.

Perls, F. S., Hefferline, R. F. and Goodman, P. (1951) *Gestalt Therapy: Excitement and Growth in the Human Personality*. London: Souvenir Press.

Raskin, N. J. and Rogers, C. R. (2000) Person-centered therapy. In Corsini, R. J. and Wedding, D. (eds) *Current Psychotherapies* (6th edition). Itasca IL: Peacock, pp. 133–67.

Robinson, J. A. T. (1963) *Honest to God*. London: SCM Press.

Rogers, C. R. (1959) A theory of therapy, personality, and interpersonal relationships as developed in the client-centred framework. In S. Koch (ed.) *Psychology: A Study of Science* (Study 1, Volume 3). New York: McGraw-Hill, pp. 184–256.

Rogers, C. R. (1961) *On Becoming A Person*. Boston MA: Houghton Mifflin.

Rogers, C. R. (1969) *Freedom to Learn*. Columbus OH: Charles E. Merrill.

Rogers, C. R. (1980) *A Way of Being*. Boston MA: Houghton Mifflin.

Rousseau, J.-J. (1993) *Emile*. London: J. M Dent. First published in 1762.

Rowan, J. (2000) *Ordinary Ecstasy: The Dialectics of Humanistic Psychology* (3rd edition). London: Brunner-Routledge.

Russell, B. (1945) *A History of Western Philosophy*. New York: Simon & Schuster.

Salzberg, S. (1995) *Lovingkindness: The Revolutionary Art of Happiness*. London: Shambala.

Schwartz, S. H. (1992) Universals in the content and structure of values: Theoretical advances and empirical tests in 20 countries. In Zanna, M. (ed.), *Advances in Experimental Social Psychology*, Vol. 25, New York: Academic Press, pp. 1–65.

Sichel, J. and Ellis, A. (1984) *RET Self-Help Form*. New York: Institute for Rational-Emotive Therapy.

Skinner, B. F. (1953) *Science and Human Behavior*. London: Free Press.

Skinner, B. F. (1969) *Contingencies of Reinforcement*. New York: Appleton-Century-Croft.

Skinner, B. F. (1974) *About Behaviourism*. London: Jonathan Cape.

Smith, R. L. (1998) *A Quaker Book of Wisdom: Life Lessons in Simplicity, Service and Common Sense*. New York: Eagle Brook.

Sober, E. and Wilson, D. S. (1998) *Unto Others: The Evolution and Psychology of Unselfish Behavior*. Cambridge MA: Harvard University Press.

Spong, J. S. (1998) *Why Christianity Must Change or Die*. San Francisco CA: HarperSanFrancisco.

Stevens, A. and Price, J. (2001) *Evolutionary Psychiatry: A New Beginning* (2nd edition). London: Routledge.

Sue, D. W., Carter, R. T., Casas, J. M., Fouad, N. A., Ivey, A. E., Jensen, M., LaFromboise, T., Manese, J. E., Ponterotto, J. G., and Vazquez-Nutall, E. (1998) *Multicultural Counseling Competencies: Individual and Organizational Development*. London: Sage.

Sutich, A. (1961) Introduction. *Journal of Humanistic Psychology*, **1**(1): vii–ix.

Szasz, T. (1973) *The Second Sin*. London. Routledge & Kegan Paul.

Thitavanno, P. (1995) *Mind Development*. Bangkok: Mahamakut Buddhist University.

Thitavanno, P. (2002) *A Buddhist Way of Mental Training* (2nd edition). Bangkok: Chuan Printing Press.

Thoreau, H. D. (1995) *Walden*. Mineola NY: Dover Publications. First published in 1854.

Tillich, P. (1952) *The Courage to Be*. New Haven CT: Yale University Press.

Waite, R. G. L. (1977) *Adolph Hitler: The Psychopathic God*. New York: Basic Books.

Walsh, R. (1999) *Essential Spirituality: Exercises from the World's Religions to Cultivate Kindness, Love, Joy, Peace, Vision, Wisdom and Generosity*. New York: John Wiley.

Walsh, R. (2000) Asian psychotherapies. In R. Corsini and D. Wedding (eds) *Current Psychotherapies* (6th edition). Itasca IL: Peacock, pp. 407–44.

Wolpe, J. (1990) *The Practice of Behavior Therapy* (4th edition). Oxford: Pergamon Press.

Yalom, I. D. (1980) *Existential Psychotherapy*. New York: Basic Books.

Name Index

Subject Index